D1446350

ANIMAL EQUALITY

ANIMAL EQUALITY

Language and Liberation

JOAN DUNAYER

Foreword by Carol J. Adams

RYCE PUBLISHING
Derwood, Maryland

2001

RYCE PUBLISHING
7806 Fairborn Court
Derwood, Maryland 20855-2227
www.rycepublishing.com

Publisher's Cataloging-in-Publication Data

Dunayer, Joan
Animal equality: language and liberation / Joan Dunayer;
foreword by Carol J. Adams
p. cm.
Includes bibliographical references and index.
ISBN 0-9706475-5-7
1. Animal rights
2. Animal welfare
3. Language and ethics
4. Animal intelligence
5. Emotions in animals
I. Title
HV4708.D86 2001
179.3—dc21
Library of Congress Control Number: 00-192984

Printed in the United States of America

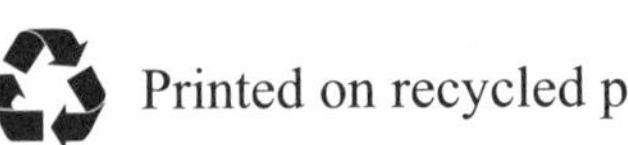

For all nonhuman animals

Contents

Foreword

by Carol J. Adams

Animal Equality is intensely powerful: groundbreaking, definitive, comprehensive, compelling. Unparalleled in scope and exhaustively researched, it is a remarkable achievement.

Joan Dunayer demonstrates that standard English usage sustains the abuse of nonhuman animals. Speciesism is a lie, and it requires a language of lies to survive. Currently, our language denies the harm that humans routinely inflict on other animals; linguistically, both the victims and the perpetrators have disappeared. *Animal Equality* exposes the language practices that constitute an important but, until now, largely unexamined part of our relationship with nonhuman animals. The book offers revelations about everyday language choices and an original, thorough exploration of the language of nonhuman-animal exploitation. If anyone ever doubted that language matters, they will doubt no more.

In exposing speciesism's lies, this important book prompts these questions: Do we wish to live lives of honesty or denial? Do we wish to cause suffering or instead contribute to alleviating suffering? Most of us probably would answer that we wish to live honestly, causing the least harm possible. But what if the harm and suffering we are causing have disappeared from our language? What if the consequences of our actions are absent from discussion? We might think we are living honestly when in fact we aren't. We might believe we are causing the least harm possible when in fact we directly or indirectly participate in harm.

This is the problem, as *Animal Equality* makes clear: a relationship exists between deception and suffering. Let's face it—most of us will respond emotionally to a description of another's suffering. Language that describes suffering shouldn't be avoided simply because of that. But most people don't want to respond emotionally. Dealing with our feelings can be difficult, especially when we ourselves directly or indirectly participate in harm to others. Deceptive language helps us deny both the suffering and the cause. Once those who suffer and those who cause the suffering are rendered absent, there is no act of violence, just business as usual.

Speciesist language enables us to disregard the suffering and abuse of nonhuman animals. How, exactly, does it work? *Animal Equality* shows us. Joan illuminates not only the terms we use but also word forms and sentence structure. Others have noticed that euphemisms disguise the killing of nonhuman animals. Joan recognizes so much more: passive verbs allow those who harm nonhuman animals to avoid acknowledging their actions; singular references to plural animals discount them as individuals; relegating mention of nonhuman victims to prepositional phrases keeps the focus off their suffering or death.... *Animal Equality* is filled with insights such as these. The book establishes speciesism and language as a field of study while providing the benchmark for the field.

Six of *Animal Equality*'s twelve chapters examine a particular type of speciesist abuse: hunting, sportfishing, zoos, "aquariums," vivisection, and "animal agriculture." These chapters vividly describe the maltreatment of nonhuman animals and show, through compelling examples, that deceptive language perpetuates this maltreatment. The book's other chapters are equally rich. Brimming with evidence of nonhuman thought and emotion, one chapter demonstrates that similar human and nonhuman attributes commonly are given different names, as a way of conceptually distancing us from other animals. Another chapter brilliantly critiques the problem of standard pronoun references to nonhuman animals and presents solutions. *Animal Equality* also contains valuable style and vocabulary guidelines. The thesaurus of speciesist terms and suggested alternatives is wonderful; I anticipate its being repeatedly cited and reprinted.

Sweeping yet precise, *Animal Equality* is an outstanding piece of scholarship and writing. Joan has gathered together an enormous amount of information, and she always documents her statistics and claims. At the same time, her writing flows; it is polished and strong. This book has life!

Animal Equality has much to offer animal activists, ecofeminists, other environmentalists, moral philosophers, language specialists, students and teachers of human–nonhuman relationships, and anyone else interested in the politics of language or the way we treat others.

If I were you, I'd pick up a second copy along with this one. You're going to want to lend one out or give it away, but you won't want to be without one yourself. You'll want to return to *Animal Equality*'s insights and let them roll over you again. I know. On several occasions, I've been given the opportunity to read the manuscript that became this book. Each time, I've been moved by Joan's writing, awed by her research, and impressed by her wisdom. Each time, I've come away amazed at what she has accomplished and anxious to share it with others. One extra copy? I'm thinking of stocking five to ten at a time! You, too, might find that one extra copy isn't enough. Nothing like *Animal Equality* exists, and nothing will surpass this work for years, if ever.

Animal Equality is a giant step for animalkind. Joan believes that we can change our language. She believes that we can end the needless speciesist practices that cause so much suffering and death. So do I. I believe *Animal Equality* will accomplish its purpose. As more and more readers spread its message, it will bring us closer to justice and compassion for all beings—closer to animal equality.

Acknowledgments

"Thank you" to everyone who helped bring *Animal Equality* into print.

Terry Sayler and her staff at the University of Maryland's Interlibrary Loan Office obtained hundreds of books and articles that I requested during my research.

Dozens of other people kindly provided requested source materials: Rachel Anastasi, Gene Bauston, Virginia Bollinger, Katherine Brant, Karen Davis, Margaret Eldon, Richard Farinato, Lise Giraud, Steve Kestin, Eric Kleiman, Pat Klein, Florence Lambert, Kay Mannes, Donna Marsden, Shirley McGreal, Barbara Orlans, Norm Phelps, Suzanne Pope, Heidi Prescott, Susan Rich, Naomi Rose, Suzanne Roy, Becky Sandstedt, Randolph Sargent, David Spratt, Valerie Stanley, Martin Stephens, and Mary Beth Sweetland.

Phyllis Dunayer, Mary Finelli, Stephen Kaufman, and Debbie Leahy brought useful source materials to my attention and provided them with special generosity.

University of Kansas biology professor Daphne Fautin repeatedly took time to answer questions about gender and sentience in sponges, cnidarians, and other marine invertebrates.

The Culture and Animals Foundation, headed by Tom Regan, and the Justice for Animals Fund, directed by Stephen Kaufman, awarded much-appreciated grants that expedited *Animal Equality*'s completion.

Carol Adams, Evelyn Pluhar, and Tom Regan read the manuscript and made invaluable suggestions. They also expressed strong support. *Animal Equality* owes a great deal to their guidance and encouragement. With characteristic generosity, Carol offered to write the book's foreword.

Eric Dunayer, my spouse, gave moral support throughout my efforts on *Animal Equality*, which greatly benefited from his editorial advice and scientific expertise. Eric hasn't eaten flesh since he was thirteen. While a University of Pennsylvania veterinary student, he refused to practice surgery on a healthy dog who then would be killed. Eric and classmate Gloria Binkowski requested a nonexploitive alternative. When the university refused, they sued. With law professor and animal rights advocate Gary Francione acting as their legal advisor, Eric and Gloria won their case. For their required practice surgery, all Penn veterinary students now perform ovariohysterectomies on dogs available for adoption. Today Eric is an emergency veterinarian. In both his professional work and his vegan lifestyle, he saves nonhuman animals and advances their well-being.

Finally, I'm grateful to all the nonhuman persons who have given me friendship and love or otherwise enriched my life with their presence. I hope that *Animal Equality* honors them and all other nonhuman animals.

Prologue

From Vivisection to Animal Rights

A gorilla stood alone in a concrete cell. Our eyes met, and his expressed deep anger and grief. My grade-school class was visiting the zoo, a place I found heavily oppressive. Four at a time, my classmates climbed onto a camel for a ride. Because she looked burdened and miserable, I refused. At age seven or so, I saw a boy intentionally stomp a caterpillar. "It would have been a butterfly!" I cried. My childhood companions included a red-eared slider turtle, parakeets, and dogs. I loved each of them intensely, and when they died I intensely mourned. Yet, throughout childhood I ate nonhuman animals' flesh, milk, and eggs and wore their hair and skin. Decades later as a graduate student, I used rats in experiments.[1] Somehow the child who had mourned a turtle, pitied a camel, and protested the killing of a caterpillar had become a vivisector.

What enables such contradictions? To great extent, evasive and deceptive language. When we indirectly participate in nonhuman victimization, the victims usually are visually absent. Standard linguistic usage keeps them verbally absent as well. As a child, I ate "bacon" and "ham" without giving a thought to pigs. If anyone had spoken of pig flesh or remains, I might have considered their slaughter. As a graduate student, I ordered ten rats, like so many test tubes, for experimental use because they were "laboratory rats" and I was a "researcher." Those labels permitted self-disguise. I didn't see myself as an abuser—not yet.

Then I observed vivisection for the first time. At the University of Pennsylvania every veteran vivisector in the psychology department treated rats with callous indifference. I heard rats scream as their ears were hole-punched for identification. I saw them flung by the tail into metal boxes that fit them like coffins. There they stayed 23 hours a day, unable to look out. So that they would work for food, some rats were kept half starved. Others received electric shocks.

Still others were subjected to painful injury such as stomach puncture. Termed "procedures" and "methods," all forms of torture escaped moral judgment.

Initially, like the department's other vivisectors, I viewed rats as mine to use. My experiments (which my advisor called "the world's most benign") didn't cause pain, but they did entail deprivation. By nature, rats are social, lively, and curious. They eat a wide variety of foods. Individually confined to small wire cages, "my rats" endured isolation, inaction, and an unchanging environment. Two hours a day they had access to one type of food pellet, always the same.

In addition to sharing the same monotonous surroundings and routine, all ten rats belonged to the same albino strain and had been born the same day. In the language of vivisection they were "standardized." But each had a highly distinct appearance, intelligence, and personality. Brutus had an overbite, Horace a nick in one ear that gave him a rakish look, Rufus a face so round that he resembled a harp-seal cub. Marcus immediately learned the experimental task; Terence never did. Only Livy ever creased his brow and looked cross. Cato was easygoing, Pliny tense. Long and muscular, Zeno moved boldly, unlike Virgil, who was small and frail.

The more I saw the rats as individuals, the more I considered their desires and needs. I arranged for bigger cages. Still too small. I put a chew toy inside each cage. Not good enough. When the experiments ended, the rats had no more use as "tools," so my advisor instructed me to have them killed. To me, however, the rats were persons.[2] To kill them would be morally wrong: murder. I obtained permission to adopt all ten.

The rats reacted to increased freedom and variety with excitement. Eagerly they explored my apartment and ate new foods. At his first taste of cantaloupe, Rufus somersaulted with joy. When I had handled them in the lab, the rats always had been gentle, however harsh and stressful their circumstances. Now they showed affection. If I sat on the floor and called his name, Rufus would scurry to me from across the room. If I sat on the couch, Virgil would climb up to perch on my shoulder. Brutus liked to sit in my lap and be petted. Thinking about the use of rats in vivisection, I felt grief, disgust, and shame.

Someone recommended Peter Singer's *Animal Liberation*. All sentient beings warrant moral consideration, Singer reasoned; a nonhuman's suffering should count no less than a human's. But humans regularly attach little or no importance to other animals' suffering, he demonstrated. They show species bias: speciesism.[3] The word had a powerful effect. Out of speciesism I had failed to consider most nonhuman animals, the vast majority of the world's living beings. Institutionalized speciesism takes many forms, Singer noted. In particular, he exposed the speciesism and cruelty of vivisection and "animal agriculture." My actions had displayed as arrogant, self-serving, and self-deceiving a mindset as sexism or racism.

The concept of nonhuman rights completed my shift in worldview. No conscious being should be treated like an exploitable thing, Tom Regan argued in *The Case for Animal Rights*. He stressed the moral rights of individuals, nonhuman and human. Currently the law recognizes only human rights. Regan proposed changing nonhuman animals' legal status from property to person (rights-holder). Yes, I thought. Universally, humans exploit and kill other animals because legally they can. As history shows, humans readily take advantage of those with less power. Because they receive little moral consideration from humans and lack political power, nonhumans are especially vulnerable to concerted abuse.

Combining Regan's ideas with Singer's, I concluded: Sentience entitles nonhuman animals to legal rights, which must protect them, as individuals, from speciesism. I left the psychology program, stopped eating flesh, and soon avoided all animal-derived food.

Having previously worked as a writer and editor, earned master's degrees in English education and English literature, and taught high school and college English, I returned to a focus on language and worked as a writer-editor, primarily on college English textbooks. Increasingly I noticed that standard English usage legitimizes, trivializes, and conceals speciesist injustice.

As a feminist, I knew that words can foster oppression or liberation, deception or truth. Sexist and speciesist language share certain features, I found—such as pronoun use, metaphors, and syntax that discount the experiences of those deemed inferior. In *The Sexual Politics of Meat* Carol Adams linked sexism and speciesism. She also cited evasive and speciesist language that serves the flesh industry. Her analysis prompted me to think more about connections between nonhuman and human oppression, and about the role of euphemism and definition in keeping nonhumans oppressed.

I began to write this book. As I examined the discourse of people who exploit nonhuman animals, persistent falsehoods emerged: denial of nonhuman sentience and individuality, disingenuous claims of necessity, a habit of blaming the victim. But the problem was larger; speciesist language pervaded human discourse. Individuals who never would utter a sexist or racist word spoke of nonhuman animals with careless contempt. Unwittingly, even animal rights advocates used speciesist language—including me.

Language can perpetuate or combat speciesism. Whether nonhuman animals are property or persons is a matter of definition. A single word, such as *speciesism*, can enlighten. The term *animal rights* points the way to justice. To achieve justice for all beings, we must overcome speciesism's linguistic ploys. We think in words and act them out. Equitable laws and practices require equitable language.

When I told a friend this book's title, he questioned the phrase *animal equality*. Did I really mean to say that all animals are equal?[4] Yes, I did. I hope the chapters that follow will show why.

1

Speciesism and Language

> This is the oppressor's language.
>
> —Adrienne Rich

Through massive and sustained exploitation, humans cause other animals enormous suffering. Nonhumans are bred for show, racing, fighting, and servitude. They're forced to perform in circuses, terrorized and injured at rodeos, imprisoned in zoos. Each year in the U.S., millions are killed for their fur; at least tens of millions are subjected to cruel experimentation; at least hundreds of millions are murdered for sport; billions go from severe confinement to slaughter; so that their flesh can be sold as seafood, billions more are wrested from U.S. waters.[1]

How do we justify our treatment of nonhumans? We lie—to ourselves and to each other, about our species and about others. Deceptive language perpetuates speciesism, the failure to accord nonhuman animals equal consideration and respect. Like sexism or racism, speciesism is a form of self-aggrandizing prejudice. Bigotry requires self-deception. Speciesism can't survive without lies. Standard English usage supplies these lies in abundance. Linguistically the lies take many forms, from euphemism to false definition. We lie with our word choices. We lie with our syntax. We even lie with our punctuation.

Often the verbal subterfuge involves speciesist language, which denigrates or discounts nonhuman animals. Conventional pronoun use, for example, terms nonhuman animals "it," erasing their gender and grouping them with inanimate things. At other times, misleading language legitimizes or sanitizes speciesist attitudes and practices without entailing speciesist usage. Relatively few humans hunt for sport, but sport hunters claim that "instinct" "compels" them to hunt.

Lesser Beings?

Current usage promotes a false dichotomy between humans and nonhumans. Separate lexicons suggest opposite behaviors and attributes. We eat, but other animals feed. A woman is pregnant or nurses her babies; a nonhuman mammal gestates or lactates. A dead human is a corpse, a dead nonhuman a carcass or meat.

Everyday speech denies human–nonhuman kinship. *We* aren't animals, primates, or apes. One animal species among millions, we declare ourselves alone. The same species hubris that has led sexist men to reserve "mankind" for men has led humans to decline linguistic membership in "animals."

Nonhuman-animal terms insult humans by invoking contempt for other species. The very word *animal* conveys opprobrium. *Human*, in contrast, signifies everything worthy. Like the remark that a woman has "the mind of a man," the comment that a nonhuman is "almost human" is assumed to be praise. Both condescend.

Translating biological diversity into a political hierarchy, humans have labeled other animals inferior—"lower." Along with scorned humans, nonhumans are "subhuman."

Standard usage purveys the view that nonhumans are less intelligent than humans. Metaphors like *jackass*, *birdbrain*, and *goose* equate nonhuman with stupid. Dictionary definitions contrast "human intelligence" and "animal instinct." Because human culture features verbal language and technology, speciesists assess intelligence in terms of these capacities. However, if we define intelligence as evidence-based perception undistorted by bigotry and myth, humans compare unfavorably to other animals. While despising nonhumans as mindless, members of "the rational species" riot over the outcomes of soccer games; smoke, eat, and drink themselves to death; poison the air, water, and soil on which they rely; and believe that other religions are false but theirs is true. We can't fully detect or appreciate nonhumans' mental powers. But even by conventional human standards, a mature brook trout is in many ways more cognizant than a newborn or senile human, and the average pigeon or rat possesses greater learning and reasoning ability than many humans with mental disabilities.

Speciesists assume that nonhumans feel, as well as think, less than humans. Analogously, racists have contended that people of color feel injury and deprivation less than whites. Behavioral and physiological evidence, evolutionary history, and the importance of not mistaking sentience for insentience (and causing suffering as a result) warrant regarding any creature with a nervous system as sentient. From dogs to red octopuses, many nonhumans obviously feel intensely both physically and emotionally. Nonhumans may suffer *more* intensely than humans in similar situations. Nonhuman victims of inescapable human abuse can't make sense of their plight, change their circumstances, or foresee an end to their suffering. Being able to understand or partially control one's fate makes adversity more bearable. Humans are good at rationalizing ("It's God's will," "My suffering will be rewarded"). What consoles the zoo-imprisoned orangutan, the vivisection-tortured rat, the hooked and suffocating bass? By downplaying nonhuman sensitivity, speciesists downplay the need for nonhuman liberation.

Especially in the sciences, many writers balk at attributing emotions to nonhuman individuals, however familiar and closely observed. Even when abundant evidence clearly indicates a nonhuman's mental state, they hedge: "she *seemed* afraid," "he *appeared* to grieve." Whereas human animals love their families and friends, nonhuman ones merely "bond" and "mate," acting out social "instincts" and sexual "drives."

In much mainstream writing, nonhumans "think" and "feel" only in quotation marks. As reported in *The Washington Post*, language studies are exploring how orangutans "'think.'"[2] The *Post*'s quotation marks around *think* exhibit speciesism, not reasonable caution. To doubt that orangutans think, a person must either be ignorant of evolution, comparative neurophysiology, and a massive amount of behavioral evidence or willfully ignore their implications.

While portraying nonhuman animals as lesser in cognition and feeling, standard usage also pronounces them morally inferior: beasts and brutes. Our language transfers human viciousness and "brutality" to other species. The ruthless, we say, "claw" their way to the top; they're vipers, rats, skunks, and sharks. Sexual offenders are "predators." The most violent criminals are "animals." Most nonhuman animals inflict serious harm only out of immediate and direct survival need, as when a lion kills prey. Because nonhumans who do cause needless harm may have no sense of wrongdoing, they too should be regarded as innocent. In contrast, most humans are guilty. While boasting of "human kindness," our species treats nonhumans (and often humans) with extreme injustice and cruelty. Directly or indirectly, most humans routinely, knowingly participate in unnecessary harm to nonhumans, including their torture, imprisonment, enslavement, and mass murder.

To speciesists, however, unjustified killing is murder only if the victim is human. In "animal agriculture" and numerous other forms of institutionalized speciesism, nonhuman animals literally are slaves: they're held in servitude as property. But few people speak of nonhuman "enslavement." Many who readily condemn human victimization as "heinous" or "evil" consider moralistic language sensational or overly emotional when applied to atrocities against nonhumans. They prefer to couch nonhuman exploitation and murder in culinary, recreational, or other nonmoralistic terms. That way they avoid acknowledging immorality. Among others, Nazi vivisectors used the quantitative language of experimentation for human, as well as nonhuman, vivisection. Slaveholders have used the economic language of "animal agriculture" for nonhuman *and* human enslavement. Why is such morally detached language considered offensive and grotesque only with regard to the human victims? Cruelty, injustice, and other moral issues call for moralistic language whatever the victim's species.

In the end, the notion of nonhuman inferiority is not only false but morally irrelevant, an illogical excuse for abuse. Although human persecution based on gender, race, or some other biological characteristic commonly entails much talk of inferiority and superiority, few people would welcome laws that protected humans in proportion to their abilities or contributions. In a democracy the law protects all human animals whatever their degree of intelligence, sensitivity, or altruism. A democratic society deprives humans of freedom or life only if they're believed to have knowingly wronged others. Among humans, justice is based on innocence and guilt, and a person is presumed innocent unless compelling evidence indicates otherwise. Why doesn't the same principle apply across species? Why don't nonhuman animals—who are innocent—enjoy a legal right to freedom and life? Speciesism rests on a double standard.

Most humans consider other animals less important, and their language reflects this bias. With rare exception, traditional usage places male before female: "his and her," "boys and girls," "men and women." Similarly, standard word order announces that humans come first: "Jill and her dog Pete," "humans and animals," "neither man nor beast."

As reported by *The Sun* (London),

> A terrified 19-stone husband was forced to lie next to his wife as two men raped her yesterday.[3]

Largely through syntax, the sentence attaches importance only to men. Instead of the raped woman, her spouse gets first mention, subject position, and the description "terrified." Relegated to "his wife," the primary victim is buried midsentence inside a prepositional phrase ("next to his wife") and dependent clause ("as two men raped her yesterday"). Dismembered while fully conscious, a lobster received equally dismissive treatment from the Associated Press:

> Katie Couric looked away as [the chef] pulled off the lobster's claws, chopped off its tail, removed its innards, sliced the upper body in half and threw the pieces into a hot frying pan with olive oil and garlic.[4]

The lobster suffered a violent death. Couric merely was present. Yet Couric is the sentence's subject, mentioned first. Hidden midsentence inside a dependent clause ("as [the chef] pulled . . ."), the lobster is alluded to only indirectly, in reference to her body parts ("the lobster's claws, . . . tail, . . . innards"). Accorded the final word, garlic gets more emphasis. Such human-centered syntax is the norm.

The media rarely acknowledge nonhuman suffering. Only human misfortune garners strong words like *tragic* and *terrible*. When thousands of cattle, left in the blazing sun on parched land, die from heat and lack of water, reporters note the losses "suffered" by their enslavers.

Belittling words minimize nonhuman suffering and death. As expressed in a *New York* magazine caption, antivivisectionists "oppose testing on *any* creature—even a mouse."[5] The word *even* ranks a mouse below humans in sensitivity and importance. There's no reason to believe that mice experience deprivation and pain less sharply than we do or value their lives less. But our language removes them from moral consideration. Who cares if millions of mice and rats are vivisected each year? They're "only rodents." What does it matter if billions of chickens live in misery until they die in pain and fear? They're "just chickens."

With punning and other wordplay, the press makes light of nonhuman suffering and death. A *Washington Post* writer who intentionally drove over a squirrel recounted the murder under the headlines "A Haunting Tail" and "Fur Whom the Bell Tolls." "The Buck Stops Here" and "The Story of BAM-bi," the paper jeered after a white-tailed buck fatally collided with a car. When a tractor-trailer en route to a slaughterhouse hit a guardrail, the impact hurled thousands of chickens from a ramp to a parking lot 50 feet (15 m) below. Those not killed outright lay there in severe cold, many with broken bones. Portland's *Oregonian* ran this headline: "How Did the Chickens Cross the Road? Well-Scrambled." Who would mock human suffering and death in such ways?[6]

Individuals or Things?

Each sentient being is physically and mentally unique, but speciesist language negates nonhuman individuality. The term *specimen* turns a unique individual into a generic species representative. If their species faces extinction, nonhuman individuals are called "endangered" even if they're personally safe. Just as racists have spoken of blacks as "the Negro" and Jews as "the Jew," people speak of all members of a nonhuman group as if they were a single animal, implying that they're all the same: they refer to cheetahs as "the cheetah" and bees as "the bee." Popular usage merges nonhuman individuals into a single substance: "amount of turkeys," "how much deer." Common expressions—*head of cattle*, *pieces of game*—reduce living nonhumans to parts.

Belying victimization, the language of speciesist exploitation renders nonhuman animals mindless and lifeless. They're metaphorical "crops" and "machines." Like plants, they're "watered" rather than given water. While alive, they're already "trophies" or "meat." In vivisection and "animal agriculture" they literally become "tools" and "stock." A *New York Times* writer syntactically equates dogs and cats with vegetation and machines: "A typical home has a dog, a cat, a green lawn and two cars."[7]

Convention teaches us to classify nonhuman beings with inanimate things. According to standard pronoun use, a nonhuman individual is "something," not someone. "A noun is a person, place, or thing," we recite as children, excluding nonhumans from "person."

Style manuals advise putting quotation marks around nonhuman animals' personal names. Why? Because nonhumans are given their names? So are we. Because nonhumans don't recognize their names? Many do. As much as the human name Barbara Bush, the canine name Millie Bush identifies a unique individual. Quotation marks around their personal names discourage us from seeing nonhumans as persons.

In both everyday speech and the law, "persons" and "individuals" don't include nonhuman individuals; "animals" don't include human animals. And "animals" have no legal rights. The Tenth Commandment enjoins against coveting a "neighbor's" house, "wife," manservant, "maidservant," ox, ass—any "thing" that is "his." The message: women, male servants, nonhuman animals, and inanimate things belong to men (who alone qualify as neighbors). Speciesist language continues to categorize "animals" as human property.

In the same way that a sexist man might say "my woman" (nonrelational noun) instead of "my spouse" (relational), people say "my dog" instead of "my dog companion" or "my dog friend," as if they owned a dog's very being. (The "master" or "mistress" demands obedience.) Formerly, owners of enslaved blacks spoke of "our Negroes." Today vivisectors, food-industry enslavers, and others who exploit and kill nonhumans speak of "our animals." Pressed to substitute a relational noun and acknowledge their stance toward nonhuman animals, what could they say? "Our victims."

Self-Justification

Victimizers seek justification. Claims that vivisectors "create" and "engineer" nonhuman animals rob nonhumans of autonomy and legitimize their exploitation and murder.

Labels born of exploitation indicate that nonhuman people exist for our use. *Furbearer* tags a nonhuman person a potential pelt. *Circus animal* suggests some natural category containing hoop-jumping tigers and dancing bears, nonhumans of a "circus" type. The verbal trick makes deprivation and coercion disappear. *Companion animal* reduces a dog, cat, or other nonhuman to the role of companion. Minus that role, the term implies, such an animal has no place; if they aren't some human's companion, or their companionship fails to please, they can be abandoned or killed.[8]

Tacitly, terms like *overhunting* and *overfishing* endorse less-rampant hunting and fishing. They normalize and naturalize the murder of nonhuman beings. The nonspeciesist word for hunting or fishing that decimates a population is *genocide*.

Evil gathers euphemisms: *the Final Solution*, *ethnic cleansing*. Over millennia, speciesism has compiled a hefty volume. *Wildlife management* legitimizes the bureaucratized killing of free-living nonhumans ("wild animals" must be "controlled"). *Leather* and *pork* serve as comfortable code for skin and flesh. *Domestication* softens captivity, subjugation, and forced breeding.

Positive words glamorize humans' ruthless genetic manipulation of other species. Horses inbred for racing are "thoroughbreds." Severely crippled and susceptible to heart failure, the fastest-growing, most top-heavy chickens are "improved." However afflicted with disabilities, dogs inbred for human pleasure and use are "purebreds," while the fittest mixed-breed dogs are "mongrels" and "mutts."

Semantic reversal pervades speciesist exploitation and killing. Each year, U.S. "shelters" kill millions of healthy cats, dogs, and other nonhumans; we call the murder "euthanasia." Officially approved murder of free-living nonhumans poses as "conservation." Designating a particular season for the killing, or specifying how many animals a hunter or fisher may legally kill, constitutes "protection."

False claims of necessity preserve the speciesist habits that cause so much harm. Whereas veganism (true vegetarianism) promotes human health and longevity, consumption of animal-derived food correlates with life-threatening conditions such as heart disease, cancer, and hardening of the arteries. Still, the lie persists that humans must eat products from nonhuman bodies. As if we possessed a lion's or shark's physiology, thoughtless cliché places us "at the top of the food chain." Educating people about disease prevention, increasing their access to medical treatment, and conducting benign human-based research remain the most cost-effective ways of improving public health, but proponents call vivisection a "necessary evil." Apologists for black slavery in America used the same phrase.

Complimentary self-description exonerates humans of wrongdoing. Food-industry enslavement and slaughter cause suffering and death of colossal magnitude. A major cause of worldwide deforestation and the primary source of U.S. water pollution, "animal agriculture" also entails environmental devastation. Growing plants for human food requires far less land and energy. Yet, consumers of flesh, eggs, and nonhuman milk count themselves among "animal lovers" and "environmentalists." Cattle enslavers, vivisectors, and others who directly abuse nonhuman animals masquerade as "animal welfarists."

In speciesism's fictitious world, nonhumans willingly participate in their own victimization. They "give" their lives in vivisection, hunting, and the food industry. Cocks "like" to fight to the death, their "handlers" allege. Then, why are fatal confrontations between cocks rare in nature? Why do cockfighters condition cocks to be aggressive, incite them with stimulants, repeatedly thrust the "opponents" toward each other, and force cocks to keep fighting when they attempt to flee? Cocks don't gladly suffer slashed muscles, broken bones, punctured lungs, and gouged eyes. Cocks don't want to die.

Blaming the victim provides another way of evading guilt. Rats find sustenance in our discarded food and take shelter in our debris. When our accumulated garbage attracts too noticeable a number, they're condemned for "infesting" the area. Although sanitation remains the most effective means of reducing rat reproduction, "pest control" employs cruelty. Poisons cause rats to die, over days, from internal bleeding. Spring traps break their backs. Glue traps grip them by their limbs; they escape maimed, suffocate, or starve. The justification for this treatment? Rats are "vermin."

The way we speak about other animals is inseparable from the way we treat them. Although nonhuman people don't perceive the disparagement and threat in speciesist words, those words legitimize abuse. By discounting nonhuman sentience, individuality, and worth, speciesist language sanctions cruelty and murder.

Patriarchal men have tried to silence women. Racist whites have tried to silence blacks. But humans *will* speak. Speciesists have an easier task. Their victims cannot, through their own voices, alter oppressive language. Humans have a verbal monopoly. And our language inscribes our prejudices. Speciesism pervades human communication, from scholarly jargon to street slang. Whereas racial slurs rightly elicit censure, people regularly use, and fail to notice, speciesist language. Unlike sexist language—which many book publishers, professional organizations, and government agencies now proscribe—speciesist language remains socially acceptable even to people who consider themselves politically progressive. Unable to gainsay speciesism's lies, other animals suffer from human abuse of linguistic power. Considered in relation to the plight of nonhuman beings, Adrienne Rich's feminist words express a terrible absolute: "This is the oppressor's language."

Because the lies that sustain speciesism desensitize people to violence and injustice, those lies harm human as well as nonhuman animals. Language that encourages a callous, exploitive view of nonhuman beings jeopardizes us all. Bigotry of any form corrupts a society's character and impairs its judgment. Nonhuman-animal epithets like *insect* and *snake* breed contempt for nonhumans *and* humans. Applied to members of politically vulnerable human groups, such as religious and ethnic minorities, "animal" epithets abet human oppression and genocide.

All sentient beings deserve equal moral consideration. *Animal equality* is a synonym for justice. Because animal equality threatens longstanding habits and beliefs, efforts to eliminate speciesist language will be ridiculed and decried. Apart from inevitable resistance to change, achieving nonspeciesist language will be difficult. Initial attempts will involve much rethinking and rewording. But nonhuman emancipation urgently requires new language. At long last, we must speak truthfully of our nonhuman kin. Lies have denied them liberty and life. Honest words will grant them the freedom and respect that are rightfully theirs.

2

False Categories

How We Define "Us" and "Them"

> *Man*, n. An animal so lost in rapturous contemplation of what he thinks he is as to overlook what he indubitably ought to be. His chief occupation is extermination of other animals and his own species, which, however, multiplies with such insistent rapidity as to infest the whole habitable earth and Canada.
>
> —Ambrose Bierce

Dictionaries provide conflicting definitions of *animal*: "a multicellular organism of the kingdom Animalia" and "an animal organism other than a human being."[1] The second definition is political. Segregating humans from all other species legitimizes a human monopoly on moral and legal rights. When we say "animals and humans," we deny that we too are animals. The verbal ruse preserves the speciesist fantasy that chimpanzees, snails, and tree frogs are more alike than chimpanzees and humans.

Like *animal*, the words *primate* and *ape* commonly refer only to nonhumans. Biologists now classify gibbons, orangutans, gorillas, bonobos, chimpanzees, *and humans* as apes. Nonhuman apes are more closely related to humans than to monkeys. If nonhuman apes and monkeys are primates, so are we. African nonhuman apes (gorillas, bonobos, and chimpanzees) share a more recent common ancestor with humans than with Asian nonhuman apes (gibbons and orangutans). Also, both bonobos and chimpanzees share more of their genes with humans (about 98.4 percent) than with gorillas (97.7 percent) or orangutans (96.4 percent). We belong in the same genus (*Homo* or *Pan*) as bonobos and chimpanzees.

"Lower" Animals

When humans admit to being animals, they label other animals "lower" or "subhuman." Two *Washington Post* writers scoff at people who would save "minks, research rats and other subhuman organisms."[2] Both *subhuman* and *organisms* reduce nonhuman animals to beings too lowly to warrant concern. Humans too are organisms. Why are we exempt from the term?

Our species occupies one of countless branches on the evolutionary bush. Life hasn't evolved along a single stalk, with nonhumans mired at its roots and humans blossoming at its tip. Nor is species something stable and fixed. The human species, like all others, continues to undergo variation. A cockroach or flamingo embodies as long a period of evolution as a human: since the beginning of life on Earth.

Humans and nonhumans share now-extinct ancestors. No living group of nonhuman animals—no extant species of invertebrate, fish, amphibian, reptile, mammal, or bird—is ancestral to humans. Long extinct, a jawless fish with bony armor spawned all vertebrates. Like us, modern fishes radically differ from this common ancestor. Roughly 375 million years ago, the evolution of humans began to follow a course separate from that of any fish alive today. The most recent ancestor shared by humans and amphibians lived some 350 million years ago. No frog, toad, or salamander ever was our forebear. The ancestral path to modern reptiles and mammals split about 280 million years ago. Although we have reptilian ancestors, we didn't descend from reptiles of any extant species. The first lizards, snakes, crocodiles, and turtles appeared after the first mammals. No bird ever was our ancestor. Birds and mammals evolved from different groups of reptiles. Mammals first appeared about 200 million years ago, 50 million years *before* birds. Today's nonhuman apes don't represent earlier stages in human development. Our common ape-like ancestor lived some 15 million years ago. About 6 million years ago, human and chimpanzee evolution parted. Chimpanzees didn't prepare the way to humans any more than we prepared the way to them.

Species don't evolve toward greater humanness but toward greater adaptiveness in their ecological niche. With supreme arrogance, humans call the biological traits that they possess "advanced" and those that they lack "primitive." The first fishes possessed skeletons of bone, but sharks, skates, and rays have skeletons of cartilage, unjustifiably termed "degenerate." If evolution tends toward humanness, why did cartilaginous fishes arise from our shared bony ancestors? Why did birds come to exist after mammals?

The notion of higher and lower beings lacks scientific validity. In an 1858 letter, Charles Darwin expressed his intention "carefully to avoid" referring to some animals as "higher" than others. Elsewhere he pencilled this reminder to himself: "Never use the words higher and lower." As stated by neuroscientists Euan Macphail and William Hodos, ranking species in some linear order that suggests evolutionary progress makes "no sense" and has "no scientific status." Hodos recommends replacing *subhuman* with *nonhuman*.[3]

Even the word *nonhuman* divides all animals into two, seemingly opposed categories: humans and everyone else. With equal validity we could categorize all animals as giant squids and non-giant-squids. Still, *nonhuman animal* avoids labeling other animals inferior and emphasizes that humans too are animals. Also, for now we must speak in terms of humans and all other animals because all other animals lack legal rights.

Supposedly Superior "Man"

Among species names, sexist pseudogeneric *man* stands alone. Whereas other species' names appear as plurals ("palm cockatoos") or follow *the* ("the palm cockatoo"), *man* does not. Frequent capitalization literally elevates Man above other animals. Functioning like a proper name, *Man* personifies our species as an adult male.

Through its male imagery, *mankind* too excludes women from humankind. The sexism of pseudogeneric *man* and *mankind* works by way of speciesism. Their power to lower women's status rests on the premise that those outside our species don't merit equal consideration and respect. Patriarchal men linguistically appropriated humanness because it represented superiority and privilege to their speciesist minds.

Definitions of *man* assert human superiority. Falsely they define humans as the sole possessors of powerful brains, speech, and abstract thought.

"A highly developed brain"

Our species is "distinguished by a highly developed brain," the *American Heritage Dictionary* claims under the term *man*. In reality, "a highly developed brain" means little more than "our kind of brain."

Humans pride themselves on possessing a large brain. On average the Neanderthal's was larger. Elephants and many cetaceans have bigger, heavier brains than ours, with more nerve cells. For their body weight, many small birds and mammals—such as canaries, house sparrows, and pygmy tree shrews—have heavier brains than humans. Further, the brains of many small vertebrates show greater neural density and interconnectedness. "Larger brains are not necessarily more efficient and more powerful than smaller brains," Harvard University neuroanatomist Terrence Deacon notes.[4]

Humans boast that their brain contains many anatomically and functionally distinct areas. However, differentiation generally increases with brain size. A smaller brain, Deacon explains, doesn't require as many distinct areas to process information with equal ease and speed. Human perception of an integrated visual image involves numerous brain areas specialized for detection of shape, brightness, movement, and other visual properties. A squirrel's brain registers and coordinates visual properties in only a few areas. Structural complexity doesn't automatically signify brain "advancement," Deacon cautions.[5]

In any case, some brain regions are organizationally *simpler* in humans than in other animals. As neuroanatomists note, the pretectum (involved in visuomotor behavior) is more "differentiated" and "elaborated" in birds, reptiles, and fishes than in humans. Many fishes generate electric fields with which they detect objects and signal; their cerebellum is "far more complex" than ours. Numerous nonhuman animals possess brain structures that humans entirely lack.[6]

Even so, humans and all other vertebrates so far studied possess the same basic cerebral circuitry, with nerve-cell populations that correspond in their chemistry, connections, and apparent functions. Popularly regarded as lowly creatures, sharks exhibit cerebral "organization comparable to that of other vertebrates, including mammals."[7]

Most humans assume that invertebrate brains are inferior to those of vertebrates. Individual nerve cells tend to be "more complex" in *invertebrate* brains. Typically, vertebrate nerve cells project only a single axon whereas invertebrate ones branch out with several axons, each capable of independent action. Also, invertebrates of numerous species possess a brain with many specialized regions. As a neurobiologist has remarked, the brains of insects, spiders, crustaceans, and other arthropods show "a high order of organizational complexity."[8]

Standard definitions of *man* transmit speciesist propaganda. All vertebrates and many invertebrates have "a highly developed brain." In differing ways, all brains manifest life's long history.

"Organized speech"

According to the *American Heritage Dictionary*, "the ability to communicate by means of organized speech" further distinguishes "man" from other species. The definition of *man* again exaggerates human uniqueness.

Since 1977 psychologist Irene Pepperberg has studied the human-language ability of an African gray parrot, Alex, who lives in her university laboratory. In English, Alex requests various foods and toys; solicits information; identifies more than a hundred objects by name, shape, material, number, color, and size; and expresses such emotions as frustration, regret, and love.[9] Alex learned the word *gray* when, viewing his reflection, he asked the color of his feathers. "Wanna go gym," he announces whenever he wishes to visit his play area of ropes and wooden rods. Asked if he'd like to return to his cage, he answers "Yeah" or "No."[10] "I want popcorn," he requests. "You tickle me?"[11] Some years ago Alex needed surgery, so Pepperberg brought him to a veterinarian. Unfamiliar with his surroundings, Alex called out when Pepperberg started to leave: "Come here. I love you." "I'm sorry," he pleaded. "Wanna go back."[12] Parrots don't just "parrot."

The chimpanzee Lana can "talk" by pressing keys that display geometric symbols representing particular words. Lana has produced sentences like "Please, machine, give piece of apple." Desiring an orange but knowing no word for this fruit, Lana improvised with "the apple which is orange."[13] Selecting among dozens of word symbols, the gorilla Koko can "speak" via a keyboard linked to a voice synthesizer.[14] The bonobo Kanzi taps out messages from hundreds of symbols for nouns and verbs.[15]

Chimpanzees, orangutans, and gorillas have learned American Sign Language (ASL), whose signs they combine and alter in innovative ways. Lucy, a chimpanzee, creatively described watermelon as "drink fruit." Chantek, an orangutan, termed contact-lens solution "eye drink." Koko called a Pinocchio doll "elephant baby," a ring "finger bracelet," and a cigarette lighter "bottle match."[16]

Taught "dirty" as the sign for urine or feces, nonhuman apes have extended its application to naughty behavior—demonstrating an ability to "speak" metaphorically. The chimpanzee Washoe so completely absorbed human-taught ASL that she spontaneously instructed her adopted son, Loulis, in that language.[17] Once, Loulis playfully swiped a magazine from Washoe and ran off with it. "Dirty, dirty," Washoe signed to herself.[18]

In ASL, nonhuman apes fib and joke. After Koko damaged a kitchen sink by sitting on it, her companion Francine Patterson asked, "What happened here?" "Kate there bad," Koko lied, blaming one of her teachers. Another time, Koko signed that a white towel was red. "You know better," a human friend reproved her. "What color is it?" "Red, red, red," Koko insisted, making the gesture larger and larger. Grinning, she then removed a speck of red lint from the towel and held it before her friend's eyes. "Red," she signed triumphantly.[19]

"When do gorillas die?" a human friend once asked Koko in ASL. "Trouble, old," she answered. "How do gorillas feel when they die? Happy? Sad? Afraid?" her friend continued. Koko replied, "Sleep." When a beloved kitten whom Koko had named All Ball was killed by a car, Koko sobbed. Asked about All Ball three days later, she gestured "Cry" and "Sleep cat." More than five years later, seeing a photo of All Ball, Koko signed, "That bad. Frown. Sorry." Nonhuman apes don't just "ape."[20]

Nonhuman primates appear to possess all the basic neural circuits required for "organized speech," but the position and shape of their larynx, tongue, palate, and jaw preclude production of many human speech sounds. Poignantly, Kanzi often seems to be trying to speak. Looking at a human, he makes short, high-pitched sounds. If the human speaks in response, he squeaks more and more, becoming increasingly frustrated.[21]

Mark Twain called *dumb beast* a "lying phrase." A hen calls her chicks to come eat a worm and warns them of a hawk, he noted. "A hen *has* speech." Unlike chickens, however, humans are poorly equipped to comprehend that speech. "It is just like man's vanity and impertinence to call an animal dumb because it is dumb to his dull perceptions," Twain observed.[22]

Many nonhuman animals—among them, chickens, robins, and eastern chipmunks—give different alarm calls depending on whether a predator is approaching by ground or air. Through barks, coughs, and other distinct calls, vervet monkeys specify an eagle, leopard, snake, baboon, jackal or hyena, unfamiliar (potentially dangerous) human, or human known to be harmless. Each call elicits appropriate action. After "eagle" the monkeys hide in bushes; after "leopard" they climb a tree.[23] Gunnison's prairie dogs vocalize in ways that identify other animals by group membership—for example, as a human, dog, coyote, or hawk—but also as individuals.[24]

Humans are just beginning to detect and decipher much nonhuman "speech." Small rodents such as rats, mice, hamsters, and gerbils communicate in ultrasound, too high-frequency for us to hear without technology's assistance. Larger nonhuman animals like alligators, hippos, elephants, and fin whales vocalize in infrasound, too low-frequency for our unaided ears. Infrasound carries miles over land and thousands of miles through ocean. Although they lack vocal cords, fishes of at least hundreds of species "talk." In ways that include vibrating their air bladder, grinding their teeth, and rubbing bony parts of their body together, they produce sounds ranging from buzzes and clicks to yelps and sobs. But humans can hear most such sounds only through hydrophones. Also, we have difficulty perceiving the units of nonhuman speech. Vervet-monkey grunts that sound the same to humans convey different meanings to vervets. Avian vocalizations too rapid or close in pitch for humans to distinguish are easily discriminated by birds.

Despite dictionary claims, the "capacity for articulate speech" isn't unique to humans.[25] Like many other birds, Alex can speak another species' words. Many humans can't speak at all. No human has mastered a language of another species as Washoe, Koko, and Kanzi have. Who, then, are the truly amazing communicators?

"Abstract reasoning"

According to dictionary definitions of *man*, a "capacity for abstract reasoning" also distinguishes humans from other animals.[26] Many nonhumans form abstract concepts.

In addition to grasping the concept of a symbol, nonhumans taught human languages conceptualize word classes and their relationships. Given a noun–verb instruction like "Cone toss," a California sea lion named Rocky takes appropriate action. Given an adjective–verb instruction like "Gray toss," she takes no action. Rocky recognizes adjective–verb combinations as nonsense (we can't toss a gray). Like Rocky, the bottlenose dolphins Phoenix and Ake comprehend complicated instructions communicated in symbolic hand and arm gestures that represent particular words and result in ever-new sentences. Demonstrating a concept of syntax, they understand that "Bottom Frisbee fetch surface hoop" means "Take the Frisbee at the bottom of the pool to the hoop at the surface" whereas "Surface hoop fetch bottom Frisbee" means "Take the hoop at the surface to the Frisbee at the bottom."[27]

Nonhuman animals also possess an abstract concept of number. Alex answers the question "How many?" for one to six objects, even when those objects form a subset within a mixed collection. Shown four pompoms and three keys and quizzed "How many key?" he responds, "Three."[28] The chimpanzee Sheba adds and subtracts. From cards marked "0" through "8" she selects the one that represents the number of objects in an array or the sum of two Arabic numerals.[29] In one test Sheba views one to four oranges, which then are covered with a box. One or more of the oranges are removed through a hole, displayed to her, and placed out of sight. Asked how many oranges remain in the box, Sheba chooses the correct numeral card.[30]

Rocky can identify the smaller or larger of two objects. What's more, if the smaller object is removed and the larger object is paired with one still larger, she recognizes that the originally larger object is now the smaller. Alex too possesses the abstract concept smaller/larger. Presented with two objects differing in color and size (say, a green bead and a red cup) and asked to name the color of the smaller or larger, Alex answers correctly. The first time he was asked "What color smaller?" about two objects of *equal* size, Alex retorted, "What's same?" When his teachers persisted ("First you tell us what color smaller"), he applied a concept learned in other contexts: he answered, "None."[31]

One evening Koko asked to go outside and her request was denied. The following day, asked if she wished to go out "later," she petulantly recalled, "Want[ed] yesterday." Whenever Koko is told she can go outside the "next" day, she gets ready at the appointed time (for example, by gathering her sweater and leash). Instructed "Before you say ear, say eye," she answers, "Eye, ear." Temporal concepts aren't limited to humans.[32]

Nonhumans also conceptualize same/different. Asked "What's same?" or "What's different?" about two objects (such as a blue paper triangle and blue paper square), Alex correctly answers "color," "mah-mah" (material), "shape," or "none."[33] Decades ago the chimpanzee Sarah learned to identify two objects as "same" or "different" using plastic words as symbols. She also applied a concept of equivalence to visual and functional relationships. By selecting the appropriate figure or object, Sarah completed analogies. Shown a small red triangle, a large red triangle, and a small green square, she chose a large green square. Shown a key, lock, and can opener, she chose a can.[34] Numerous nonhuman animals—including pigeons, coatis, bottlenose dolphins, chimpanzees, rhesus monkeys, and rats—have demonstrated that they can comprehend and communicate "same" and "different" without any training in a human symbolic system. Following presentation of a visual object, sound, or smell, they indicate (in a wordless way like pecking a key or pressing a bar) which stimulus in a set matches or differs. Whether confronted with new or familiar stimuli, they perform well because they've grasped the principle behind the task.

Different, but Equal, Beings

Even if every nonhuman lacked the capacity for human language and human-like reasoning, nonhumans wouldn't be inferior. Why equate so-called human characteristics with superiority? Because *we* possess them? In the same self-serving and otherwise arbitrary manner, an individual might pronounce, "I have great physical strength, so strength signifies superiority." Many humans can't produce "organized speech." Anyone who regards them as inferior fails to recognize the difference between an individual's abilities and the individual themselves. Inferior speaker doesn't mean inferior person. Someone who can't speak experiences the world differently (not more, not less) than someone who can.

Nonhumans shouldn't be required to act like humans. After being drilled on the ASL gestures for various parts of the body, Koko offered this reproach: "Think eye ear eye nose boring."[35] Alex too gets bored with testing. Irritated by repetitive questions, he often rebels. "I'm gonna go away," he announces, and he walks off.[36] Or he shouts "No!" and turns his back. Once, asked to name the green object among six objects on a tray, Alex named every object *except* the green one. Then he flipped the tray to the floor.[37] Koko and Alex aren't too "dumb" to always produce human language on demand. They're too smart.

Standard ways of categorizing and defining nonhuman and human animals falsify. As popularly used, *animal*, *primate*, and *ape* remove our species from animalkind. Hierarchical terms like *lower animals*, *subhuman*, and *degenerate trait* distort evolution, equating nonhuman with inferior. Dictionary definitions of *man* exaggerate human uniqueness and present characteristics typical of humans (such as verbal ability) as marks of superiority, especially superior intelligence.

Over decades, guided by the earth's magnetic fields, sea turtles experience vast stretches of ocean. Swimming through endlessly varied tropical color, fishes see forward, above, below, and behind. Alert to the faintest electrical pulse, sharks detect the heartbeats of smaller fishes hidden in sand. Soaring in rhythm with the rest of their flock, birds navigate over hemispheres; they sense the beating of waves against distant shores and hear the shape of mountains. Nonhuman animals have their own ways of knowing.

3

Animal Attributes

The Verbal Dichotomy

> If an animal does something we call it instinct; if we do the same thing for the same reason, we call it intelligence.
>
> —Will Cuppy

Kept hungry and individually confined to small, nearly barren laboratory tanks, three common octopuses—Albert, Bertram, and Charles—learned to pull a lever for food. With each pull, they lit a lamp suspended just above the water and received part of a sardine. Whereas Albert and Bertram virtually ignored the lamp, Charles often yanked it underwater. Floating in place, Albert and Bertram moved the lever gently. Latching onto the tank's side with several tentacles and grasping the lever with others, Charles "applied great force" until, after ten days of repeated bending, the lever broke.[1] Of the three octopuses, only Charles habitually waited, eyes just above the water's surface, for a human to approach and then squirted them with water.

Baffled by Charles' behavior, the experimenter reported, "The variables responsible for the maintenance and strengthening of the lamp-pulling and squirting behavior in this animal were not apparent."[2] This language suggests that external stimuli ("the variables responsible") cause octopus behavior independently of mind. The experimenter failed to consider octopus anger, frustration, or fear. The three octopuses experienced nearly identical environments, but Charles behaved in a singular way. The experimenter overlooked the most likely explanation: individual temperament. When the octopus report appeared in 1959, behaviorism dominated experimental psychology. Behaviorists take pains to report nonhuman behavior with minimal attribution of thought and feeling. Although waning, behaviorism has strongly influenced writing on nonhuman animals, especially science writing.

As expressed by a nature writer, octopuses show "signs of" fear and rage, "reactions that are perhaps easiest to describe as emotions, for lack of a better term."[3] If octopuses react *as if* they're feeling emotion, why shouldn't we suppose that they *are*? Behaviorists invoke Morgan's Canon, an 1894 dictum of comparative psychologist C. Lloyd Morgan: "In no case may we interpret an action as the outcome of the exercise of a higher psychical faculty, if it can be interpreted as the outcome of the exercise of one which stands lower in the psychological scale."[4] The dictum, however, doesn't enjoin against attributing *some* "psychical faculty." Also, how can we rank mental capacities? Is learning a string of associations "higher" or "lower" than feeling fear? In any case, why should the default interpretation be scant awareness? If we dispense with Morgan's Canon, we might overestimate some animals; but if we adhere to it, we'll surely underestimate many. It makes the most sense to consider all available information about any particular animal and interpret their behavior accordingly.

The journal article "Personalities of Octopuses" presents laboratory evidence of marked, lasting behavioral differences between individual red octopuses. Informed of this evidence, participants in a 1991 International Ethological Congress workshop nevertheless contended that researchers should restrict the word *personality* to humans.[5] Given the evidence, octopus personality almost certainly exists. A refusal to accept the most probable explanation for nonhuman behavior is political rather than scientific. Recognition of octopus personality would blur the speciesist line between "persons" and "animals."

In academic circles, anyone who violates Morgan's Canon risks the charge "Anthropomorphism!" Used accurately, *anthropomorphism* refers to the false attribution of uniquely human characteristics. It isn't anthropomorphic to believe that owls, iguanas, and orangutans have thoughts, feelings, and personalities. It *is* anthropomorphic to believe that they should wear shoes, would benefit from a college education, or must have human thoughts, feelings, and personalities or none at all.

Early in her career Jane Goodall encountered much criticism for attributing "motivation," "excitement," and "mood" to chimpanzees. "Even worse was my crime of suggesting that chimpanzees had 'personalities,'" she writes. "I was . . . guilty of that worst of ethological sins—anthropomorphism." Chimpanzees, she adds, "show many human characteristics."[6] That is, chimpanzees and humans show many of the same *animal* characteristics. Motivation, excitement, mood, and personality aren't exclusively human or primate.

However, human supremacists resist applying the same vocabulary to humans and nonhumans. Separate lexicons help maintain a false dichotomy that bolsters human conceit and soothes human conscience. The greater the apparent psychological distance between nonhuman and human animals, the more secure humans' assumption of species superiority and uniqueness. This assumption provides a rationale for exploitation.

"Animal Instinct" v. "Human Intelligence"

Whereas terms largely reserved for our species compliment and aggrandize, those assigned to other animals belittle and anathematize. While signifying other negative qualities, the adjectives *animal*, *bestial*, and *brute* denote unreasoning. Dictionaries and common parlance oppose "animal instinct" and "human intelligence." The polarization credits all humans, and no other animals, with the capacity to learn, reason, and plan. Limiting nonhuman behavior to instinctive response denies individuality as well as thought, because instincts are genetically inherited and shared by all members of a species or other biological group. In reality, both nonhuman and human behavior reflect a combination of instinct and intelligence.

While a family of North American beavers slept in their lodge, a man tore a large hole in their dam. Water escaped with such force that their pond soon would drain. When naturalists Hope Ryden and John Miller discovered the vandalism, Miller began piling rocks underwater at the breach to slow the outpouring. But his makeshift wall remained riddled with gaps. In *Lily Pond: Four Years with a Family of Beavers*, Ryden describes the beavers' response to the crisis.

Emerging from the family lodge at his usual time of early evening, the father beaver, whom Ryden had named the Inspector General, rapidly swam to the dam and observed its condition "with a wild eye."[7] Quickly he crossed the pond, felled a large shrub, dragged it into the water, towed it to the break, and wedged it into the top of the rock-pile wall. Only once he repeated this process, which failed to stanch the outflow. The Inspector General's next action amazed Ryden and Miller. By sight and sound the pond's water loss was obvious only at the surface, yet the Inspector General addressed underwater damage. He started to uproot lily plants (usually reserved for eating) and began using them to plug the dam's underwater leaks. Soon the young beavers Blossom, Buttercup, and Huckleberry emerged from the lodge and hurried to assist their father. Together the four worked to repair the dam with vegetation, mud, and sticks. Whenever dissatisfied with his offspring's placement of sticks, the Inspector General repositioned them for greater tightness and stability. The beavers labored throughout the night.

The next day while the beavers slept, Ryden, Miller, and other volunteers carried sticks to the dam. When the Inspector General emerged from the lodge at his usual time, he again did something extraordinary: he pulled a log from the lodge's roof and towed it to the dam. Clearly, he remembered the urgent need for building materials. With cries of joy, he discovered the pile of sticks left by human well-wishers and started putting them to use. Soon Blossom, Buttercup, Huckleberry, and a fourth sibling, Lotus, arrived, towing logs they too had removed from the lodge. Of those beavers able to help, only the mother, Lily, stayed behind, to care for newborn kits. In addition to making the dam leak-proof, the beavers added 6 inches (150 mm) to its height so that future rainfall would raise the pond's water level.

As Ryden remarks, the beavers' actions weren't merely "instinctive."[8] They demonstrated reasoning and foresight. In this incident the only unthinking individual was the man whose vandalism nearly destroyed the ecosystem on which the beavers and other nonhumans depended. All too characteristic of our species, his senseless violence contrasts with the beavers' rational, constructive behavior. Those who equate "human" with "intelligent" ignore the prevalence of human folly.

Ryden's language shows a tension between seeing the beavers as persons and categorizing them as supposedly lower animals. Ryden calls the beavers "individuals,"[9] gives them personal names, and refers to them as "who," "he," and "she." ("It," she notes, would equate them with inanimate things.)[10] But she also calls them "subhuman."[11] And the name Inspector General caricatures the father, reducing him to a single role.

Ryden believes in, argues for, and reveals beaver intelligence. At the same time, she uses overqualified language that casts doubt on that intelligence. In her view, the Inspector General showed foresight when he removed a log from the lodge. From that location he couldn't see, feel, or hear the dam's leakage, Ryden points out in answer to behaviorists: "This then was no automatic response—conditioned or inherent—to the presentation of visual, tactile, or auditory stimuli." Still, she hedges: "Some higher psychic function *seemed* to be involved" (emphasis added). Ryden expresses uncertainty even that the Inspector General remembered the emergency. "It would appear" that he remembered, she writes. In retelling the incident, I didn't equivocate: "Clearly, he remembered." That conclusion has compelling evidential support and explanatory power. Why undermine it with qualified language?[12]

Upon discovering the sticks left by Ryden and others, the Inspector General repeatedly cried out and "swirled" through them.[13] Observing this reaction, Miller commented, "I hesitate to say this, but that animal sounds like he's rejoicing."[14] Miller hesitated to voice even a noncommittal comparison ("sounds like"), the mere possibility that the Inspector General (depersonalized as "that animal") felt joy. My own language ("cries of joy") confidently communicates an interpretation supported by the context and the similarities between the Inspector General's behavior and that of joyful humans. In attributing joy, I indirectly attribute thought as well: the Inspector General felt joy because he realized that the sticks were a great boon.

Reluctance to attribute a particular mental state to a nonhuman person isn't always speciesist. When uncertain about human thoughts and feelings, we use qualifiers like *probably*, *appeared*, and *seemed*. However, if we qualify or withhold mental attribution that explains a nonhuman's behavior, fits the available evidence, and accords with our knowledge of biology (such as neurophysiology and evolution), the reason probably is speciesism, especially if we would make the attribution in the case of other animals, human or nonhuman, behaving similarly.

In *Raccoons Are the Brightest People* Sterling North shows the accuracy and ease with which nonhumans (unafflicted with Morgan's Canon) make cross-species mental attributions. Members of the same household, playmates, and close friends, the cocker spaniel Rusty and raccoon Snoopy demonstrated much mutual understanding. North recounts behavior repeatedly witnessed by their human companion Carl Marty:

> Rusty *wanted* to get into the house, but could not open the screen door. Carl was busy with other matters, *so* Rusty went to the woods and soon came back with Snoopy waddling behind him. Snoopy opened the door *for* his friend, and let the dog into the house. *His mission accomplished*, he turned and waddled back to the woods.[15] (emphases added)

The italicized language attributes intention, therefore intelligence, to Rusty and Snoopy. North writes of them as we write of humans, in a way that portrays their actions as purposeful. When we attribute a particular thought or emotion to a person (nonhuman or human), we may err. However, if we withhold mental attribution, we risk depicting animals as mindless, which is both misleading and harmful. Although lighthearted, North's description of raccoons as "the brightest people" reminds us that keenly perceptive people needn't be human.

Speciesists assume that nonhuman intelligence correlates with biological relatedness to humans. For this reason they may recognize intelligence in nonhuman mammals but not in birds. This is biological classism. Closely related species such as chimpanzees and humans do share more of their evolution (including the evolution of their mental traits) than distantly related species, but all animals are kin. Also, the same capacities often evolve independently along different ancestral lines. Less closely related to humans doesn't mean less intelligent, especially given that there are different ways of being intelligent.

Because Len Howard regularly fed the birds in her garden, a blue titmouse knew her as a friend. One day the titmouse flew into Howard's cottage. Crying out, she hovered in front of Howard while looking her in the eye. The titmouse's mate waited outside, watching "intently."[16] As soon as Howard left the cottage, the female titmouse stopped crying out. With Howard following, the two birds flew ahead, periodically pausing to look behind. The couple led Howard to their nest box. A cat or other animal had pulled out the nesting material, leaving twelve eggs exposed. Howard quickly restored the nest, and the female titmouse flew in to resume incubating her eggs, which later hatched into healthy chicks.

It was "obvious" that the female titmouse "was asking for my help," Howard writes. "What else except thought could have made her act thus?"[17] Howard's knowledge—of the context, this particular bird, and blue titmice more generally—warrants confidence in her interpretation. The titmouse acted contrary to instinct, which would prompt her to keep humans *away* from her nest, Howard notes. Having come to know and trust Howard, the titmouse surmised her human friend's ability and willingness to help. Birds not only think; they also infer what others are thinking.

A small body doesn't mean a small mind. Partly because of insects' size, small-minded humans reflexively ridicule any positing of insect intelligence.

After catching a fly nearly her own size, a wasp lightened her load by detaching her prey's abdomen and head. Grasping the remaining thorax, she attempted flight. A breeze caught the wings still attached to the fly's thorax and blew the wasp about. She landed, bit off the impediments, and flew away with the streamlined body part. Erasmus Darwin witnessed this behavior at the end of the eighteenth century. Foreshadowing his grandson Charles' theory of evolution, he noted mental continuity between biologically distant species. The wasp, he wrote, showed "reason . . . as it is exercised among men." Unable to take flight while holding a grasshopper's body several times her own size, another wasp (a yellow jacket) dragged the body about 30 feet (9 m) to a tree, carried it to the top, and leaped off into flight. Reporting this incident in 1878, the Academy of Natural Sciences of Philadelphia credited the wasp with "intelligence," "reasoning," and "judgment"; "There was more than instinct in this act." Finding caterpillar prey too heavy for takeoff, a third wasp split the body in two, flew off with one half, and soon returned for the rest. Writing in 1880, an eyewitness interpreted this behavior as "evidence of intelligence."[18]

Before Morgan's Canon and twentieth-century behaviorism, the scientific establishment more readily acknowledged wasp intelligence. Instinct can't account for the flexibility and variability of wasp behavior. Faced with different problems, three wasps found different, efficient solutions. Their behavior indicates insight and a capacity to learn from experience, such as the experience that it's easier to remain airborne after leaping from a height than it is to become airborne via liftoff. A stimulus–response explanation would be forced, requiring an elaborate, serendipitous combination of preprogrammed reactions. Problem-solving ability has survival value for wasps as well as humans.

Unreasonably, speciesists assume that animals whose form greatly differs from ours must be unreasoning. In their view, six or more limbs evince inferiority rather than marvelous coordination.

As with wasps, prejudice disallows that spiders think. When a storm destroyed her web's bottom connecting strands, a spider descended to the ground by a thread, crawled over to some wood fragments, chose one, brought it back to her web, and hung it from the bottom. With the wood as ballast, her web survived the storm. Good weather having returned, the spider mended her web and broke the thread holding the wood, letting the now-useless aid fall to the ground. In 1867 the author of *The Reasoning Power in Animals* recounted this behavior as evidence of spider "sagacity" and "ingenuity." In 1874 under the heading "Ingenuity in a Spider," *Nature* published an eyewitness report of similar behavior in another spider, who used a stone to secure her web.[19]

Science journals like *Nature* no longer print such reports, now dismissed as anecdotes. The word *anecdote* suggests an odd, singular occurrence, but the nonhuman behavior reported in an anecdote may be highly representative. Much devalued in the twentieth century, anecdotal evidence is inherently no less valid—in some ways, more valid—than experimental evidence.

Experimenters (especially laboratory researchers) manipulate nonhuman behavior, which they observe under artificial conditions at predetermined times. In general, they shy away from reporting behavior that appears anomalous or challenges the view of nonhuman cognition in which they've been schooled. Overlooking the behaving individual, experimenters commonly examine behavior at the micro level of action units or note a behavior's frequency within nonhuman groups. In the laboratory an invasive, exploitive stance interferes with empathy. Laboratory reports' technical, behavioristic language removes nonhumans from the natural and familiar and reduces them to objects.

Anecdotes relate nonhuman behavior that occurred within a more natural environment, in the course of a nonhuman's ongoing activities. They describe behavior as normally perceived in our daily lives: at the level of individuals. Anecdotes' narrative style and everyday vocabulary help us understand and empathize with nonhuman animals. Much as experimental findings can be replicated, the type of behavior reported in anecdotes can be corroborated by other accounts—if the anecdotes are published. The scientific establishment's rejection of anecdotes has assisted nonhuman oppression by privileging experimentation over sympathetic, nonexploitive observation of nonhuman animals.

To most humans with no vested interest in believing otherwise, numerous nonhumans clearly satisfy dictionary definitions of *intelligent*: able to "acquire and apply knowledge," having "the faculty of thought and reason," "showing sound judgment and rationality."[20] If no nonhuman animal can solve complex equations or write a treatise, neither can most humans. Some humans can't use numbers or words at all. Humans differ widely in their cognitive abilities, which overlap with nonhuman ones. Also, nonhumans possess cognitive abilities that humans lack. Intelligence is an animal trait characteristic of both nonhumans and humans. So is instinct. Linking intelligence only or primarily to humans, and instinct only or primarily to nonhumans, preserves a false dichotomy.

"Maternal Instinct" v. "Motherly Love"

Along with nonhuman intelligence, standard usage discounts nonhuman love, especially motherly love. Supposedly, nonhuman mothers merely display "maternal instinct." The word *instinct* implies rote behavior devoid of feeling.

When the gorilla Patty Cake was six months old, her arm was broken in an accident. So that the injury could be treated, Patty Cake was taken from the Central Park Zoo (Manhattan) and her mother, Lulu. Initially Lulu reacted with "frantic distress," daily observer

Susan Kohn Green reports.[21] Lulu barely ate. Despondency alternated with frenzy. With a blank stare, Lulu would sit motionless. Suddenly she would dash around the cage in an apparent search for her daughter. Then she would crumple again.

After three months Patty Cake was returned to the zoo. While Lulu was confined outdoors, Patty Cake was placed in an indoor cage separated from Lulu's by a mesh wall. Then Lulu was allowed inside. She raced over to the mesh, saw Patty Cake, and started to scream. Her eyes fixed on Patty Cake, Lulu ran back and forth along the wall, shrieking. Next she rushed toward a closed door keeping her from Patty Cake and stood there, impatiently shifting her weight from foot to foot. A zoo worker opened the door, and Lulu bounded toward her daughter. Patty Cake collapsed in terror. Lulu froze. Green describes Lulu's next actions:

> She took one deliberate step forward, stopped, then moved again, one step at a time. With unbelievable restraint she came to her child. Tenderly she squatted down beside her trembling baby. Slowly and tentatively she moved her hand above the infant's back. The baby screamed! Lulu withdrew her hand.[22]

After some time, Lulu gently kissed her daughter's head. Again Patty Cake screamed. Waiting for Patty Cake's fear to subside, Lulu repeatedly retreated and approached until, at last, she held her daughter close.

Instinct doesn't involve such hesitation and restraint. Lulu's feelings for Patty Cake proved stronger than impulse. In categorizing these feelings as "mother love," Green compellingly explains Lulu's behavior, so like a loving human mother's.[23] By presenting gorillas as persons throughout her narrative, Green also indicates less directly that they can love. Her book's title, *Gentle Gorilla: The Story of Patty Cake*, announces nonhuman biography. Her syntax animates Lulu and Patty Cake and implies their importance. In the above excerpt they occupy the subject position of every sentence and the most emphatic position (beginning or end) of every sentence but one. Some readers might consider Green's use of the word *child* anthropomorphic, but English lacks a species-specific term for gorilla young. Words like *kit* and *cub* apply to multiple species. Why shouldn't *child* extend beyond humans?

As acknowledged by the mentalistic language of a veterinarian writing in 1836, bovine mothers too love their offspring. Mooing "piteously," a cow ran up to a man walking across a field. Looking at him "earnestly," she started back the way she had come. When the man failed to follow, the cow repeated her actions, regarding him "anxiously." This time she led him to the field's far end. There, in a water-filled ditch, her calf was drowning. The man rescued the calf, and the mother gamboled with "joy." The cow didn't merely react instinctively to her calf, who was absent during her efforts to gain assistance. She showed "reasoning" and "affection."[24]

Today cow exploiters rarely speak of bovine emotion, even with tepid terms like *affection*. With the word *instinct* they minimize a cow's feelings for her calf. Remove a calf within 24 hours of birth to prevent "maternal instincts" from intensifying, a cow-milk industry textbook warns.[25] By definition, instincts don't strengthen over time; love does. When separated, both the cow and calf bawl in distress, the cow often for days. As long as they remain within sight or smell of each other, a cow frantically tries to reach her calf. Bred continually, cows suffer the anguish of birth and separation every year. No wonder their enslavers are more comfortable with *maternal instinct* than with *motherly love*.

"Mating" v. "Romantic Love"

The common expression *humans' animal nature* equates *animal* with the purely physical or base. Human rape of a nonhuman is called bestiality. Many humans readily engage in sex devoid of emotion or respect; still, we say that human animals make love whereas nonhuman ones mechanically "mate."

In *The Hidden Life of Dogs* Elizabeth Marshall Thomas tells of love between two huskies, Maria and Misha. When Misha first entered the house where Maria lived, they immediately leaped about in play, noticing no one but each other. A week later, "their faces gentle and smiling," they made love. From the beginning Maria and Misha ate together, went outside together, and slept so that their bodies touched. But Misha's stay was temporary; his owners lived in another state. After more than a year of intense closeness, Misha and Maria were separated. Futilely Maria tried to follow Misha out to the car. From a window seat, she watched as he was forced inside and driven away. For weeks Maria watched and waited at the window. Then, apparently realizing that Misha never would return, she became listless. She never regained her former exuberance. Pointing to Misha and Maria, Thomas rejects the claim that it's anthropomorphic to speak of canine "romantic love."[26]

For years the pugs Violet and Bingo lived in the same household as Maria. At age twelve Bingo was carried out to the car so that he could be brought to a veterinarian for surgery. Violet frantically tried to follow. Then she stationed herself under a table from which she could watch the door. That evening she refused to eat. That night, for the first time ever, she howled. When Bingo returned several days later, Violet yelped and leaped with joy. However, Bingo soon was taken away for another operation. Again Violet set up watch. This time Bingo died. Except to eat, drink, and relieve herself, Violet never again left her spot under the table. There she waited for Bingo, looking at the door and listening, until, in about a year, she too died. Thomas bravely refers to Bingo as Violet's "beloved."[27]

With quotation marks a review of Thomas's book disputed that dogs can be "in love."[28] Writer Roger Caras has criticized Thomas for speaking of "love" between dogs instead of a "bond."[29] The word *bond* doesn't do justice to dogs' intense feelings for their companions. Because dogs love as well as mate, other male canine companions failed to console Maria. Breeders and other dog exploiters may see dogs as replaceable, but Maria cherished Misha as an irreplaceable individual. The word *love* credits the uniqueness of canine individuals and their relationships. The *American Heritage Dictionary* defines romantic love as "a feeling of intense desire and attraction toward a person with whom one is disposed to make a pair." Until *person* includes nonhumans, that definition will falsely limit romantic love to humans.

When the elderly rats Trouble and Max first met, Trouble "kissed" Max all over his face. From then on, the couple spent much of their time snuggling. Soon Trouble suffered a stroke. "Agitated," Max groomed Trouble, who lay on her side. Trouble's ears and nose were pale, her eyes dim, her back legs paralyzed. In time Trouble regained the use of her back legs, but she remained uncoordinated and disoriented. Max would lead her about the cage as she held his tail. Then Trouble died. The night of her death, Max refused even the most appetizing food and appeared limp with despair. The next day, with a shudder and gasp, he died.[30]

Before telling the love story of Trouble and Max, their provider, Mary Macdonald, anticipates that some readers might consider her narrative anthropomorphic. She can convey the two rats' "seeming" feelings only by "translating their reactions into human emotions," she writes defensively. "I say in my anthropomorphic fashion that [Max] died of a broken heart," she remarks in closing. Apart from the words *loneliness*, *agitated*, and *disturbed*, Macdonald's narrative contains no unqualified language that attributes emotion to either rat: Max "seemed" more confident after meeting Trouble; he "seemed depressed" when she died. Feelings like loneliness and depression aren't uniquely human. The evidence supports attributing such feelings to rats. Why did Max stop eating immediately after Trouble's death and, having previously shown no sign of illness, soon die? The most plausible explanation is that grief caused, or at least precipitated, his death. Macdonald's language isn't anthropomorphic; it's unduly apologetic and qualified.

In *The Human Nature of Birds* psychologist Theodore Barber describes parakeet love at first sight. While the male parakeet Blue Bird was in another room, the female parakeet Blondie was placed in his cage. When Blue Bird flew back to his cage and saw Blondie, he burst into excited calls and aerial acrobatics. Landing on the cage again, he chirped to his new companion. The two soon became ardent lovers. Often they sat cuddling and twittering. Blue Bird, who spoke and understood numerous English words and phrases, would lavish Blondie with endearments. "Pretty Blondie, give me a kiss," he would say, after which they would rub their beaks together or open them and kiss with intertwined tongues.[31] Frequently Blue Bird sang to an enraptured Blondie or delighted her by flying in impressive zigzags. They made love face to face while Blue Bird embraced Blondie with one wing. After seven years with Blondie, Blue Bird died. Blondie turned lethargic and unsociable. When a parakeet named Lover joined the household, Blondie rejected his company. They never became lovers or friends.

Blondie and Blue Bird shared a deep, enduring, passionate love. Yet, as Barber notes, ornithology textbooks speak of avian lovemaking as mechanical: birds don't kiss and make love; they "engage in false feeding" and "rub their cloacas together."[32] Under the guise of science, such language distorts and conceals. Blondie wouldn't accept a "substitute" mate because, like Maria, she had loved a particular individual with a unique personality. Blue Bird and Blondie behaved so much like humans in love that we're justified in inferring comparable emotion. What Barber calls "the human nature of birds" is an animal nature that birds and humans share.

Instructed to capture some birds for a zoo, naturalist Loren Eiseley entered an abandoned cabin at night. Flashing on a lamp, he grabbed a female sparrow hawk. With a cry her mate bit and clawed Eiseley's hand, enabling her to escape. Eiseley captured the male and shut him in a small box. The next day Eiseley brought the box outside, opened it, and—moved to compassion—placed the hawk onto the grass. With invisible speed the hawk vanished into the bright sky.

> Straight out of the sun's eye, where she must have been soaring restlessly above us for untold hours, hurtled his mate. And from far up, ringing from peak to peak of the summits over us, came a cry of such unutterable and ecstatic joy that it sounds down across the years. . . .
>
> I saw them both now. He was rising fast to meet her. They met in a great soaring gyre that turned to a whirling circle and a dance of wings. Once more, just once, their two voices, joined in a harsh wild medley of question and response, struck and echoed against the pinnacles of the valley. Then they were gone forever somewhere into those upper regions beyond the eyes of men.[33]

The hawks' mutual devotion surprised Eiseley. Humans tend to think of nonhuman individuals (especially those they harm) as isolated objects rather than social beings. If two birds are life partners, not just mates, you harm both in harming one. Instead of depriving a single bird of happiness, you deprive two. Use of the phrase *avian love* would acknowledge the strength of emotional ties that humans casually sever.

Titled "The Bird and the Machine," Eiseley's 1959 essay juxtaposes the animate and inanimate. Before and after his narrative on the hawks, Eiseley notes society's growing enthusiasm for robotics and artificial intelligence. "I'll still stick with the birds," he writes. "It's life I believe in, not machines. Maybe you don't believe there is any difference." Conveying intense avian emotion, Eiseley's poetic prose highlights the difference: a "machine does not bleed, ache, hang for hours in the empty sky in a torment of hope to learn the fate of another machine, nor does it cry out with joy nor dance in the air with the fierce passion of a bird."[34]

Nonhuman animals experience. To the extent that it deadens living beings, behavioristic language falsifies. *The Times* (London) called Eiseley's book "true science" and "great literature."[35] In driving a wedge between the two, behaviorists lose both.

"Affiliative Behavior" v. "Friendship"

Because friendship goes so far beyond the physical, some speciesists deny its existence in nonhuman animals. Avoiding reference to nonhuman individuals and their feelings, behaviorists speak of nonhuman "affiliative behavior" rather than friendship. No less than humans, nonhumans who seek each other's company and well-being deserve the name friend.

The gorillas Caroline and Joanne had been caged together at the Central Park Zoo for more than 30 years, during which they had remained incompatible. Occasionally, snarling a warning or screaming in protest, they competed for space or food. Otherwise they ignored each other. Caroline had a very different relationship with Lulu, Patty Cake's mother, from whom she was permanently separated by a metal wall with small peepholes. Once, Caroline discovered a piece of straw, a precious find. After briefly toying with it, she passed it through a hole to Lulu. Peering through to watch Lulu play with the straw, Caroline hooted with delight. Another time, Caroline began to eat some hard rolls, a special treat she loved, and then realized that Lulu was near the wall. Caroline pulled off part of a roll and poked it through a hole. When Lulu took the offering, Caroline hooted excitedly. She tore off piece after piece and pushed it through the hole, until she had given Lulu all the remaining bread. Caroline and Lulu often sat at the front of their cages, on opposite sides of the wall, and held hands through the bars. Watching the gorillas day after day, Green had no doubt: "Lulu and Caroline were friends."[36]

Two male rats of different breeds were already adults when brought to a "shelter" as a pair. Aware that rats form deep attachments, I adopted both. Vegan, who was the older and larger, proved very protective of Nori, who was blind. Although their cage was 8 feet (2.4 m) long, they usually stayed side by side, snuggling. Once, my cat companion Chi peered inquisitively into their cage while only Nori was near the front. I saw Vegan, startled, rush forward. Pushing Nori behind him, Vegan positioned himself as a shield. His eyes glittering, he confronted Chi. Rebuffed, Chi left the room. When Vegan died two years later, Nori drastically changed, becoming listless and withdrawn. For the rest of his life, he visibly mourned.

I wrote "visibly mourned" rather than something more qualified like "appeared to mourn" because a rat's mourning *is* visible, in collapsed posture, dulled eyes, decreased activity, reduced appetite.... Over the years, 38 rats have been my companions, and I've read much about their species. My language reflects confidence in interpreting Vegan's and Nori's behavior.

Far from lauding rats as devoted friends, common usage denigrates them as selfish, vicious "rats." Rats don't betray one another; they care for orphaned young, those too old to fend for themselves, and other rats in need. Rat communities exemplify peaceful cooperation. Speaking of "rat friendship" would help to dispel a false and pernicious stereotype.

Like other kinds of love, friendship isn't limited to mammals. The dog Kim and magpie Orphée grew up together in the Roulet household. One day in 1992 Kim disappeared. For four days Orphée refused to eat. Then he too disappeared. The next morning, Orphée reappeared at the Roulets' open bedroom window. Unwilling to come inside, Orphée screeched until Mr. Roulet went outside to follow him. Orphée led Roulet 2 miles (3 km), into the woods. There, with a snare around his throat, Kim lay dying. In an effort to reach home, he had dragged himself some distance. Accompanied by Orphée, Roulet carried Kim home for nursing. Kim recovered and Orphée again thrived.

Highly social, magpies form strong, lasting relationships. Orphée stopped eating as soon as Kim disappeared, acted in an uncharacteristic way that prompted Roulet to follow him, went "straight to Kim," and resumed normal behavior when Kim recovered.[37] Friendship is the most plausible explanation.

As reported by zoologist Maurice Burton, two hens of different breeds walked, ate, dustbathed, sunbathed, and slept together. One, Aggie, was elderly and nearly blind. The other (unnamed) was younger and could fend for two. During the day the younger hen would guide Aggie around the garden and place food before her, clucking an invitation to eat. At night she would lead Aggie back to their roost. When Aggie died, the younger hen stopped eating, "was dejected," and rapidly deteriorated.[38] Within a week she, too, died.

Humans caricature chickens' interactions as negative and rigid "pecking orders." Our species' massive, needless violence toward chickens requires seeing them as unfeeling things, not individuals who can love and grieve. Whether or not she died from grief, the younger hen was Aggie's friend.

Affiliative behavior and other pseudoscientific terms that substitute for *nonhuman friendship* falsify. With such jargon, skeptics remain safely at the surface of nonhuman lives, whose depths they deny.

"Brutishness" v. "Human Refinement"

"*Brutish* stresses marked lack of human refinement," the *American Heritage Dictionary* notes. *Webster's* defines *brutish* as "relating to animals as opposed to man" and "utterly without sensitivity"; the dictionary's usage examples include "brutish aesthetic apathy." Only humans possess an aesthetic sensibility, many speciesists contend. In truth, animals other than humans prize and create beauty.

Observed by primatologist Geza Teleki, two male chimpanzees climbed opposite slopes of a hill. At the top, the chimpanzees spotted each other. Immediately both stood and hurried through the tall grass. Panting lightly and nodding, they greeted each other with an enthusiastic handshake. Then they sat down together and looked out over Lake Tanganyika, lit by a brilliant sunset. The chimpanzees remained there until dusk, contemplating the view. Never again "would I regard chimpanzees as 'mere animals,'" Teleki writes. "I had seen my species inside the skin of another."[39]

While Teleki conveys empathy, his wording is problematic insofar as it casts chimpanzees as honorary humans. To the extent that chimpanzees resemble *us*, it implies, they rise above "mere animals." Like Goodall's reference to chimpanzees' "human characteristics" and Barber's reference to birds' "human nature," such language equates sensitive with human.

Skeptics might dispute that the chimpanzees took pleasure in a sunset. Teleki, however, had a strong holistic impression, so strong that it changed his view of chimpanzees. Since then, years of further knowledge and experience have reinforced his conviction that the chimpanzees were enjoying natural beauty.

North tells of a free-living raccoon who loved classical music, especially by Beethoven and Bach. Neighbors of North frequently would play a recording of Beethoven's ninth symphony. "Almost always" the raccoon would arrive from the woods within minutes of the symphony's start, open a screen door, and sit in front of a speaker to listen. As soon as the music ended, he would depart. Before he witnessed this behavior, North was "somewhat skeptical," even though his raccoon companion Rascal also had shown "preferences" for particular musical pieces.[40] The strict correlation between the music and the visits of the woods-dwelling raccoon warrants an inference of aesthetic sensitivity. Unlike many humans, raccoons can appreciate art created by individuals outside their own species.

By watching their elders and practicing, male bowerbirds of Australia and New Guinea learn to construct elaborate bowers decorated to individual taste. Using a sapling stem as a center column, orange-crested gardener bowerbirds build a domed hut, open in front, from twigs that they tightly interweave. They cover the sapling column with dark green moss and adorn its front with objects carefully arranged in a three-part mosaic: on the left they might display beetle remains of iridescent blue; down the middle, yellow orchids; on the right, gleaming snail-shell fragments. In front of their hut they maintain a lawn of strewn flowers, keeping it free of windblown leaves and replacing flowers when they wilt. The lawn ends at a fence that they construct of plaited twigs and ornament with red and yellow fruit.

Naturalist Heinz Sielmann has observed one of the birds at work:

> Every time the bird returns from one of his collecting forays, he studies the over-all color effect. He seems to wonder how he could improve on it and at once sets out to do so. He picks up a flower in his beak, places it into the mosaic, and retreats to an optimum viewing distance. He behaves exactly like a painter critically reviewing his own canvas. He paints with flowers; that is the only way I can put it. A yellow orchid does not seem to him to be in the right place. He moves it slightly to the left and

> puts it between some blue flowers. With his head on one side he then contemplates the general effect once more, and seems satisfied.[41]

Because art is a product of individual creativity, the passage's focus on a particular bird (who is the subject of every sentence but one) helps to convey avian artistry, as do active, mentalistic verbs like *studies* and *contemplates*. Comparison to human artists ("like a painter," "He paints with flowers") further attributes conscious artistry. As translated here from German, the passage ends with tentative "seems satisfied." Sielmann's original concludes with more conviction: "is satisfied" (*ist zufrieden*).[42] Resemblances between bowerbird behavior and human artistry entitle Sielmann to attribute aesthetic judgment and satisfaction to the bird he observed. Like the art of individual humans, a bowerbird's art becomes more sophisticated and individualized over time and isn't restricted to particular materials; bowerbirds "paint" with flowers or fruit, on bower or fence. Avian art challenges the speciesist assumption that human lives are richest. Many birds are brilliant visual or musical artists.

Individual male European blackbirds compose multiple unique songs rich in rhythmic variation, melodic development, and other musical devices. Discarding some musical ideas and refining others, they painstakingly craft each song. A professional musician, Len Howard has noted a wide range of blackbird musical ability, including "imaginative genius." In the process of perfecting one of his melodies, an especially gifted blackbird named Fields inserted a semitone between two eighth notes, creating a triplet that Howard found "graceful and charming." After several days, Fields tried replacing the triplet with four sixteenth notes. He sang the new version several times. Then he returned to the triplets—an artistic decision with which Howard concurred.[43]

Like bowerbirds, blackbirds learn their art partly by following older birds' example. One evening Howard saw Fields, perched high in a tree, singing toward the setting sun. A younger male blackbird flew to the tree, perched within several yards of Fields, and gazed at him with a rapt expression. The younger bird edged closer. In exact imitation of Fields, he faced the sun and puffed out his feathers. Fields adjusted his posture; the younger bird did the same. For half an hour, Fields sang on. Sometimes he briefly glanced at his engrossed listener, whose eyes remained fixed on "the master musician." During the performance both birds remained nearly still, with looks of deep contentment.[44]

Able to appreciate Fields's virtuosic composing and singing, Howard uses "master musician" literally. Artistry epitomizes individuality. To recognize avian artistry, we must recognize avian individuality, as Howard does in her book, aptly titled *Birds as Individuals*.

Nonhuman persons like Fields not only possess unique minds; they create unique beauty. While rendering much of the world ugly and noisy—"brutish"—humans have claimed a monopoly on aesthetic sensitivity, which extends far beyond our species.

"Brutality" v. "Human Kindness"

Like aesthetic sensitivity, kindness allegedly finds no place among "brutes." Used as metaphors, *animal*, *beast*, and *brute* accuse humans of violent and depraved cruelty.

According to the *American Heritage Dictionary*, "brutal" traits such as "unfeeling cruelty" are "more characteristic of lower animals than of human beings." But the usage example cites human behavior: "brutal" bullbaiting and cockfighting.[45] The example reveals the ironic truth: humans are the brutes and nonhumans their victims. Overwhelmingly it's humans who needlessly hurt and kill. Nonhuman predators aren't cruel; they kill to survive. Sport hunters and fishers wound and kill for fun. Nonhuman predators don't unnecessarily prolong killing. From vivisectors to bullfighters, many humans routinely torture to death. Each day, flesh purveyors kill millions of birds, mammals, and fishes for profit. For mere convenience and taste, consumers eat the remains. Every moment, millions of nonhumans enslaved by humans live in cruel confinement. How many humans feel anger, sorrow, or pain for the caged hen, the whale confined to a tank, the elephant in chains? In "unfeeling cruelty," humans have no rivals.

Yet, the definition of *human* vaunts moral superiority: "having or showing those positive aspects of nature and character that distinguish human beings from the lower animals: *an act of human kind-*

ness."[46] *Humane* means kind; *inhuman* and *inhumane* mean cruel. Many nonhuman animals are more "humane" than most humans.

The free-living raccoon Blacky was accustomed to accepting food from naturalist Virginia Holmgren. One day Holmgren saw Blacky lead another raccoon to her house, a starving stranger she soon would name Boy. Holmgren hurried outside with bread, but Boy hid in the bushes. Directing a "reassuring" glance at Boy, Blacky came forward. He took one nibble (enough to display trust) and turned to Boy "with a look that said more plainly than words, *See, this is a friend. Come, eat.*" Boy ventured a step closer. Holmgren tossed him some bread and went inside to watch. While Blacky stayed beside him, Boy devoured the bread. After drinking from a bowl of water, the two raccoons left together. Boy became a regular visitor.[47]

Does Holmgren anthropomorphize Blacky when she puts words into his mouth? Humans successfully read the body language of other animals (human and nonhuman) all the time. An experienced and sensitive observer, Holmgren possesses detailed knowledge of raccoons in general and Blacky in particular. Most likely she has translated his gestures and expressions accurately. Before Boy's appearance the only raccoons who regularly visited Holmgren were Blacky, his mates, and their offspring. Blacky welcomed a needy adult male into his thriving family group and shared food with him. Holmgren reasonably interprets this behavior as benevolence.

In a desert area of southern Africa during intense heat, a springbok (a small gazelle) guided a wildebeest. The wildebeest's face was severely swollen, probably from a snakebite. She couldn't see or smell. Sometimes, lagging behind the springbok, the wildebeest would whimper. The springbok would pause, wait for the wildebeest to catch up, then gently nose her along. In this way the springbok led the wildebeest to a water hole. A human observer shot the wildebeest to end her suffering.

My narration of this incident contrasts with E. M. Menmuir's *African Wild Life* report from 1952, behaviorism's heyday:

> a low intermittent whimper was heard. . . . a solitary springbok was seen approaching, followed by a wildebeest. From the way the wildebeest moved its head continually from side to side they [human observers] concluded something was wrong. It was evi-

> dent that the springbok was guiding it, for whenever the wildebeest uttered its low sound the springbok would stand and wait for it to come up and then nose it in a reassuring manner. Finally the strange pair disappeared behind a dune. Later . . . the wildebeest and springbok were seen at a drinking hole. Then the springbok bounded away alone. Investigation proved that the wildebeest was blind.[48]

In my narrative, most sentences have the springbok or wildebeest as their subject; verbs such as *guided, would wait*, and *led* highlight the springbok's purposeful action; and the pronoun *she* endows the wildebeest with gender and personhood. (I chose a feminine rather than masculine pronoun arbitrarily, as explained in Chapter 10.) In Menmuir's account the springbok and wildebeest rarely are the subject; verbs such as *was heard, was seen*, and *concluded* emphasize human thought and perception; and *it* renders the wildebeest genderless and inanimate. In keeping with his highly human-centered writing style, Menmuir calls the shooter's action "merciful" but fails to credit the springbok with compassion, even though he can offer no other explanation for the springbok's "strange" behavior.

Most humans are even less willing to acknowledge compassion in birds than in nonhuman mammals. Missing one foot, a chaffinch hopped toward a garden spot where chaffinches and sparrows had gathered to eat crumbs. As the lame bird approached, the others drew aside and let him eat first. To Burton, "it looked as if they were standing back out of compassion." But fear may have motivated them instead, he speculates.[49] Given how easily a group of healthy birds could overpower a lame one, the fear explanation is farfetched.

Burton also witnessed starlings rapidly converge on a pile of food but refrain from eating until another starling, with an injured leg, hobbled over and ate her fill, after which the other birds "jostled to grab what they could." The group may have paused "by accident" rather than "design," Burton conjectures. The entire group? For precisely as long as it took the injured bird to finish eating? The evidence does "seem to indicate that even birds are capable of true altruism," Burton begrudgingly concedes. The word *even* signals a classist assumption that compassion is primarily mammalian.[50]

Blackie, a severely deformed Moor goldfish, could barely swim. Big Red, a larger Oranda goldfish, apparently sensed Blackie's helplessness. As soon as Blackie was added to Big Red's pet-store tank, Big Red started looking after him. Regularly, Big Red would gently take Blackie onto his back and swim him around the tank. The movement enabled Blackie to breathe. Whenever food was sprinkled overhead, Big Red would carry Blackie to the water's surface so that both could eat. In a newspaper interview, the pet-store owner reported that Big Red's assistance to Blackie already had lasted a year. To what did he attribute Big Red's behavior? "Compassion."[51]

Speciesists will scoff, but the evidence supports the pet-store owner's view. Intensely social, goldfishes commonly sicken or die when separated from a companion. Numerous observers, including first-time visitors to the pet store, were moved by Big Red's behavior, which struck them as compassionate. Whereas Big Red assisted Blackie, three other tankmates ignored his plight. The singularity of Big Red's deeds suggests more than some preprogrammed reaction. He chose to help.

When we deny that other animals show compassion, it's easier not to show it ourselves. The question is not whether nonhumans can be altruistic, but the extent to which humans can. Believing themselves morally superior to nonhuman animals, speciesists are particularly immoral; they selfishly seek to preserve massive injustice and abuse.

By humans' own definitions, nonhumans think; love their offspring, mates, and friends; appreciate beauty; and display compassion. But speciesist words assign all admirable traits to humans and all contemptible ones to nonhumans. In distancing ourselves from other animals, we distance ourselves from the truth.

Our language's false characterization of nonhuman animals as devoid of positive thought and emotion provides an excuse for depriving them of liberty, well-being, and life. The excuse is logically inconsistent given that the law protects all human animals, whatever their intellectual or emotional capacity. Because the lie of nonhuman inferiority doesn't suffice to justify our treatment of other animals, speciesist abuse requires additional lies. The language that propagates these lies ranges from the everyday and universal to the highly specialized. From sport hunting to "animal agriculture," each traditional form of speciesist abuse has developed its own dialect of deception.

4

Victims Mistaken for Game

The Language of Hunting

> Hast thou named all the birds without a gun?
>
> —Ralph Waldo Emerson

Shot geese were "everywhere." They flew with dangling legs. Their sides streamed blood. Their bellies showed wounds of widening red. They smashed into trees and crashed into the ground. They walked dragging broken wings or stumbled about, dazed. They lay crippled, dying, or dead. Most of the geese remained silent. Some called or screamed. Many of the shooters laughed. This slaughter, witnessed by a U.S. Fish and Wildlife Service agent in 1969, occurred at South Dakota's Sand Lake National Wildlife Refuge. That autumn, shooters at Sand Lake killed an estimated 50,000 geese, 20,000 of whom went unretrieved.[1]

Each year in the U.S., hunters kill more than 125 million nonhuman animals, excluding untold millions killed illegally or left fatally wounded.[2] To preserve their "sport," hunters verbally camouflage suffering and death.

"Humane" Wounding and Killing

Understatements and outright lies conceal hunting's cruelty. Hunters don't "always" shoot with "perfect" skill, hunting spokesman Jim Posewitz says.[3] Hunters routinely fail to kill cleanly. They aim too low or too far back. They shoot birds so distant that shotgun pellets lack sufficient force to kill on impact. They fire at mammals who are running or are partly concealed. On one Tennessee hunt, a European wild boar cornered by dogs suffered hits from at least five shooters. Each of three times that bullets knocked him down, the boar struggled to his feet. Before he died, he was shot thirteen times.[4]

"There will be times when the first shot is not instantly fatal," Posewitz continues.[5] A brain shot that kills instantly is rare in gun hunting and virtually nonexistent in bowhunting. Most hunters of large mammals don't aim for the head, but the heart–lung area. Unconsciousness and death are rapid (but not immediate) only if a gunshot or arrow ruptures the heart or aorta.

According to bowhunter Stewart Edward White, an arrow that strikes a nonhuman animal anywhere, including the belly, causes "prompt death."[6] After a shot to the heart–lung area, bowhunters generally wait at least half an hour before tracking, to allow time for the wounded animal to die from blood loss. After a belly shot they wait eight to twelve hours.[7] Animals who escape with lesser arrow wounds commonly die, over days or weeks, from painful bacterial infection.[8] The California Department of Fish and Game has denied that arrow wounding is "inhumane."[9]

At least half of the elks and white-tailed deer shot with arrows go unretrieved, studies indicate.[10] Bowhunter Clare Conley saw a bowhunting companion shoot a doe through the neck. After waiting an hour, the hunters began to follow her trail. Pools of blood marked places where she had collapsed before stumbling on. "At last we found her," Conley relates. "She was dying. She was on her knees and hocks. Her ears . . . were sagging. Her head was down. Her nose was in her blood." From 15 feet (4.6 m) away, the Class A archer who had wounded the doe aimed at her head, and missed. "Somehow the doe lurched up. Stumbling, bounding, crashing blindly into the brush," she disappeared. The hunters never found her.[11] Bowhunter Glenn Helgeland dismisses bowhunting's "supposed inefficiencies and cruelties."[12]

To Helgeland the belief that an arrow causes pain is "baloney, mostly." Another bowhunter has described the pain that an arrow inflicts as "slight, about the same as a clap on the shoulder." Really? When Conley shot a rabbit through the chest, she screamed, stumbled, and jumped until Conley stomped her to death.[13]

A bullet to the heart–lung area "feels like a bee sting," a deer hunter contends.[14] As humans can attest, having ribs broken or the chest wall penetrated is excruciating. An animal gun-shot in the lungs suffers intense pain and suffocates when the lungs collapse or fill with blood.

An animal shot anywhere other than the brain, heart, or a major blood vessel endures prolonged suffering, especially if left wounded (as are an estimated one-fifth of white-tailed deer hit with shotgun slugs).[15] One hunter recalls a young buck shot in the spine. Bleating loudly, the buck dragged himself through the snow by his forelegs. One of his hind legs dangled by a tendon.[16] A hunting proponent denies "the 'cruelty' involved in hunting deer."[17]

A belly shot causes extreme pain. Gut-shot mule deer and pronghorn antelopes have dragged their stomach and intestines along the ground.[18] His abdomen shot open, a desert bighorn ram attempted to jump a cactus. The spines caught his exposed stomach and yanked it out.[19] When a white-tailed buck was shot in the stomach by bowhunter Ted Nugent, his entrails fell out.[20] But, say Nugent and Helgeland, gut-shot nonhumans only "feel sick."[21]

Shot, up close, by a "game ranch" bowhunter, a tame Corsican ram jumped when the first arrow pierced his rump. A second struck his back; a third, one of his rear legs. The ram started to limp away, but two more arrows hit him in the rump, knocking him down. The ram managed to rise. Dripping blood, he ran to a wire fence that prevented escape. With arrows sticking out of him, he stood shaking, gazing beyond the fence. A sixth arrow pierced his belly. Still he stood, shaking and looking out. Then he collapsed. He kept thrashing, trying to stand. Finally the bowhunter borrowed a rifle and shot the ram from 4 feet (1.2 m) away. Five minutes more the ram thrashed. He was still alive when the shooter began to yank the arrows from his body. At last, with a long, slow exhalation, he died.[22] White calls bowhunting, even by beginners, "humane."[23]

Bird hunter Vance Bourjaily, too, contends that "hunting is humane."[24] Along with the pain of being shot, many wounded birds suffer slow death by starvation or gangrene. Studies indicate that more than one-fourth of mourning doves and bobwhite quails shot by hunters go unretrieved, and more than one-third of ducks.[25]

Before a British-style foxhunt, hunters block fox holes and other burrows to increase the chances that a hunted red fox will run to exhaustion. Pursued by about 35 hounds, the fox initially runs fastest; but, bred for stamina, the hounds gain as the fox weakens. The chase may last more than two hours. By the end, some foxes can only drag themselves.[26] According to the U.K.'s Countryside Alliance, in hunts "all foxes are either humanely dispatched or escape without injury."[27] A fox caught by hounds is ripped apart. As inadvertently witnessed by a horrified woman in 1998, a fox running from hounds was "covered in blood," a "huge gaping hole" in her side. Caught once more, the fox screamed as she was "torn apart."[28] A fox who flees into a burrow is dug out and either shot or tossed alive to the hounds. Or, still inside, the fox is attacked by terriers sent below; the underground fight, in which terriers too may be badly wounded or killed, usually ends with the fox's death. In 1999 a fox overtaken by hounds was bitten on his neck and rump before he escaped down a rabbit hole. Hunting opponents rescued the fox, whom they named Copper, and took him to a veterinarian. Without treatment Copper would have died from shock, the veterinarian reported.[29] Each year in the U.K., thousands of red foxes die in foxhunts;[30] numerous others may escape only to die from wounds or shock. Red foxes live in stable, loving family groups; the death of one red fox strongly affects others. Summer–autumn foxhunting targets cubs several months old. Spring foxhunting frequently kills one or both parents of nursing cubs. Normally the father brings the nursing mother food. If he is killed, she and the cubs are less likely to survive. If the mother is killed, the cubs starve. Supporters call foxhunting "humane."

Coupling *humane* with any sport hunting—any chasing, wounding, or killing for fun—empties *humane* of meaning.

"Fair Chase"

Proponents claim that hunting is fair as well as humane. "The concept of fair chase is important to hunting," Posewitz states.[31] Its importance lies in public relations and self-justification.

Hunting's only chase is by dogs or motorized vehicles, and it's never fair. Frequently the chase lasts hours. In the U.S., radio-collared dogs chase cougars and black bears while the hunters, often in cars, follow the signals. Dogs terrorize and bite a cornered bear or feral pig until the hunters shoot. When a wounded raccoon or black bear tumbles from a tree, the dogs below attack. In cars, hunters scout for turkeys; before shooting, they drive right up to the birds. From slow-moving and parked cars, hunters shoot partridges, grouses, and deer alongside the road. From boats they shoot marsh birds and moose. In snowmobiles and all-terrain vehicles, they chase wolves, deer, elks, antelopes, and caribous. Flying low in helicopters, they chase polar bears, wolves, and bighorn sheep. Wild-eyed, their tongue hanging out, the terrified and exhausted victims pant or cough blood.

Hunters use binoculars and high-powered rifles with telescopic sights. They use compound bows with range finders, string silencers, and mechanical releases. They use decoys, scent lures, and tape-recorded calls. Hunters shoot nonhumans at water holes. They bait deer with corn, ducks with grain, and bears with flesh and sweets. To preserve the pretense of fairness, hunters call baiting "feeding."

Animal-shooting operations involve no tracking or pursuit, but *hunting ranch* gives "aim and fire" an aura of fair chase. Released immediately before a shoot, pen-reared pheasants can fly only in short spurts if at all. On some shooting operations, to make the pheasants stay where they're placed, operators rock or spin them so that they become dizzy, or press their chest until they faint. Sometimes the pheasants are released by being tossed from a tower; the most disabled crash to earth before the assembled shooters fire.[32] On at least hundreds of U.S. shooting operations, nonhuman mammals are confined to fenced pastures, corrals, or cages. Many of the animals offered for killing were bottle-fed in infancy. Among the lions and tigers are former pets who greet customers with friendly licks. Pigs are shot at their food troughs and black bears in their cages.

Field & Stream executive editor David Petzal defines fair chase as "stalking an animal on its own terms."[33] An animal's own terms are "Don't hunt me." In sport hunting, fair chase doesn't exist. Fairness requires comparable consequences for all "players." Imagine a betting situation. If I lose, I pay you $50; if I win, you pay me $50. Fair, right? But how about this? If I lose, I pay you $5; if I win, you pay me $500. Not fair, unless you and I agree to such unequal terms. A sport hunter who "loses" suffers only some disappointment, until their attention shifts to some harmless activity or another potential victim. But if the human wins, the nonhuman dies. In hunting, nonhuman animals even pay for their "opponent's" ineptitude: poor shooting and retrieval skills leave them wounded. Fairness also requires the same rules for all players. In hunting, these rules apply for the human: You may be assisted by vehicles and companions; you'll have a weapon; you'll possess foreknowledge of the "game." These rules apply for the nonhuman: Most likely you'll face your assailant(s) alone; in your defense you'll have only your own body and wits; the "game" will begin without warning. Most importantly, fairness requires mutual consent. Opponents in tennis, soccer, or any other game agree to compete. In hunting, only the humans want to "play"; the nonhuman is simply a victim.

To maintain the guise of sportsmanship ("fair honest rivalry"), hunters pretend that their victims willingly participate.[34] The fox is a "good opponent," a "real sport" who "runs because he loves to run."[35] Even a pen-reared pheasant can be a "challenging adversary."[36] Hunters describe their premeditated murder as a "confrontation between man and animal."[37] Do rabbits, ducks, and deer confront their attackers? Hunters also claim to "interact" with their victims. They call "game animal" birth and death "recruitment" and "attrition," as if the animals signed up to be hunted and turned in letters of resignation from life. After slaying a deer, Richard Nelson "whisper[s] thanks to the animal for giving itself to me," even if the deer had started to flee.[38] Ted Kerasote likes to believe that hunted animals "sacrifice" themselves as part of an "accord" with him and "permit themselves to be taken."[39] This kind of hallucinatory drivel fills hunting books and magazines.

In truth, even severely injured nonhumans want to live. After gunshot shattered one of his wings, a young snow goose began to starve; he no longer could fly, with other geese in his marsh, to a cornfield half a mile (nearly a kilometer) away. Finally, emaciated, he walked the entire distance.[40]

Categorizing hunting as "sport" or "recreation" hides its violence and injustice inside a trivial context of play and completely discounts the nonhuman perspective. Being chased, wounded, or killed isn't recreation to the victim. When a human attacks or kills an innocent human, we rightly consider the act assault or murder. Hunting, too, inflicts suffering and death on innocent victims. Hunters kill *for* sport, but their actions don't qualify as *a* sport. Hunting is ritualized murder.

"Wildlife Management"

Whereas the designation *sport* portrays hunting as harmless (and fair) play, *wildlife management* sanctifies hunting as serving some grand plan. The term reflects the speciesist premise that "wild" non-humans can and should be "managed" by humans.

Often called "the father of wildlife management," hunter Aldo Leopold advocated "managing" "game animals" so that humans annually could kill as many as possible.[41] In the U.S., maximum "yield" remains the goal of most "wildlife management." Largely composed of hunters and fishers, state wildlife agencies (often named the Game Commission or Department of Fish and Game) dedicate themselves to Leopold's scheme. As of 1990 most of these agencies were devoting more than 90 percent of their funds to "managing" populations whose members are hunted or fished.[42]

To give hunters more ducks to shoot, states release at least tens of thousands of pen-reared mallards each year. Within two years most are dead. This is "waterfowl management."[43]

To boost the number of deer available for hunters, state wildlife agencies burn acreage and clear-cut forests down to browse. The initially profuse food supply causes deer to reproduce at a high rate. Hunters then announce that shooting is necessary to reduce the deer population. But they continue to kill many more bucks than does. The skewed sex ratio leaves does with more than their natural share of available food, so once again they give birth at an inflated rate. And the shooting cycle continues. This is "game management."[44]

According to the Countryside Alliance, "No-one disputes that fox numbers have to be controlled."[45] Among many others, I do. Able to reabsorb embryos, vixens give birth to fewer cubs when food is scarce. "Responsible fox management includes maintaining a healthy population at a level at which it can thrive without threatening livestock or other wildlife," the Countryside Alliance states.[46] From both a scientific and a moral perspective, *responsible fox management* is an oxymoron. Fox populations are sustained and limited by their environment. Of necessity, foxes kill "other wildlife"; they're predators. Red foxes primarily eat rabbits and rodents. Few humans resent this predation because it reduces the number of small mammals who eat crops. Hypocritically, people who shoot birds do resent fox predation on pheasants, partridges, and other "gamebirds." Similarly, those who send nonhumans to slaughter resent fox predation on chickens, lambs, and other "agricultural animals." While humans needlessly kill nonhumans in massive numbers, foxhunters condemn foxes for "threatening livestock." When a fox kills an enslaved animal, the problem is enslavement, not the fox. Unlike humans, foxes must eat flesh. Fox predation needs no justification; blood "sports" and "animal agriculture" have none. Foxhunters call fox predation "ruthless" and foxhunting "natural."[47] The reverse is true.

Applied to predators, *manage* is a straight euphemism for *kill*. In the U.S., Carnivore Management and Strategic Wolf Management pogroms (I mean, programs) target wolves because they prey on deer, elks, moose, and caribous. "Removal of predators" increases the number of animals available for hunters, two "managers" cheerfully note.[48]

In hunting, *control* too signifies killing. "I'm all for wolf control," an Alaskan hunter has declared. "Let's kill them all." A New York State Division of Fish and Wildlife biologist gleefully has described the way to "control" deer herds: "shoot the hell out of them."[49]

The Congressional Sportsmen's Caucus applauds the "planned management" of "renewables"—that is, the slaughter of nonhuman animals.[50] To hunters and their manager cronies, free-living nonhumans are exploitable, replaceable resources. Agencies with names like Department of Natural Resources and Wildlife Resources Commission "allocate" and "ration" nonhuman animals like so many gallons of gasoline. Hunters may "deplete" populations, but wildlife managers hope they will, instead, remove only "surplus" that otherwise would be "wasted." This language communicates the arrogant, false belief that humans fully understand nature's complex interrelationships and are qualified and entitled to categorize some nonhumans as "excess." Meanwhile an ever-multiplying human population continues to destroy the natural world.

Nonhumans contribute to their communities and ecosystems. Bear mothers love their cubs. Geese and wolves love their mates. Nonhumans matter to other nonhumans. Like us, nonhuman animals value their own lives. But the language of "wildlife management" declares nonhumans worthless apart from their use to humans.

Free-living nonhumans can't be "stored as other products are," hunter Clyde Ormond states.[51] *Wildlife production* often substitutes for *wildlife management*. Whether born free or pen-reared, nonhuman animals are "stock." By species, hunters "inventory" the available "supplies." Free-living nonhumans are consumer goods, items to be purchased for a license fee. At shooting operations, customers select victims price-listed by species and selling points, such as a "lion with good mane." Viewing living beings as commodities obliterates their sentience. While critical of "wildlife" merchandising, hunter Ted Williams himself sees nonhuman animals as aesthetic objects. In his view, pen-reared mallards miserably fail to measure up. He scorns them as "fake ducks."[52] No, they're real, Mr. Williams. So is their suffering.

Whether hunters regard nonhuman animals as resources or commodities, they regard them as human property. In general, hunters detest predators, whom they see as killing *their* "game." Coyotes and other predators might "take your trophy," Helgeland tells bowhunters.[53] Revealing a sense of entitlement, hunters ask each other, "Did you get your buck?" not "Did you get *a* buck?" The common phrase *our wildlife* conveys the proprietary attitude that prevails among humans. To *Field & Stream* conservation editor George Reiger, someone who shoots a member of an endangered species is a "vandal."[54] To *New Mexico Wildlife* editor John Crenshaw, a "poacher is a thief who steals . . . from a public resource."[55] If Reiger and Crenshaw saw nonhuman animals as thinking, feeling individuals rather than human property, they would see the so-called vandals, poachers, and thieves—and all other hunters—as murderers.

"Wildlife Conservation"

Hunters claim to "conserve" nonhuman animals. *Conserve* means, first, to protect from harm or preserve. Clearly, hunters don't protect nonhuman animals. They kill them. Hunters rightly regard animal protectionists as their opponents. Safari Club International—whose contradictory motto is "Conservation of Wildlife and Protection of the Hunter"—has urged members to keep "protectionists from gaining any ground."[56] Along with animal protection, Safari Club rejects "preservation, or non-use."[57] The oxymoron *shooting preserve* makes sense when reversed; hunters preserve shooting, not animals. In the U.S., public-land "preserves" permit hunting, and thousands of commercial "preserves" offer a chance to kill tame birds or mammals for a fee. Hunters don't even allow nonhuman animals the safe haven of so-called refuges. Today hunting occurs on more than half of the U.S.'s 500-plus national "wildlife refuges."

Do hunters kill individuals yet somehow safeguard species, as they love to claim? Sport hunters have pushed numerous species and subspecies toward extinction, from whooping cranes and polar bears to California condors and Florida panthers.[58] The fewer a species' members, the greater a "trophy hunter's" desire to kill one. In 1977 hunter Jack O'Connor fumed, "Anti-hunters were behind the provisions of the so-called Endangered Species Act" (ESA).[59] As a group, hunters have opposed the ESA and have tried to prevent animals they view as game, such as leopards and African elephants, from gaining or keeping ESA protection.[60] Not that illegality deters trophy-seeking hunters. They're notorious for killing members of endangered species. Routinely the culprits receive "conservation" awards.[61]

Nor do hunters abide by *conserve*'s second definition: "to use carefully or sparingly, avoiding waste."[62] In a three-year undercover investigation, a U.S. federal agent saw only one duck hunter forgo a chance to exceed the legal kill-limit.[63] Before attempting to retrieve wounded doves, hunters often shoot more, sometimes competing to be the first to kill a hundred.[64] Sport hunting has nothing to do with genuine conservation because this "use" of other animals has nothing to do with need. By its very nature, wounding and killing for sport is neither careful nor sparing, but wanton.

Applied to living beings, *conservation* means killing. Becoming "involved" in bighorn "conservation"—that's what one hunter calls killing a California bighorn sheep.[65] In any case, the idea of "conserving" animals, as if they were inanimate resources or commodities, should arouse disgust. The phrase *wildlife conservation* reveals a deeply speciesist viewpoint.

"Harvesting"

Because evolution indicates human "kindredship with the animals," anyone who believes in evolution "may conclude that killing of animals constitutes murder," James Whisker reflects in *The Right to Hunt*.[66] He's decided not to believe in evolution.

To avoid seeing themselves as murderers, hunters apply separate vocabularies to violence against humans and violence against nonhumans. Hunters' guns never should be called "weapons" but "firearms," one hunter exhorts. As expressed by another, a shotgun is a "weapon capable of savage carnage" when handled in a way that endangers humans but a "delightful tool" when fired at a nonhuman.[67]

According to hunting apologists, a "total package of recreational satisfaction" distinguishes hunting from killing. That is, killing accompanied by other fun activities isn't killing—when the victim is nonhuman. Hunters call themselves sportsmen and outdoorsmen. In this lingo, promotion of hunting becomes utterly benign "pro-outdoor activism." "Sportsmen . . . are all under attack," a hunter sputters, although no one is objecting to baseball or golf.[68]

"I hate the word *killing*," a trophy-seeking hunter complains. He shuns this "murderous term," which "ruins everything." "I'm not a killer," he insists while conceding, "Killing, unfortunately, is part of hunting."[69] Instead of serial killers or mass murderers, hunters are "users of wildlife." Hunting doesn't entail killing, just "user actions." Hunting's opponents are "antiuse."

In a phrase like *bag a goose*, *bag* means to kill and place in a bag. The euphemism acknowledges only the second action. Hunters also "bag" animals too large to be bagged, such as bears and moose. Often *bag* simply substitutes for *kill*, as in "deer bagged with bow and arrow." Taking one baby step toward enlightenment, hunter Sydney Jarkow ponders, "Odd, now that I think about it, that game hunters talk in terms of 'securing' or 'filling' a bag rather than shooting or killing animals."[70] Such evasion isn't odd at all; it's a necessary component of unjustifiable behavior.

In addition to being "bagged," nonhuman animals are "gathered" and "collected." These euphemisms too jump directly to lifeless bodies, omitting the step of killing. Even when a single animal is slain, *collect* replaces *kill*: "collect a javelina [collared peccary] with his handgun."[71]

Another replacement for *kill*, *cull* falsely suggests that hunters primarily kill the frail and infirm. Instead they create what naturalist Edwin Way Teale has called "evolution in reverse."[72] Hoping to kill the "big boss" or "big boy," hunters prefer to shoot dominant male deer, elks, turkeys, and sheep—the males most likely to guide others, defend others, and father offspring who thrive. True predators selectively kill the weak, sick, and disabled. The word *cull* naturalizes sport hunting and implies benefit to nonhuman communities that actually are harmed.

The euphemism *harvest* is especially popular with hunters and, like other hunting lingo, has been adopted by the U.S. government and media. *Harvest* discourages sympathy for nonhuman animals by equating them with plants, disguising the fact that killing a nonhuman being inflicts suffering and destroys a mental world. Calling a deer hunt "a harvest, not a kill," hunter Sam Fadala states, "An arrow harvests game by the bleeding process."[73] Although *harvest* means gather, hunters speak of "harvesting" even a single individual. The oxymoron *unretrieved harvest* signifies nonhuman animals left wounded. Would anyone say that harvesting apples includes leaving them on the ground? Making anti-hunting activists sound irrational, hunters describe them as "antiharvest." Whisker rejects any analogy between "the wanton killing of human beings and the harvesting of animals."[74] So do I. The parallel is between the wanton killing of human beings and the wanton killing of nonhuman beings.

In supreme doublespeak, murder becomes its opposite. Hunters pronounce their unnecessary killing "life-giving." "When I kill an animal," a hunter has said, "I'm celebrating life."[75]

Human "Predators" and Nonhuman "Game"

While acknowledging that humans needn't eat flesh (a truth that he considers "unfortunate"), one hunter terms the desire to kill "prey" a human "need" shared with "other carnivores." Another hunter has stated that humans are "predators, as much as a mountain lion or a coyote." Such language falsifies. Unlike mountain lions and coyotes, humans thrive as pure vegetarians. We don't possess a carnivore's teeth, digestive system, or anatomy.[76]

Just as calling humans "carnivores" or "predators" disguises choice as necessity, designating members of particular species "game" or "recreational animals" creates the illusion that some animals naturally, inherently, and inevitably exist to be hunted for sport. This belief clashes with evolutionary reality. Deer antlers didn't evolve to provide humans with trophies. They evolved because they increased a buck's likelihood of reproducing, not his likelihood of being killed. "Game animals are animals which may be or even should be hunted," Whisker states. Their existence implies "the existence of hunters."[77] Of course it does. Hunters invented the category "game animal." When hunting apologists speak of a "right" to "kill game animals," they mouth empty circularity. The very label *game animals* legitimizes killing members of certain species for sport. Unlike the scientific designation *vertebrate*, the classification *game* is strictly political.

If classified as "varmints" (a colloquial variant of *vermin*), unglamorous mammals like coyotes, raccoons, and prairie dogs can legally be killed in any number at any time, including when they have dependent young. "Varmints" don't live in an area; they "infest" it. The word *varmint* transforms speciesist genocide into a public service.

The "nuisance" label is equally lethal. To gain public support for the hunting of grizzly bears near Grand Teton and Yellowstone National Parks, the Fish and Wildlife Service termed them "nuisance" bears.[78] Whenever human "development" and tourism encroach on nonhuman territory, the nonhumans are condemned. If death sentences were handed out with equal alacrity to humans who annoy, inconvenience, or compete with others, how many of us would remain alive?

Asked "Is hunting cruel?" a British foxhunter answered, "No, the fox is a pest." (While calling red foxes "pests," foxhunters maintain coverts for them.) To Ormond, porcupines and western ground squirrels are "pests," black-tailed jackrabbits "another pest," striped skunks "another pest-predator," and wolverines "a larger pest." Because many suburbanites consider their areas too densely populated with white-tailed deer, some hunters have started calling whitetails—the supposedly quintessential "game animal"—a pest. Like *varmint* and *nuisance*, *pest* legitimizes killing. The pest tag has authorized the murder of jaguars, cougars, and other non-"domesticated" cats. A wildlife biologist has explained why he objects to this killing: "wild felines" are too useful in "pest control to be considered pests." In other words, pests who kill pestier pests stop being pests.[79]

Pejorative labels like *varmint*, *nuisance*, and *pest* blame the victim by transforming murder into just punishment. Other hunting language, too, blames the victim. Feral pigs are gentle unless attacked, but hunters vilify them as "vicious," "malicious," and "bad to the bone."[80] While labeling great horned owls "killers" and "wildlife murderers" because they prey on pheasants, Bert Popowski enjoyed killing pheasants *and* great horned owls.[81] Scenting a hunter and his guide, a caribou initially bolted. When the caribou returned, the guide hissed, "Shoot the stupid bastard! He's got it coming."[82] Five lions peaceably eating seemed "disdainful" to a hunter because they didn't raise their heads at his approach. Bwana promptly shot one.[83]

Shooting at "Species"

Displaying speciesism's hallmark trait, hunters deny nonhuman individuality. Shooting woodcocks feels like killing "the same bird over and over," a hunter says.[84] Just as racists see individual humans as embodiments of a particular race, hunters regard nonhumans as mere species representatives: "specimens."

An insistence that nonhuman animals matter only at the species level pervades hunting. This aggregate view of other animals leads to massive abuse. One by one, millions upon millions, nonhumans can be killed without compunction, provided others of their species remain available for future hurting and killing. Without apology, Bourjaily declares hunters "indifferent to the lives of individual creatures."[85]

"Animals are not correctly thought of as individuals," a hunter asserts. Both physically and mentally all sentient beings are individuals. In nature "the species is everything and the individual nothing," another hunter contends. To the contrary, evolution proceeds through mutations manifested in individual organisms. Sexual selection favors individuals with certain traits. Reproductive success depends on cooperation and competition among individuals as well as species. If many nonhumans have little effect on natural history, the same is true of many humans.[86]

Hunter-sociologist Richard Hummel is so oblivious to individual nonhumans that he wrongly describes the animal rights viewpoint as "all living species are citizens," rather than "all living beings." Hunters commonly speak of killing species, not individuals. A trophy-seeking hunter has killed "thirty-four different species of deer," Kerasote writes. "Deer of thirty-four different species" would be accurate and equally concise. Fortunately, individual hunters don't single-handedly kill off entire species, although some have tried. Whenever the media report that someone has killed "an endangered animal" or "an endangered species," they too confuse individual and species. *Any* animal threatened by a gun or arrow is endangered. Hunters kill *members* of endangered species.[87]

Referring to multiple nonhuman animals with singular word forms perpetuates a view of them as one collective thing. Hunting abounds with collective nouns like *wildlife*, *game*, *quarry*, and *prey*, which usually appear with singular verbs. The plural of *deer* or *moose* is uninflected (identical to the singular). The names of many other "game" birds and mammals have uninflected as well as inflected plurals: *quail* or *quails*, *grouse* or *grouses*, *elk* or *elks*. As noted in *The Merriam-Webster Concise Handbook for Writers*, hunters prefer the uninflected forms.[88] Hunters often refer to sport-hunted animals with uninflected plurals even when they're incorrect: "had hunted crocodile," "who kills the most bear."

Hunters speak of nonhuman animals as nonindividuated substance. Incorrectly they boast about "how much" they shot rather than how many, the "amount" of deer or ducks rather than the number. An African big-"game" hunter talks about shooting "toothy stuff such as lion, leopard, bear, puma, boar, and jaguar."[89] Another hunter has killed "zoological material, principally mammals."[90] As if nonhuman individuals were so much lumber or salt, hunters refer to a particular size or weight "of" animal. They "outfox . . . several square yards of bear" and "look down the sights at a half ton or more of moose."[91] Would they describe a homicide as "bringing down 150 pounds of human"?

Speaking of nonhuman animals as part of some entity negates their individuality. When a pheasant hunter says that he retrieved "the first half" of his "double," he means the first of two shot pheasants.[92] Hunters kill "a piece of game" rather than one animal. Together they shoot nonhumans "by the millions of units," not simply by the millions, which would hit with uncomfortable impact.[93]

"Physical Objects"

Fatally shot, a collapsed buck raised his head and licked the hand of his killer, who felt such remorse that he renounced hunting. "The deer was no longer an object" but "a living being," the ex-hunter has explained. Hunters can kill sentient beings for sport because they mentally reduce them to inanimate things, "physical objects" in Leopold's speciesist words. Hummel defines animal rights as the belief that "natural things have rights like human beings." Animal rights isn't about things; it's about sentient beings.[94]

Reductive metaphor reinforces hunters' tendency to regard nonhuman beings as insentient things. Hunters regularly refer to nonhuman animals as crops: "the annual fawn crop," "bumper crops of pheasants." Deer are "a harvestable crop," a hunter has stated. "It's not a whole lot different than going into the field and harvesting apples every year."[95] It *is* "a whole lot different." Unlike apples, deer think and feel.

Perceived as inanimate targets, animals can't be murdered. Feigned crow calls keep "a stream of fresh targets flowing toward the blind-hidden shooter," Popowski states. By saying "It's just a target," Fadala prodded his son to shoot a deer.[96]

Hunters see living nonhumans as already dead. They shoot "food" and "wild protein." As expressed by Whisker, to hunt is to "kill meat."[97] Viewing living nonhumans as "meat," hunters frequently shoot to preserve flesh rather than kill as quickly as possible. After wounding a white-tailed buck, a hunter rejected a companion's advice to shoot again. "No use wasting meat," the shooter said, expecting the buck to collapse without another bullet that would damage more flesh. The buck ran off and never was found.[98] One hunter saw another "cutting off the hindquarters of a wounded doe while she watched."[99]

Deer hunters anticipate "shooting the trophy when he comes sauntering into the open."[100] Hunters verbally reduce nonhumans to body parts, especially parts assessed for trophy value. Depending on the number of points that their antlers bear, male deer and elks are "spikes," "forkhorns," "three-by-threes," or "four-by-fours." Viewed through a hunter's sights, a white-tailed buck becomes "the rack of a lifetime picking its way through the blowdowns."[101] In hunting vernacular, a hunter of pronghorn antelopes "killed one of the most perfectly sculpted pronghorn heads."[102] Hunters aim with the goal of leaving "trophy" body parts undamaged. Rather than fire at a leopard's head, "ruining it as a trophy," Jarkow decided to "guess" the location of the leopard's heart and aim there.[103] He shot the leopard in his belly. Before ending the leopard's suffering, Jarkow trailed him for nearly three hours.

Victims of "Love"

Advocating "all-out war" against some bird species, Popowski divides all birds into "game" and "pests." He has killed numerous red-winged blackbirds (whom he despises as "villains"), starlings ("filthy"), great horned owls ("killers"), magpies ("murderous" and "fiendish"), and sparrows ("obnoxious nuisances"), as well as 80,000 or more crows ("destructive"). He is, he says, a "bird lover."[104] Semantic reversal casts hunters as "animal lovers." "I have so loved them that I longed to kill them," a bowhunter has said of his victims.[105]

Respect for a living being precludes killing them for sport, yet hunters claim to respect, admire, even revere their victims. In Whisker's twisted view, when a hunter *refrains* from shooting a nonhuman animal, "he is saying, no, I do not respect you, and therefore I will not kill you."[106] To hunters, *respect* (like *love*) means its opposite.

Hunters embellish their pretense of love and respect by suggesting that they do their victims a favor. Having killed a tame bontebok (an antelope) on a shooting operation, a hunter initially admitted, "It was brutal." Then he attempted self-justification: "I elected to *immortalize* that animal" (by displaying his remains). As expressed by another hunter, shooting a doe "allows" her to "complete" her "life cycle." Is shooting a human also an act of kindness?[107]

Like other bigotries, speciesism is a failure to empathize with those outside one's own group. Hunters consider only how *they* feel. Their victim's experience doesn't matter. Having shot a white-tailed buck in the hip, a bowhunter complained, "You should have seen the bastard take off. Lost an arrow." Bourjaily confesses little regret about inflicting "agony." (Yes, the same man who claims elsewhere that "hunting is humane.")[108]

Overwhelmingly, hunting accounts are first-person autobiographical narratives punctuated with *me*, *myself*, and *I*. Their point of view belies the fact that the most important event—wounding or death—befalls the nonhuman victim. Popowski remembers the day that he first killed a fox as "my 'First Fox Day.'"[109] He never would see it as The Fox's Last Day. Hunting literature is the moral equivalent of boastful homicide accounts written by the killers.

Applying the word *victim* to nonhuman animals discomfits hunters. After admitting that hunters select a "victim," Jarkow partly retracts the word: "if you want to call it that." Hunters prefer to regard only humans (especially hunters such as themselves) as victims. One hunter has pitied a "victim" of nervousness who, overanxious, shot a pheasant too far back. The real victim, of course, was the wounded bird. Hunters call themselves victims when animal rights activists attempt to prevent them from shooting nonhuman animals. In that case, muggers intending to stab someone must be victims when brave bystanders intervene.[110]

A hunter who accidentally shoots another human should be imprisoned for causing suffering or death and showing a "flagrant," "callous" disregard for life, Petzal states.[111] But he himself hunts. He too causes suffering and death, which are no less real when they befall nonhumans. Doesn't killing for sport show the most flagrant disregard for life? Isn't it more callous to kill intentionally than to do so accidentally?

In common parlance, *victims mistaken for game* and *hunting fatalities* refer only to humans. Those phrases perfectly describe all the nonhumans whom hunters wound and kill.

5

Cruelty by Deception

The Language of Sportfishing

> angling—the cruelest, the coldest, and the stupidest of pretended sports
>
> —Lord Byron

A tarpon leaped six times when hooked, then raced off. Soon she was exhausted. Reeled in alongside the boat, she circled weakly. The boat's captain reached over with a thick, hand-held hook. Stabbing the tarpon through the lower jaw, he yanked her upward. She struggled to breathe. Her mouth gaped and gill plates flared. Heaved partly over the boat's side, she flopped there, head hanging down. Then she dropped onto the boat's floor, where she lay gasping. Over the next twenty minutes, lying in her own blood and feces, she died.[1]

Annually U.S. sportfishers kill at least hundreds of millions of fishes and leave countless others permanently disabled.[2] Deceptive language, which shares many of hunting's linguistic ploys, disguises sportfishing's cruelty and destructiveness.

"Gentle Art"

Biochemically and structurally a fish's nervous system closely resembles ours. Fishes possess abundant pain receptors and produce chemicals known to counter pain and fear. Traditionally portrayed as "the gentle art of angling," fishing is no more gentle than hunting is humane.

Artificial lures generally hook fishes in the jaw, mouth, lip, or snout—areas rich in nerves. When the hook penetrates, fishes shake their head, jump, and dive. Carps react the same way if electrically shocked in the roof of their mouth.[3] Yet, according to *The Game Fishing Bible*, fishes find the hook merely "annoying."[4] Trouts caught on a barbless hook suffer "little more damage" than humans do from a pinprick, two fishers claim.[5] Then, why do many trouts die from the injury that a barbless hook inflicts?[6]

A sportfisher scoffs at those who term fishes' experience on hook and line "torment."[7] In their violent struggle to escape, many fishes drastically overheat. The soar in body temperature, as much as 15 °F (8 °C) in tunas and marlins, often kills. Under severe physical strain, fishes lack adequate oxygen as they burn muscle glucose. As a result, lactic acid painfully accumulates in their bloodstream. The buildup can leave them paralyzed. In experiments, carps hooked and held on a taut line for at least several minutes spat gas from their air bladder (a gas-filled elastic membrane that enables fishes to stay buoyant and, in some species, assists breathing). When the line went slack, they sank. Carps also spit gas and sink when subjected to severe, sustained electric shock.[8] If anything, *torment* too weakly describes a fish's ordeal on hook and line. *Torture* is more apt. But fishers prefer that references to their "sport" be free of moral implications.

To obtain oxygen, fishes draw water over their gills. Hooked fishes struggle to breathe. After attempting to flee, they must recover oxygen by swimming slowly with their mouth open. Fishers prevent this recovery by pulling the line from different angles, keeping the fish's head turned and never allowing them to rest. Many fishers intentionally prolong fishes' ordeal. Instead of hauling them in as quickly as possible on heavy line, they use the lightest possible line, for sport. Gradually they weaken a fish enough to pull them in without snapping the line. A *Field & Stream* writer has extolled a fisher who pressured a swordfish for nearly five hours.[9] In sportfishing lingo, fishers "play" or "exercise" fishes to weakness or exhaustion. These euphemisms disguise a fish's life-and-death struggle as harmless fun or physical activity beneficial to the fish. Exertion, pain, and fear so drain many fishes that they lose the ability to stay upright. "Played out," they float belly up.

A fish's air bladder becomes conditioned to a particular depth. If water pressure plummets, the bloodstream can't absorb air-bladder gas as rapidly as it increases in volume. Hauled up from a substantial depth, fishes undergo excruciating decompression. The intense internal pressure frequently ruptures their air bladder or pushes it out through their mouth. The pressure may also pop a fish's eyes from their sockets or cause organs to hemorrhage. Having yanked a trout from far below the ice, a fisher mocks his suffering. Flopping on the ice, his eyes bulging and quivering, his body distended, the trout has "the ultimate tummyache and bends."[10] From an adult perspective, children often exaggerate hurt. If we think the fish must have been in agony, we do the same, the childish word *tummyache* suggests.

To "land" a fish sounds innocuous. Depending on their species and size, many fishes are grabbed by their lower lip, gill plates, midsection, or eye sockets. Others are lifted on board as they dangle from a rod or pole; these fishes feel their full weight bear down on the hook. Fishes need water to support their bodies. Hoisted into the air, they suffer often-fatal injury as organs stretch and shift, blood vessels tear, and connective tissues rip.

In sportfishing, as in other forms of speciesist abuse, specialized terms can make violence toward nonhumans seem qualitatively different from comparable violence toward humans. To "gaff" a fish means to stab one with a thick hand-held hook (a gaff). The term's technicality assists emotional detachment. Also, by saying that fishes are "gaffed" but humans "stabbed," fishers avoid seeing the parallel. Typically, larger fishes are stabbed in their jaw or neck. Streaming blood, they're lifted at the wound.

Commonly, large fishes are bludgeoned to death. Excuse me—subdued, as when a fisher "subdued" a king mackerel with a baseball bat.[11] *Subdued* transforms beating a helpless victim into heroically overcoming some powerful opponent. *Persuader* is the snide euphemism for the club often used.

Other fishes bleed to death. Many are still conscious when their scales are scraped off, gills slashed, tail cut off, belly slit, or body sliced in the first motions of "filleting." Many fishes are eviscerated when a swallowed hook is ripped out. Strung together with any other caught fishes and dangling in or out of water, fishes may survive for hours on a rope threaded through their mouth and one gill-opening, or on a chain with giant safety pins, one of which impales them through the jaw. "Probably" fishers "sometimes get a little careless" with fishes they've caught and fail to kill them immediately, a fisher says in colossal understatement.[12]

Most fishes caught in sport suffocate. Dropped into a live-well, they struggle to breathe as the water fills with waste. The more fishes thrown into the live-well, the less oxygen available for each. Writhing, fishes suffocate on a boat floor or pier—often, like one bass, "still gasping" after an hour out of water. Peacock basses removed from water "don't relax easily," a fisher states. Relax? They're dying.[13]

While "catch and release" sounds harmless, even generous, to fishes, the practice is far from benign. At a minimum, catching and releasing a fish inflicts pain, terror, and temporary disability. Often it permanently disables or kills. Many caught and released fishes die slowly, over a period of weeks.[14] Being caught and released leaves muskellunges "tired" but "none the worse for wear," a fisher has contended.[15] At summer's height in Nogie's Creek (Ontario), research indicates, about 30 percent die from the experience.[16]

Many fishes are released brain-damaged or in shock from oxygen deprivation. Lactic-acid poisoning commonly kills fishes several or more hours after their overexertion, hours during which they may remain completely paralyzed. "Overplayed" fishes have been tortured beyond their ability to recover. The euphemism *overplay* sanctions *some* "playing." From a nonspeciesist perspective, any playing is overplaying, totally unnecessary and therefore cruel. Like *overhunt* or *overfish*, *overplay* actually is redundant.

Netting and handling remove portions of a fish's delicate, transparent surface skin. Mucous coated, this outermost layer protects against potentially fatal infection. Clumsy handling easily leaves fishes internally injured or blind.[17] Hook removal causes tearing. Fishes hooked in the tongue, esophagus, stomach, gill, or eye are unlikely to survive.[18] A fish with a severely lacerated mouth may starve. Many fishes are released with a gaping hole where they were stabbed and held aloft for photos. A *Field & Stream* editor has called catching largemouth basses, weighing them as they hang from a flesh hook through their lower jaw, and then releasing them "catch, wound, and release."[19] Wounding is the minimum harm inflicted on any hooked or handled fish.

"Fisheries Management" and "Conservation"

Catch and release "revitalizes" fish populations, fishers claim. In a 1993 study that simulated standard sportfishing methods, 32 percent of native cutthroat trouts caught in two Washington State river systems died within three days of hook removal. The Alaska Department of Fish and Game investigated characteristic catch and release of coho salmons: 69 percent died within five days. Fishers who catch and release may kill more fishes than those who catch only the number they're legally allowed to keep. A Minnesota Department of Natural Resources fish specialist explains: "Take a bass angler who lands 50 fish but doesn't keep any. If 80 percent survive, 10 will die. That's worse than if the guy caught his limit and quit fishing." If fishers truly wished to revitalize fish populations, they would leave them alone. Through semantic reversal, fishers (like hunters) pretend to promote rather than destroy life.[20]

To keep U.S. fishers well supplied with victims, state and federal hatcheries "produce" at least hundreds of millions of walleyes, trouts, and other fishes each year.[21] By mixing eggs and sperm of different species, hatcheries crossbreed fishes who never would mate in nature: saugers and walleyes, white basses and striped basses, northern pikes and muskellunges. Through inbreeding they afflict fishes with disabilities. Many hatchery-born trouts have deformed gill plates, lips, and jaws. Many are light-sensitive albinos (intended for easy detection by fishers). Hatchery conditions further debilitate trouts, who abrade themselves in crowded concrete troughs and learn to expect pellet rations. Hatchery-reared fishes fare poorly after release. Relatively few outlast one fishing season. Fishers tout all this manufactured suffering and death as "management."

Throughout the U.S., "managers" have placed hatchery-reared fishes in alien waters, including coldwater fishes in warm waters and saltwater fishes in freshwater lakes. In many cases, hatchery-reared fishes have bred with or replaced native fishes. "Stocking" reduces biodiversity and contributes to species extinctions. Sometimes "managers" dump fishes into waters after killing the previous residents by draining or poisoning. In 1997, to exterminate northern pikes (who prey on trouts and salmons), the California Department of Fish and Game poured barrels of the "pest"-icide rotenone into Lake Davis.

All fish inhabitants suffocated. The department then "restocked" the lake with rainbow trouts for sportfishing. The term *fisheries management* turns ecological havoc into order, and mass murder and environmental destruction into benign intervention.

As loudly as hunters, fishers proclaim themselves conservationists. They, too, oppose Endangered Species Act protections that would curtail their "sport." For example, they've fought endangered status for Atlantic salmons.[22] Sportfishers have hastened the demise of numerous fishes, from sharks, tarpons, and bluefin tunas to snappers, groupers, and muskellunges.[23] While claiming to "cull," fishers attempt to catch, and tend to keep, the largest fishes, primarily females of superior fitness and high reproductive capacity. Often sportfishers catch more fishes than legally allowed and leave them to rot.[24] Fishing tournaments are slaughters. Of 1,558 walleyes caught during a three-day catch-and-release tournament, 98 percent died, three-fourths of them before being weighed in.[25] Some fishers compete to catch and release the most fishes within a given period. In a single day, one ship of fools caught 83 sailfishes, each hurriedly released by cutting the line.[26]

"Objects" of Abuse

Fishers share hunters' penchant for regarding nonhuman beings as insentient things. Their victims are "recycled" (caught and released) or "harvested" (killed). Like consumer goods, fishes are "damaged" rather than injured or hurt. They're "crops," "renewable resources," and "stock"; "natural objects" or hatchery "products"; "natural commodities" or "manufactured" ones.

Fishers mentally reduce living fishes to corpses: flesh or objects of display. Upon reeling in a channel catfish, a fisher drops "another tasty meal" into the live-well. Muskellunge fishers "hook into a true trophy."[27]

As in hunting, the victims are "specimens" with no individual identities. One fisher attributes unique "personality" to each fish species, not each individual fish.[28] Instead of catching individuals, fishers hook, boat, hold, and photograph "species" and "strains." Captured fishes blur into the "string" or "catch." Fishers catch "little or nothing" instead of few or none. They release "a portion of their catch" instead of some fishes among those caught. Avoiding noticeably plural references to basses, trouts, and other fishes, they kill "bass," "trout," and other "fish," even multiple "marlin" and "shark." All such language conveys the same speciesist message: Individual fishes don't matter; they either exist for human pleasure and use or have no right to exist at all.

The victims are categorized accordingly. They're "gamefish," "bait," or "trash." Like *game animal*, the designation *gamefish* or *sportfish* misleads. Depending on particular fishers' preferences, "gamefish" may leap or dive when hooked, be easy or hard to catch, and have flesh considered delicious or inedible. In the words *gamefish* and *sportfish*, *game* and *sport* describe human attitudes, not fishes.

While a fisher was using a live minnow as bait, her infant son repeatedly yanked the minnow from the water and announced, "I've got a fish." "No, that's a minnow," the fisher responded, conditioned to see live minnows as bait, not fishes.[29] Bait is far from a natural category. Animals used as live bait range from shrimps, lizards, worms, and frogs to mackerels, salmons, crickets, and crabs. "Baitfish" are hooked so that they won't die quickly: through their lips, their nose, their eye sockets.... If large, they may be impaled on two or three hooks. Sometimes, to reduce drag, fishers sew a fish's mouth shut before towing them as bait. Because a fish who struggles and bleeds is especially likely to attract predators, fishers often break a "baitfish's" back, cut their fins, or notch them with multiple razor slits.

Other fishes are labeled "nuisances." Why? A *Field & Stream* writer enlightens us: because "they interfere with the popular gamefish" or "just because they're there."[30] As in hunting, *nuisance* licenses genocide.

Afforded no legal protection even at the species level, "trash fish" (also called "rough" or "coarse" fish) are viewed as trash because fishers don't want to catch them. As with "gamefish," just who is a "trash fish" depends on the era, place, and individual fisher. But they're all treated like garbage. When caught, "trash fish" often are yanked from the hook and thrown, either back into water or onto land. As laughingly related by one fisher, someone who catches a perch while seeking a walleye might, with a whip of their fishing pole, "splat" the perch onto the ground, step on their head, and "rip out" the swallowed hook. Another fisher remembers firing bullets into a school of carps. "All carp were trash," he writes. Once, he beat a carp to death with a branch, reviling her as "garbage."[31]

Speciesist labels such as *sportfish*, *bait*, and *trash fish* depict willful, gratuitous harm as natural and inevitable.

"Fair Fight," "Innocent Game"

After being tortured for 32 hours by a succession of fishers, a blue marlin supposedly "won" when they cut the line.[32] Surely she failed to survive. But the language of competition provides a façade of fairness. Fishers speak of their "one-on-one contest" with a fish, who is a "foe," "adversary," or "antagonist." Those labels suit a hooked fish no better than a rape victim.

As if there were mutual aggression, the words *fight* and *battle* pervade sportfishing. Fishers call their various weapons and aids "fighting equipment." The swivel chair bolted to the deck of a sportfishing boat bears the hokey name "fighting chair." To hold a rod more easily, fishers insert it into the socket of a "fighting belt" worn around the waist. Under tension the rod bends into a "fighting curve." To "fight" a fish sounds so much nicer than "slowly kill." Upon reeling in a salmon, a fisher discovered her to be fatally wrapped in the line. "For most of the time," we're told, the fisher had been "fighting a dead fish."[33] In fishing, all fighting is imaginary.

Like hunters, fishers view and report the world through the lens of first-person narrative. Me, me, me—not you, the fish. Even when he catches dozens of smallmouth basses, a fisher considers the number "not important"; what matters is his "sense of levitation."[34]

Disregarding their victims, fishers sometimes call fishing "innocent" or "harmless." Sportfishing epitomizes the needless infliction of suffering and death. Defining cruelty as "the voluntary infliction of unnecessary or avoidable pain," avid fisher A. A. Luce categorizes all catch-and-release fishing as cruel; to avoid cruelty, he argues, a fisher must catch fishes for food, as quickly and painlessly as possible.[35] The only person who must fish is someone who otherwise would starve. Because humans don't need to eat flesh to survive in good health, virtually all fishing is unnecessary and avoidable.

Whether for food or vainglory, fishing satisfies Luce's own definition of cruelty.

In attempting to justify their "sport," fishers use the same means by which they catch fishes—deception.

6

Freedom Denied

The Language of Zoos

> The language of the [zoo] promoter is always suspect, often disingenuous. The word “habitat,” for example, has replaced “cage.”
>
> —David Hancocks

Picture “a rectangular enclosure with bars in the front and back and chain link on the top” containing two tigers. “Many people” would call this a cage, but that’s “inappropriate,” Gary Clarke stated while director of the Topeka Zoo; when referring to a cage in a zoo, people should say “home.”[1] Connoting comfort and security, *home* signifies the place where one belongs. To call a zoo cage a nonhuman’s “home” naturalizes displacement and confinement. Like other speciesist institutions, zoos survive through verbal deception, including euphemism, false definition, and semantic reversal.

“Natural Habitats”

Zoos increasingly term all enclosures “habitats,” even “natural habitats.” The most manufactured environments bear names that evoke nature. The Bronx Zoo’s JungleWorld features fiberglass trees, concrete rocks, and plastic vines.[2] Intending no irony, one zoo director has commented, “Technology is reaching higher levels. There’s an increasing public demand for natural environments.”[3]

While zoo visitors experience what the industry calls "habitat immersion," the inmates experience exhibit imprisonment. Their worlds extend no farther than transparent plastic walls, invisible electrified wire, or scarcely perceptible mesh. "Cold concrete walls" surround the animals kept inside the Tropical Forest at Franklin Park Zoo (Boston).[4]

Beyond spectators' view, conditions are worse. Hidden behind exhibits with expansive names like African Plains, you'll find barred concrete cells.

Among more than 2,000 licensed U.S. exhibitors of nonhuman animals, fewer than 9 percent have sought and received accreditation by the American Zoo and Aquarium Association (AZA).[5] Most U.S. zoos comprise hellish confinement units incarcerating physically and psychologically deprived animals.[6] Inmates usually are confined indoors every night and throughout wintry weather. Typically, they spend sixteen hours a day in small, barren cells.[7] Many—especially invertebrates, birds, reptiles, amphibians, and small mammals confined behind glass—never go outside. Yet, as with enclosures, the language applied to exhibiting institutions suggests freedom and naturalness. While keeping many birds in small cages, a Miami zoo calls itself Parrot Jungle and Gardens.[8]

In 1993 the New York Zoological Society changed its name to the Wildlife Conservation Society and asked the public to drop the word *zoo* because of its negative connotations. Under the Society's management the Central Park (Manhattan), Prospect Park (Brooklyn), and Queens Zoos have become Wildlife Centers. Whereas *zoo* evokes images of forcible displacement and confinement, *wildlife center* suggests a largely natural environment located within nonhumans' native habitat. Only public resistance prevented a permanent change from Bronx Zoo to International Wildlife Conservation Park. The new name would have transformed urban imprisonment of individuals into global preservation of species.

~~Captivity~~ "Freedom"

According to Michael Robinson, director of the National Zoo (Washington, D.C.), it's "biologically ignorant to think of zoos as prisons."[9] The *American Heritage Dictionary* defines prisons as places of "confinement," "forcible restraint," or "captivity." That exactly describes zoos.

"Animals in the wild are as confined by territorial boundaries as zoo animals are by their enclosures," Robinson claims.[10] A rabbit behind glass that she has heavily scratched in frantic attempts to escape; a bald eagle in a small, rusted cage; a snow leopard in a corncrib cage—do these animals find their enclosures no more confining than natural territorial boundaries?[11] At Robinson's own institution, two Andean condors are caged so that they barely can fly and never can soar; restricted to glass cases or to cells with low ceilings, numerous reptiles, birds, and small mammals never feel a breeze or see the sky.[12] In 1997 I saw one such National Zoo inmate—a lone Geoffroy's cat confined behind glass—frenetically pacing.

Rather than admit that zoos deprive animals of freedom, some zoo professionals pretend that freedom doesn't exist. "Freedom is a meaningless abstraction when applied to the wild state of animals," Robinson contends.[13] As expressed by the Denver Zoo's director, "All animals are captives of their environment"; because nature can be harsh, "animals that are so-called 'living free' are not living free at all."[14] Whoever said that freedom means security or ease? Freedom means "liberty from slavery, detention, or oppression."[15] To prevent flight, many zoos clip birds' wings, violating their very nature. Captured and placed in a "terrarium," some snakes repeatedly strike the glass. Shipped from wintertime in Australia to summertime at the Philadelphia Zoo, a Bactrian camel covered with a thick winter coat of hair was forced to give rides in intense heat. Each day, all day, she trudged around a paddock, bearing human weight up to 400 pounds (181 kg).[16] Such forced detention and servitude are freedom's antithesis.

In his novel *1984* George Orwell depicts a totalitarian state that brainwashes the public through doublespeak, including the slogans "Freedom is Slavery" and "Slavery is Freedom." Like Orwell's fictional agents of mind control, zoo promoters work at convincing the public that Freedom is Captivity and Captivity is Freedom. Two tigers confined to a cage have "freedom" from enemies, Clarke has remarked. With equal validity, we could say that a human locked inside a room has "freedom" from muggers. According to Robinson, "For many species, zoos may offer the ultimate freedom—freedom from extinction." Individuals, not species, experience freedom or captivity. And, again, freedom means liberty, not guaranteed longevity.[17]

In any case, captivity poses its own threats. At two National Zoo facilities in winter 2000, two Grevy's zebras—members of an endangered species—died from the cold. Fed an inadequate diet, they had virtually no body fat to protect them from low temperatures. One was eight years old; the other was one. Grevy's zebras can live to 30.[18] In 1994, also at the National Zoo, a teenage boy dropped a large rock onto an Australian black swan. She died of internal bleeding.[19] Raped and beaten by an intruder at the Buttonwood Zoo (New Bedford, Massachusetts), a tame two-year-old fallow deer named Rachel suffered "head injuries, a broken jaw and severe bleeding from the rectum and vagina." She died two days later.[20] Quite apart from fatal negligence and abuse, captivity causes countless nonhuman animals to die prematurely. For example, many captured reptiles refuse to eat, and starve to death.[21]

So that inmate deaths will attract little notice, some zoos avoid giving inmates personal names known to the public.[22] Concealing the deaths of publicly known inmates requires more-drastic measures. Like many other zoos, the Philadelphia Zoo solicits contributions by encouraging the public to "adopt" zoo inmates. When a slow loris named Boris died, the zoo told his adopters only that he was "currently not on exhibit." Adopters were asked to keep contributing, this time in behalf of a loris named Cloris. Soon after, Cloris died. Instead of informing adopters of her death, the zoo acquired another loris and pretended that *he* was Cloris.[23] By emphasizing some inmates' longevity while downplaying others' deaths, zoos make captivity seem benign.

"How then can we defend zoos from the charge of overriding animals' right to freedom?" Glasgow Zoo education officer Stephen Bostock ponders. Unable to give an adequate answer, he resorts to redefining freedom as "being in an environment in which the majority of their needs are catered for."[24] Zoos fail to provide freedom even so creatively defined. They condemn a peregrine falcon to a tent-shaped cage only 9 feet (2.7 m) tall at its highest point; a polar bear to a den without light, a pool, or adequate ventilation; and chimpanzees to solitary confinement within bare concrete cells.[25] Many zoo inmates lack sorely needed medical attention. In a concrete enclosure at the Sacramento Zoo, the grizzly bear Bruno lay dying for nearly a week, bleeding and fighting for breath. Finally the zoo called in a veterinarian to euthanize him.[26] While investigating Florida zoos in 1996, veterinarian John Gripper saw numerous ailing animals such as a raccoon hobbling in obvious pain and an emaciated white-tailed deer, with an apparently long-unmended broken jaw, struggling to eat.[27] But even the finest care wouldn't compensate for loss of liberty. How many of us would consent to physically comfortable imprisonment?

"I don't like the word 'captivity,'" a zoo proponent has stated. Nor do other zoo apologists. As "suitable substitutes" for *captivity*, Bostock proposes *keeping* and *holding* (which implies that imprisonment is temporary). Robinson favors *custodianship*, which suggests that incarceration aids and protects the incarcerated.[28]

Because *captive* means "held prisoner," Robinson seeks a "simple word to substitute." The word *captive* is losing currency. Zoo apologist Colin Tudge prefers *conservation breeding* to *captive breeding*. In the 1990s the World Conservation Union's Captive Breeding Specialist Group changed Captive to Conservation.[29]

Zoos shun the candid term *captor*. Robinson would eliminate *keeper* because it has "overtones of imprisonment." He urges zoo personnel to use *caretaker* instead. With *caretaker*, zoo staff present themselves as protectors, rather than exploiters, of nonhuman animals. Having virtually absolute power over their prisoners, zoo captors can abuse them with impunity. To lessen the sexual arousal of an Indian rhino named Billy, a book on the Philadelphia Zoo relates, keepers would "whack" his erect penis with a shovel. The owner of the Natural Bridge Zoo (Natural Bridge, Virginia) reportedly has beaten monkeys so severely that afterwards they've remained lying on the floor of their cage for days.[30]

Helping zoos to escape the onus of injustice, the terms *zoo animal* and *display animal* falsely link imprisonment to a nonhuman's own nature. When *zoo* precedes *veterinarian* or *director*, it describes an individual who thinks and behaves in a certain way. But *zoo animal* actually says nothing about a nonhuman except that they're confined to a zoo. "Display animals" really are displayed animals.

Zoos avoid references to zoo "inmates" or "prisoners." Belying involuntary confinement, they call their captives "residents" and "ambassadors for their species." Nonhuman animals in zoos are political prisoners. The politics is speciesism.

"Mindless" Bears and "Hyper" Baboons

As a result of prolonged deprivation and stress, zoo captives show obsessive-compulsive behavior, including self-mutilation. Disingenuously, zoo staff downplay the pathological habits that indicate suffering.

Over and over, captive giraffes lick the walls of their cage, suck its bars, and sway their head. After the Born Free Foundation videotaped compulsive head swaying by giraffes at a zoo in Twycross, England, a zoo spokesperson called the behavior "a natural way for a giraffe to express itself."[31] Captive tigers and other cats pace, some so incessantly that they wear tracks into the ground. According to a guide at Lincoln Park Zoo (Chicago), Bengal tigers who pace aren't frustrated by confinement and inaction; "They're just exercising."[32] Free-living bears spend most of their active time foraging, hunting, or catching fishes. Captive bears compulsively bite the bars of their cage, shake their head, and sway. Some pace so much that their feet bleed. At the San Diego Zoo in 1996, inside the world's largest polar bear exhibit, the adult bear Bonnie and the cubs Chinook and Shakari continuously paced a set distance, returned, and then repeated the ritual; throughout, Chinook bobbed her head. In response to different visitors who expressed concern, a guide stationed at the exhibit repeatedly stated that the bears were pacing "because it's relaxing."[33] An animal behaviorist employed by the zoo called the pacing "mindless."[34] Then, why did the zoo consider giving the bears Prozac™, as other zoos have done to lessen bears' pacing?[35] In addition to denying pathology, describing nonhuman obsessive-compulsive behavior as "natural," "exercising," or "mindless" casts the sufferers as automatons.

Captive nonhuman primates repeatedly bite themselves, throw up and then eat their vomit, and show other pathological behavior. Born sickly, the Lincoln Park Zoo monkey Puddles (a DeBrazza's guenon) was rejected by his mother, who urinated on him. Puddles developed numerous sores. Separated from his mother and denied the companionship of any other DeBrazza's guenon, Puddles reacted to chronic deprivation by rocking himself and beating his head against the wall. A keeper labeled him "weird." Also at Lincoln Park, a mandrill (a large baboon) named Jonesie tore out her hair. The same keeper described her as "bizarre, schizzy, hyper."[36] Such language falsely indicates that emotionally disturbed zoo inmates are exceptions and that the fault lies with them rather than their cruel treatment.

"Training" and "Discipline"

During a single day, free-living elephants may travel 50 miles (80 km) and forage for twenty hours. In zoos, most elephants are kept chained at night.[37] Many are chained sixteen to seventeen hours a day.[38] (Because chained elephants are forced to stand in their own waste, many die from foot infection that spreads throughout their body.) Although intensely social, elephants often are confined alone in barren enclosures. Captive elephants compulsively sway from side to side, swing their head, and lift their feet in left–right alternation. Living free, elephants rarely are violent. But captivity causes some elephants to show aggression. In zoo parlance, captive elephants who disobey or actively defy their captors are "punished." The means range from starvation to isolation lasting months or years.[39] The word *punished* blames the elephants for behavior elicited by deprivation and abuse. Because the treatment of captive elephants is especially abusive, the language of elephant "handlers" is especially dishonest.

The African elephant Dunda had lived among a small group of elephants at the San Diego Zoo most of her eighteen years when she suddenly was separated from all her keepers and elephant companions. She was moved to a completely unfamiliar place, the San Diego Wild Animal Park (Escondido, California), and confined inside a barn. Terrified, Dunda threatened some of her new captors. Keepers then chained her legs, pulled her down onto her elbows and knees, and tied her—splayed—to the floor. Over the next two days, while Dunda remained bound and splayed, five keepers struck her on the head with ax handles more than a hundred times. Three weeks later, Dunda's face still was swollen. More than three months after the beatings, her head showed scarred and jagged skin and she continued to rub unhealed wounds.[40] A Park spokesman called Dunda's beatings "training."[41] The executive director of the Zoological Society of San Diego (which runs the zoo and the Park) called them "discipline."[42] "On a par with you hitting your German shepherd with a rolled-up newspaper," the Park's chief elephant "handler" commented.[43]

Dismissing Dunda's injuries as "superficial," he stated, "We love these animals."[44]

After 36 years in a barren enclosure at the Milwaukee County Zoo, the Asian elephant Lota faced transport to a company that "trains" elephants for circus performances. Suffering from severe diarrhea indicative of intense fear, Lota was forced toward a truck. "Handlers" yelled at her, pulled ropes attached to chains around three of her ankles, and repeatedly stabbed her with hand-held hooks. One stomped on her trunk. Lota was halfway into the truck when the chain around one of her ankles broke. Her upper body tumbled from the truck. With a thud, she landed headfirst on concrete. Lota screamed and tried to right herself. Bleeding, she bellowed and struggled as men continued to strike her legs, back, and head with hooks. Then someone drove the truck forward, causing her to fall out. Lota righted herself and started to reenter the truck. Again she fell. Again the men beat her. One used a metal rod with such force that it bent. After a three-hour ordeal, Lota, finally inside the truck, was driven away.[45]

The next day, the *Milwaukee Sentinel* printed a photo that shows a keeper swinging a crowbar at Lota. Ludicrously, the caption states that she was "coaxed" toward the truck.[46] As reported in a companion article, zoo veterinarians equated Lota's injuries with a knuckle scrape.[47] (Later a zoo spokeswoman would claim that Lota had suffered no injuries at all.)[48] The *Sentinel*'s coverage of the "loading" failed to mention that Lota was beaten, noting only that she fell repeatedly and left "bleeding and bruised."[49] A follow-up *Sentinel* article reported that hand-held hooks had been used to "guide" Lota.[50] Even the *Sentinel*'s initial statement that Lota "fell" was more than zoo officials would tolerate. A zoo representative phoned the newspaper to complain.[51] The *Sentinel* promptly printed an article relaying the zoo's claim that Lota intentionally "lay down" rather than fell.[52] At a 1991 zoo-industry conference, the zoo's principal large-mammal keeper stated that Lota "took advantage of the slack" after the chain broke and "lay down."[53] At another conference, in a presentation titled "A Lota Due about Nothing," the zoo's PR director read from the same script: Lota "took advantage of the slack and laid down."[54]

Hired to supervise Lota's move, Don Meyer operates a zoo and has worked nationwide as a keeper and elephant "handler." In a 1992 affidavit to the U.S. Department of Agriculture, zoo owner Craig Perry relates that he arranged for Meyer to "train" a newly purchased African elephant named Teaha (whom Meyer referred to with an unspecified epithet that Perry indicates is similar to *whore*). After Teaha had been with Meyer for two weeks, Perry visited Meyer's facility and was "appalled" by Teaha's many "cuts and open wounds." He questioned Meyer, who told Perry "that this was the unpublicized training of an elephant." For a week Perry watched as Teaha was "continuously abused." She was kept chained by her legs inside a barn, beaten with baseball bats and ax handles, and given 110-volt electric shocks (comparable to those from a household electric socket). Yet Perry left Teaha with Meyer for four more months, during which she apparently remained chained. When Teaha's "training" was over, she barely could walk.[55] In 1993, having used Meyer's services for more than a decade, Lincoln Park Zoo's principal mammal keeper stated, "Don is a consummate professional. . . . He has great respect for animals and a caring that goes beyond those he owns."[56]

"Education"

While demonstrating contempt for nonhuman animals, zoo professionals claim to teach respect. "We're going to save animals by being great educators," Zoo Atlanta director Terry Maple has boasted.[57] The evidence indicates otherwise.

Zoogoers view exhibits only fleetingly, studies show. At thirteen U.S. zoos the average length of time that visitors watched various nonhuman mammals ranged from fourteen seconds for Malayan tapirs to less than two minutes for orangutans. In the National Zoo's reptile building, visitors viewed each exhibit an average six-and-a-half seconds.[58]

Most comments on exhibited animals consist of little more than labeling. Visitors classify the inmates—"That's a tiger," "There's a duck"—often incorrectly. They declare them ugly, beautiful, creepy, or cute. Zoogoers rarely discuss weighty matters like evolution, habitat preservation, or nonhuman well-being.[59]

To assess the extent to which zoos impart biological knowledge, Stephen Kellert and Julie Dunlap gave written true–false tests to approximately a hundred people immediately before and after they visited the Philadelphia Zoo, Sedgwick County Zoo (Wichita), or Arizona-Sonora Desert Museum (a Tucson zoo). Most visitors scored lower *after* their visit. At various exhibits, Kellert and Dunlap also asked, "What did you learn at this exhibit?" "Nothing" was the most frequent answer at all three zoos. In addition, Kellert and Dunlap surveyed visitors' attitudes. Overall, post-zoo attitudes were more *negative*, marked by increased dislike and fear of nonhuman animals as well as a stronger desire to see them under human control and domination.[60]

In a study by Arizona State University psychologists, three groups of college students viewed seven slides, each showing a bear, snake, zebra, lion, elephant, gorilla, or chimpanzee in one type of setting: natural environment, seminatural zoo enclosure, or zoo cage. Students who saw animals in either kind of zoo environment characterized them as less graceful, less dignified, and of less value than did students who saw them in a natural setting. The evidence indicates that "displaying animals in zoos detracts from their inherent dignity in the eyes of the public," the researchers concluded.[61]

Zoos can't foster genuine understanding. The word *zoo* connotes confusion because menageries sever natural connections and impose artificial ones. Instead of offering a glimpse of beaver society, the Ferme Aqua-Zoo (Edmundston, New Brunswick) has exhibited a lone beaver in a tiny enclosure without any swimming area.[62] The San Diego Zoo has displayed an African civet, a nocturnal cat who naturally lives in thicket, in a sunny concrete pen.[63] Zoos disproportionately feature mammals, reinforcing the speciesist belief that members of our biological class are more important than other animals.

By separating humans from all other animals, zoos preach anthropocentrism rather than teach biodiversity. They promote a pre-Darwinian worldview. Humans are the privileged observers and manipulators. Nonhumans are framed objects that exist to gratify human desires. Even the PR-motivated emphasis on "education" transmits a speciesist message: The zoogoer's experience matters more than the inmate's. Touted as institutions that increase public interest in "wildlife conservation," zoos actually embody the human acquisitiveness that lies behind habitat destruction and species extinctions.

"Conservation"

"Wildlife conservation is hot!" an AZA public relations officer declared at a 1989 industry conference. Terming *wildlife conservation* "today's buzzword," she announced, "Wildlife conservation is 'our marketing ace in the hole'"; zoos "should be perceived as major players in this movement." Marketing zoos as "conservation organizations" has improved their public image, another AZA public relations officer reported six years later. Similarly, in 1992 London Zoo director Jo Gipps summarized previous management's "basic problem" this way: "Nobody realized conservation can sell tickets." Gipps began a PR campaign advertising the zoo as "Conservation in Action."[64]

Zoos don't "conserve wildlife." As expressed by the International Union of Directors of Zoological Gardens (IUDZG), some national laws and international regulations "hamper or delay" taking nonhumans from their natural habitats and putting them into zoos. The IUDZG has advocated weakening these laws and regulations, such as those restricting trade in members of endangered species.[65]

In the U.S., as elsewhere, zoos remain involved in the capture (euphemized as "collection") of free-living nonhumans. In 1996 the Woodland Park Zoo (Seattle) trapped three black-billed magpies in Washington State; through dealers, the zoo imported a tamandua (an anteater) and three crested oropendolas (blackbirds) captured in Guiana. Also in 1996, the Phoenix Zoo bought four green-and-black poison-dart frogs and four strawberry poison-dart frogs captured in Hawaii; caught a Gambel's quail, an Arizona giant hairy scorpion, a vinegarroon (a large whip scorpion), two orb weaver spiders, two green scarab beetles, two rhinoceros beetles, two stick mantises, and numerous desert leaf-cutter ants in Arizona; and purchased two Guianan toucanets (small toucans), six yellow-rumped caciques (blackbirds), and nine green oropendolas (blackbirds) trapped in Surinam. The same year, the Zoological Society of San Diego bought thirteen mammals from a dealer who captured them in South Africa: two bat-eared foxes, two desert lynxes, three Cape ground squirrels, and six rock hyraxes (who resemble woodchucks). The Society also paid dealers for 91 birds ranging from red-throated bee-eaters trapped in equatorial Africa to Steller's sea eagles caught in Russia.[66]

Zoos claim to "conserve" species through captive breeding. Largely, captive breeding is inbreeding. Many zoo inmates carry the genes of repeated incest. Highly inbred, captive-born cheetahs rarely have healthy offspring and easily succumb to infectious disease. Some zoos participate in so-called Species Survival Plans (SSPs), which attempt to minimize inbreeding but still involve severely restricted populations. To increase genetic variation, SSP zoos preferentially breed captives thought to possess genes not yet common within these populations. But rare genes aren't necessarily better. In nature, some genes predominate within any given species because those genes confer survival advantages. Human manipulation can't replace natural selection. "We don't know what genes a tiger needs to survive in the wild," one zoo professional has admitted. "We're playing God a lot. . . . It's just scary as hell."[67]

Capturing, transporting, and maintaining nonhuman animals for the professed purpose of "conserving" them is enormously expensive. As of 1990 it cost more than 46 times as much to keep one African elephant in a zoo as to safeguard sufficient natural habitat to sustain that elephant and countless other inhabitants.[68] For several hundred thousand dollars a year, an African national park can protect the nonhumans within its borders from nearly all "poaching."[69] It costs millions to build one high-tech zoo exhibit.

Many animals in zoo "breeding programs" die without reproducing. Between 1984 and 1993, 35 Sumatran rhinos—members of a critically endangered species—were caught with pit traps in southeast Asia for placement in zoos. Twelve died during or shortly after capture. As of 1995, only one survivor (already pregnant when captured) had reproduced.[70]

"We just flat out aren't going to save [SSP] animals in zoos," Maple has conceded.[71] But depicting zoos as saviors of species plays well with the public.

"I will [be] knocking on natural editors' doors to sell them on the '20th Century Ark' story," an AZA public relations officer promised colleagues in 1989.[72] She and other industry promoters have succeeded. Newspaper articles that call zoos "arks" are legion, as are books with titles like *The Ark Evolving*, *The Stationary Ark*, and *The Modern Ark*. The ark metaphor implies that captive breeding eventually will enhance free-living populations. Few reintroduction projects involving captive-bred animals have helped to establish self-sustaining populations in nature—apparently only 16 of 145 such projects documented as of 1995. Even fewer have entailed any zoo involvement. Most zoos never have participated in any reintroduction program.[73] Zoos are unsuited to preparing nonhumans for freedom. Their captives generally lack the fitness of free-living nonhumans, who are more active. Many zoo inmates also lack survival skills, especially those normally learned from a parent. The notion that humans should attempt to save species apart from their ecosystems is arrogant, simplistic, and reductionist. Black-footed ferrets bred and released by the National Zoo have been decimated by disease and a scarcity of prairie dogs, on whom they prey.[74] Zoos aren't arks; they're showboats.[75]

In the end, the word *conservation* always is telltale. Those who speak of "conserving" nonhumans regard them as exploitable things to be manipulated by and for humans. That attitude can't possibly save species; it remains the primary cause of their extinction.

"Research"

Along with education and conservation, zoo professionals cite research as justification for zoos' existence. Overwhelmingly, zoo-industry research focuses on keeping nonhumans captive.

The thousands of inmates in a major zoo span a vast anatomical, physiological, and behavioral range. No one possesses adequate knowledge to care for all of these animals. Euphemizing their trial-and-error approach as a "challenge," zoo veterinarians often express bewilderment. They "wouldn't even be able to speculate" on the cause of an animal's illness.[76] "You wish you knew what normal was."[77]

In May 1996 St. Paul's Como Zoo anesthetized an eleven-year-old giraffe, Sunny, for hoof trimming. After the procedure, his tongue swelled so much that he couldn't eat or drink. Sunny was euthanized. We "have no idea" what caused the swelling, the zoo's director stated.[78] In August a calf fathered by Sunny died soon after birth. In September the nine-year-old mother, Gigi, died of a digestive-tract ailment, again of unknown cause.[79] Although zoos first held giraffes captive thousands of years ago, the industry still lacks critical knowledge of their health needs.

Zoo promoters shrewdly portray myriad mistakes as endless investigation. Harmful ignorance becomes research. No captivity, no need for further "research."

"Exhibits"

The pursuit of knowledge never could justify imprisoning innocent individuals, of any species. But zoo professionals regard nonhuman animals primarily as objects of curiosity rather than individuals with rights. Museum terminology reinforces this view. The Virginia Living Museum (Newport News), Arizona-Sonora Desert Museum, and other zoos dub their principal keepers "curators" (Curator of Mammals, Curator of Birds) and their inmates "exhibits." The public and press have adopted zoo parlance. Following the death of Kumari, a much-publicized baby Asian elephant at the National Zoo, a school teacher complained that her students had come to the zoo "especially for two or three exhibits. One of them was her."[80] An "exhibit" also may comprise multiple animals. While Lota was one of four elephants at the Milwaukee County Zoo, the director referred to her as "25 percent of the exhibit."[81] Zoo inmates constitute "the collection."

To the industry, zoo inmates are human possessions, "precious objects" in Bostock's words.[82] "Vandals" break into zoos and injure or kill inmates. Zoo administrators see their captives as commodities: "inventory." They "shop" for tigers and use polar bears as "trading material." Zoo captives are *loaned*, *leased*, *rented*, *borrowed*, *donated*, *marketed*, and *merchandised*. The words reflect the attitude. Asked why an elephant in Monroe, Louisiana's zoo had been left with an untended broken leg, the city's mayor answered, "He was bought that way. It was a used elephant."[83]

"Breeding Stock"

Zoo professionals regard nonhumans of certain genotypes as "genetic resources": "breeding stock." Captive breeding involves invasive manipulation, such as electroejaculation, drug-induced superovulation, artificial insemination, contraception maintained with pills or implants, and surgical removal and implantation of embryos. In 1994 the

National Zoo subjected a two-and-a-half-year-old cheetah, Mazunga, to a sperm removal procedure. He died the next day.[84] Through embryo transfer, zoos have forced nonhumans to bear animals of other species. For example, a cow has borne a gaur (an Asian ox), and a horse a zebra. Zoos have begun attempts to implant embryos into free-living nonhumans as well.

To prevent or increase breeding, zoos separate longtime companions, who may be shipped thousands of miles away. At the San Francisco Zoo the orangutans Josephine and Denny and their ten-year-old daughter Violet formed a close-knit family. Then an SSP committee decreed that Josephine and Denny, being of different subspecies, must be separated: Josephine must go to the Philadelphia Zoo and mate with another Bornean orangutan; Denny must stay in San Francisco and mate with another Sumatran.[85] When Josephine left, Denny sat bawling. According to San Francisco Zoo visitors, he became disconsolate and withdrawn.[86] The zoo's director declared the separation "a great triumph for conservation."[87] At the Philadelphia Zoo, Josephine (renamed Rita) did mate and give birth, to a daughter named Jingga. Along with 21 other nonhuman primates, mother and daughter died in a 1995 fire. Referring to Josephine's and Jingga's deaths, the zoo's principal primate keeper remarked, "We basically lost an entire bloodline."[88]

"Surplus"

However young and healthy, captives judged inappropriate for exhibition or breeding are considered "excess" and usually are "unloaded" or killed. Each year, U.S. zoos label thousands of nonhuman animals "surplus" and treat them accordingly.[89]

After the Milwaukee County Zoo gave Lota away, she ended up, with tuberculosis and foot fissures, in a circus that has forced her to do hind-leg stands and other strenuous tricks.[90] Since the 1980s, hundreds of monkeys have gone from the Detroit Zoo (Royal Oak, Michigan) and Henry Vilas Zoo (Madison, Wisconsin) to vivisection facilities. At least dozens of these monkeys have been used in invasive experiments and killed.[91] Numerous zoos, many of them AZA-accredited, have sold "dispensable" animals to owners of shooting operations or nonhuman-animal traffickers with ties to such operations.[92] For at least fifteen years, fawns, bear and lion cubs, and other animals born at the Irvine Park Zoo (Chippewa Falls, Wisconsin) have been handed over to a trafficker who has transported bears to slaughter and auctioned other nonhumans to flesh brokers.[93]

Other "surplus" animals remain at the zoo, consigned to cramped enclosures hidden from public view. Still others are "euthanized." In a bungled attempt at justification, Bostock writes, "Culling in zoos is out of virtual necessity, given, certainly, that we have zoos, which is not a necessity."[94] As in hunting and fishing, the word *cull* transforms murder prompted by artificial needs into something natural and beneficial. The killing extends to members of endangered species. The Detroit Zoo, for example, has killed healthy tigers and scimitar-horned oryxes (African antelopes).[95] An SSP necessarily involves "culling healthy but extraneous individuals," a former director of the zoo has stated, terming the systematic murder a "management tool."[96] Species Survival Plans actually are Individual Death Plans.

"Specimens"

After she received thirteen red howler monkeys captured in Bolivia, San Diego Zoo principal primate keeper Diane Brockman calculated, "If only three die, we're in good shape."[97] Four died. Brockman ordered five more. Captured and transported, the additional monkeys belonged to the wrong subspecies. Brockman ordered more. To zoo administrators, nonhuman animals are "specimens," generic representatives of their species or subspecies. "Backup" animals and new inmates "replace" those who die. Only species, not individuals, are irreplaceable. "Animals come in 'sets' that we call species," Bostock writes, "sets of very similar though not identical specimens."[98] He ranks an individual tiger as less unique than either their species or a human work of art and therefore less worthy of protection. No doubt he judges individual humans more generously.

Leaving nonhumans nameless makes it easier to ignore their individuality. Two sociologists who visited dozens of zoos worldwide found that inmates who attract little public attention or live in large groups, such as herds, usually lack a personal name.[99] In 1991 a reporter noted that most Miami Metrozoo inmates were nameless, apparently because "keepers aren't supposed to anthropomorphize" or "become emotionally involved."[100] Similarly, as of 1995 the Minnesota Zoo (Apple Valley) identified all inmates only by number—except for a wolverine called Dork. A keeper at the zoo expressed a desire to avoid supposed anthropomorphism: "When you become personally involved with the animal, you don't look at him objectively. You're assigning emotions or feelings to an animal that don't exist."[101] Personal involvement with anyone (nonhuman or human) increases understanding of that individual. Exploiters guard against genuine relationships with those they exploit because empathy and exploitation are mutually exclusive.

A personal name often constitutes a zoo PR ploy rather than an acknowledgment of nonhuman individuality. The Philadelphia Zoo's ADOPT program succeeded only after the "adoptees" received personal names. A marketing director at Brookfield Zoo (Brookfield, Illinois) has cited PR as Brookfield's primary reason for naming inmates. Personal names boost Animal Adoption donations, increase public interest, and please the press, she has noted. Referring to a particular captive by number or species "just doesn't have the same pizazz."[102]

Personal names rarely appear on zoo cages, even those containing a single animal. The standard zoo sign identifies an enclosure's inmates by species (often family and order as well), describes not the imprisoned animals but their free-living counterparts, and does so in collective terms such as weight range, average or maximum life span, possible diets and habitats, and the species' geographic extent and population status (especially if the species is endangered). "The things we are exhibiting are disappearing," the director of the Wildlife Conservation Society has remarked.[103] The "things" in zoo enclosures are individuals, not species.

"We have to be concerned with species and populations rather than individuals," Robinson has stated.[104] Zoos readily sacrifice individuals to the supposed eventual good of species. Of course, the sacrificed individuals never include humans, even though human overpopulation causes environmental devastation and humans are the primary destroyers of species and ecosystems. Like all other speciesists, zoo professionals apply a double standard.

Zoo apologists contend that nonhuman rights would accelerate the extinction of species. The opposite is true. Humans' presumed right to kill nonhumans and take their land has caused the widespread extinction that zoos publicly bewail. In a society that respected nonhuman rights, it would be illegal to kill nonhuman animals for reasons other than mercy, defense, or avoidance of imminent starvation. Their habitats would be off-limits to further "development." Instead of manipulating nonhuman reproduction, humans would curtail their own.

Zoos perpetuate the speciesism that drives destruction of the natural world. Only when these institutions are abolished and nonhuman animals are accorded a legal right to liberty and life will that destruction cease.

7

More Speciesism on Display

The Language of "Aquariums" and "Marine Parks"

> The whole marine-park industry is based on deception. . . . They call their dolphins and whales "ambassadors." But they are victims.
>
> —Richard O'Barry

Three boats close in on a pod of thirteen bottlenose dolphins. Circling, they force the dolphins into shallow water. The dolphins huddle together as a web of rope surrounds them, cutting off escape. Then they realize that they're trapped. In panic, some charge the net; twisting and thrashing, they become entangled. Among those pulled below by the tightening web are a mother and her baby. A crew member dives in, cuts the baby loose, and brings him aboard. Lying on his belly, head raised, eyes wide with terror, the baby screams. In the water his mother too gives shrill, jagged cries. Freed from the net by two crew members and led just outside its perimeter, she continues to scream for her baby. On board, the baby's breathing quickens, turns irregular and thin. He has gone into shock. A crew member returns him to the water and tries to revive him. But he is dead. The mother screams as her baby's body is brought on board. Having been taken on board, examined, and released, other dolphins flee. The mother remains alongside the boat. Even as the crew hauls in its net, she stays, until the boat departs.[1] As this eyewitness account reveals, dolphin capture traumatizes and kills. Justifying such cruelty requires verbal deception.

The language of aquatic-animal captivity is both speciesist and disingenuous. The very terms *aquarium* and *marine park* euphemize. Lacking *zoo*'s negative connotations and its direct reference to nonhuman animals (*zoo-*), they draw attention to aquatic and park settings, not captives. The settings are fake (a "marine" park has no sea), the imprisonment real. So-called aquariums and marine parks actually are aquatic-animal prisons. Former dolphin "trainer" Richard O'Barry rightly calls them aquaprisons.

"Collecting"

Before capturing three bottlenose dolphins in 1989, the National Aquarium in Baltimore (NAIB) instructed staff to "put our spin on the issues." Recommendations from the PR department included replacing the word *capture* with *collection.*[2] One of the "collected" dolphins, Benni, died before reaching the aquaprison.[3] The NAIB has advised staff to substitute *collect* for *capture* whenever addressing the public or press (which obligingly has adopted the euphemism).[4] The word *collect* conceals capture's violence.

By equating nonhuman animals with inanimate objects such as coins or stamps, *collect* also encourages a callous disregard of individual lives. Using lines with baited hooks, Miami Seaquarium has "collected" sharks.[5] Before delivering one live bull shark, two lines hauled in during a Seaquarium expedition brought up four dead sharks: a bull, two blacktips, and a hammerhead. Satisfied, the crew captain remarked, "One out of five's not a bad average."[6] From a completely human-centered perspective, the result was one live shark. From a nonspeciesist perspective the result was four sharks who suffered and died and one shark who was taken captive. Having caught fishes for Seaquarium, O'Barry estimates that only one in ten survived captivity for more than a week.[7]

Urging avoidance of words with "negative connotations," Sea World of Florida (Orlando) has instructed its visitor guides to say "acquired," not "captured," to "give guests a better overall impression."[8] Like *collect*, *acquire* avoids any suggestion of violence or reference to the nonhuman perspective. The euphemism also absolves Sea World of culpability: Sea World doesn't capture animals or arrange for their capture; it just passively acquires them.

In 1989, during the season when many belugas (white whales) are pregnant or nursing, motorboat crews set out to capture the first belugas for Chicago's Shedd Aquarium. The crews searched Manitoba's Churchill River for a juvenile whale. Spotting one, they disoriented and terrorized her by yelling, thumping on the boat, and speeding back and forth. Blocking escape, they forced her into shallow water. A crew member leaped onto her back and roped her by the neck. To prevent her from swimming, another man jumped onto her tail. Still others jumped onto her to halt her thrashing. She was dragged to shore, placed in a sling, and put on a boat for transport to a holding tank. Altogether the Shedd caught at least 25 belugas, held three for observation, and kept two, later named Immiayuk and Puiji.[9] For years, *Chicago Tribune* publisher Stanton Cook has been a Shedd trustee.[10] In promoting the Shedd, *Tribune* editors and reporters rival the Shedd's own PR staff. As if Immiayuk and Puiji willingly parted from freedom and their families, a *Tribune* reporter wrote that they "exchanged" the ocean's depths for an airplane's heights and "took up residence" in an aquaprison tank.[11] In 1992 the Shedd "collected" four more belugas. For PR purposes the Shedd needed to make its assault on the whales sound gentle and protective. As described by a Shedd spokeswoman, the captors "jump[ed] into the water" (rather than onto the belugas) and "put their arms around [the belugas] to hold them."[12]

"Homes" and "Habitats"

For eighteen months after their capture, Immiayuk and Puiji remained at the Point Defiance Zoo and Aquarium (Tacoma, Washington). Although each was about 15 feet (4.6 m) long, the two shared a circular tank only 30 feet (9.1 m) in diameter.[13] A *Chicago Tribune* writer called this tank the belugas' "temporary home."[14] When Immiayuk and Puiji were moved to the Shedd, they were placed in an indoor pool only 90 feet long, 70 feet wide, and 16 feet deep (27 x 21 x 5 m).[15] Another *Tribune* writer called this pool their "permanent home."[16] Immiayuk died in her "permanent home" in 1999, at age fourteen.[17] Free, she might have lived more than twice as long. While using *home*, without quotation marks, for the tanks and pools to which belugas are confined, *Tribune* editors put quotation marks around the word in reference to taking belugas from their natural ocean environment: "from their 'homes.'"[18] Like zoo professionals, aquaprison promoters use semantic reversal to portray a situation as its opposite. With the word *home*, the site of captivity becomes whales' rightful place; the artificial becomes natural.

The Shedd designates its beluga confinement area a "habitat." A 1993 visitor saw no habitat, only a pool surrounded by "fake rocks," "fake plants," and "fake birds": "One whale did nothing but frantically swim the same circular pattern, over and over, the entire time I was there. Another drifted with her blowhole just above the water, rarely moving. Over a period of many hours, there was no variation to their behavior."[19]

Sea World of Florida's Wild Arctic is a "100 percent fake polar environment" with an "artificially cooled" polar bear pool containing "artificially salted water" and "artificially frozen icebergs," a journalist has observed.[20] In addition to polar bears, the exhibit has confined belugas, walruses, penguins, and puffins.[21] Just as industry photos leave tank and pool borders invisible (giving the impression of open ocean), industry language excludes words that signal harsh confinement. Sea World of Florida has directed its staff to replace *tank* with *aquarium*, and *cage* with *enclosure*.[22]

Monterey Bay Aquarium (Monterey) has touted its Outer Bay exhibit—a tank 90 feet long, 52 feet wide, and 35 feet deep (27 x 16 x 11 m)—as an "indoor ocean" and "world without walls."[23] Even before the exhibit opened to the public, at least four yellowfin tunas fatally smashed into the walls of the "world without walls."[24] A blue shark developed so severe an infection from rubbing her jaw against the tank's walls and floor that she was euthanized.[25]

In ocean herds of 50–100 individuals, bottlenose dolphins swim up to 100 miles (161 km) a day and routinely dive several hundred feet (100 m). The NAIB restricts bottlenose dolphins to a concrete tank, partitioned to segregate males from females, 110 feet (34 m) in diameter and 24 feet (7 m) deep.[26] During a 1997 visit to the NAIB, I asked a dolphin "trainer" whether the entire tank is barren. "It depends on how you define *barren*," he answered. "There's nothing in the tank except water?" I pressed. "That's correct," he said. The NAIB has publicized the tank as "an ideal habitat for dolphins."[27] In this "ideal habitat" at least two dolphins have experienced chronic health problems: Akai is anemic; Hailey was euthanized in 1999 after years of suffering from anorexia and liver disease.[28] The NAIB has advised staff to replace *tank* with *pool* (a word associated with pleasure) and to euphemize *cage*, *pen*, and *isolation area* as *holding area* (which avoids any imagery of confinement).[29]

At least hundreds of thousands of nonhumans are currently confined to U.S. aquaprisons. As of 1995 the Monterey Bay Aquarium alone imprisoned more than 300,000.[30] Throughout the industry, most inmates live in small tanks. In 1997 I saw a 4-foot (1.2-m) electric eel confined to an NAIB tank 5 by 5 by 3 feet deep (1.5 x 1.5 x 0.9 m). New Orleans' Aquarium of the Americas has kept alligators too cramped to "move more than one body length in any direction."[31] Free, green turtles migrate more than a thousand miles. At the National Aquarium (Washington, D.C.) in 1997, the green turtle Sea-cil was suffering existence in a semielliptical tank that scarcely allowed him room to swim. During an hour-and-a-half visit, I repeatedly returned to Sea-cil. His position and expression never changed. Staring blankly, he remained immobile in one corner of the tank. Whether you call them homes, habitats, or oceans, aquaprison tanks remain cells incarcerating the innocent.

Like their zoo colleagues, aquaprison personnel verbally reverse freedom and coercion. Captive dolphins have "freedom" from predators, whereas free-living dolphins are "driven" to find food and "have to" hunt.[32] In nature, dolphins hunt in groups and eat a wide variety of live fishes. In captivity they eat dead fishes, usually previously frozen, of one or a few species. Most captured dolphins initially refuse to eat and are force-fed.[33]

Sea World of Florida has instructed its visitor guides to avoid the word *captivity* and substitute the "more positive" term *controlled environment*. The NAIB has advised staff to replace *captivity* with *aquarium setting* or *animal care facility* when addressing the public or press. Whereas *captivity* calls attention to the prisoners' plight, *controlled environment* and *aquarium setting* remove the prisoners from view. *Animal care facility* turns unjust imprisonment into succor.[34]

"Pampered" Captives

Care has little meaning in the aquaprison industry. In 1994 the Cabrillo Marine Aquarium (San Pedro, California) received a just-captured giant Pacific octopus later named Octavia. Although her tentacles were 13 feet (4 m) long, Octavia was confined to a tank 4 feet (1.2 m) wide and 5 feet (1.5 m) deep.[35] Normally orange-red, she soon paled to nearly white. After three months of captivity, Octavia yanked her tank's drain plug from its socket. As her tank drained, she suffocated. "We believe she was better off in our care," Cabrillo's exhibit director said.[36] Before the 1996 opening of UnderWater World (Bloomington, Minnesota), staff failed to monitor water quality adequately, quarantine all newly captured fishes, and properly diagnose and treat disease. Within a two-month period, 829 of approximately 2,500 fishes in holding tanks died.[37] A "husbandry" director involved in the start-up stated, "We're giving the animals the finest possible care."[38]

During his long tenure as Shedd director, William Braker described aquaprison inmates as "pampered." Like the Shedd's penguins? A *Chicago Tribune* writer has called the low, narrow case in which they live "penguin heaven." Confined behind glass, the penguins have a strip of water for swimming and a ledge of fake rocks filthy with molt and excrement.[39]

According to Sea World vice-president Brad Andrews, orcas (killer whales) and dolphins experience captivity as one long Club Med vacation.[40] In reality they suffer ongoing stress from confinement, noise, artificial lighting, human crowds, and other aspects of imprisonment. In the ocean, orcas travel a home range of 500–900 miles (800–1,500 km), through waters teeming with life. At Sea World of Texas (San Antonio), the orca Kotar repeatedly has beaten his head against his tank's walls.[41] No human observer has reported violent aggression between free-living orcas. But close confinement, a frustrated urge to hunt, and unstable, artificial social groups can cause such aggression between captives. In 1989 an audience at Sea World of California (San Diego) witnessed a violent confrontation between two female orcas, Kandu and Corky, who had sparred before. Kandu rammed into Corky with such force that the impact broke Kandu's upper jaw and severed nasal arteries. Spewing blood from her mouth and blowhole, Kandu died. To downplay her unnatural violence, Sea World employees marshaled euphemism, oxymoronic doublespeak, and semantic reversal. They termed Kandu's attack on Corky a "physical interaction," "one-whale altercation," and "bit of playing between the two whales."[42] Captive orcas and dolphins commonly require frequent doses of antibiotics and anti-ulcer medication.[43] Most die of stress-related infection, especially pneumonia.[44] Annual mortality rates are "significantly higher" for captive orcas and bottlenose dolphins than for free-living ones of the same age and sex.[45]

Because so many aquatic animals die prematurely in captivity, their captors conceal the toll in lives. Three days after the Scott Aquarium opened at the Henry Doorly Zoo (Omaha), all moon jellies (jellyfishes) in a tank died. The aquaprison posted this sign at the tank: "Animals temporarily off display."[46] At Sea World different orcas perform under the same name (Shamu, Namu, or Baby Shamu); offstage, orcas such as Orky and Corky bear the same names as predecessors.[47] As of 1989 an orca at Marineland of Canada (Niagara Falls, Ontario) was at least the fifth named Nootka.[48] Other "marine parks" too recycle orcas' personal names.[49] The practice presents a false picture of orca longevity. In its annual reports to the National Marine Fisheries Service, Sea World omits the personal names of nearly all its marine mammal captives, making it difficult for outsiders to know which of them have died.[50] Sea World of Florida has told its guides to avoid the words *dead* and *die*. It also has recommended lying: "If people ask you about a particular animal that you know has passed away, please say 'I don't know.'"[51]

Apart from the cost in money and PR, individual nonhuman deaths give aquaprison administrators little pause. Mentally reducing nonhuman beings to things, aquaprison staff "barter" with fishes, keep them "in storage" (in some cases for more than a year), and "replace" those who die. Three giant Pacific octopuses captured by the Vancouver Aquarium died the next day. The director didn't fret: "Our divers were able to keep us well-stocked."[52] A month after their capture by the Shedd, two three-year-old belugas were injected with a deworming drug. Within minutes both died of heart failure. Questioned about the deaths, Braker commented, "Any time that you're dealing with live animals, it's a perishable commodity."[53]

~~Entertainment~~ "Education"

Boston's New England Aquarium has presented California sea lions who balance balls, stand on one flipper, and "kiss" audience members.[54] The Point Defiance Zoo and Aquarium has forced a Pacific walrus named E.T. to perform equally demeaning tricks for food, ordering him to "Speak," "Whistle," and "Roll over."[55] In standard Sea World displays of speciesist dominance, a "trainer" rides an orca like a surfboard or two dolphins like water skis.[56] At the Aquarium of the Americas, sociologist George Lundskow witnessed gimmicky abuse of an octopus. While noting that octopuses are “shy,” “gentle,” and among the ocean’s “most intelligent animals,” a sign at the octopus’s tank invited visitors to flash a bright light at her and see her change color. A crowd gathered while the octopus remained hidden behind coral. When she fully emerged, someone pressed the flash-activating button. Alarmed, the octopus changed color and bolted back into hiding. Satisfied, the crowd dispersed. Before long, other visitors gathered for another round of Scare the Octopus.[57] While encouraging contempt, aquaprisons claim to instill “profound respect,” even “reverence,” for nonhuman animals.

Aquaprisons entertain at nonhumans’ expense, but proponents say that they educate. To maintain the pretense of education, aquaprisons avoid words associated with entertainment. The director of the Virginia Marine Science Museum (Virginia Beach) has said that the Museum’s display of live animals offers a learning experience; *entertainment* is “not a word we use to describe ourselves.”[58] According to a Shedd “naturalist,” the Shedd’s shows with belugas and Pacific white-sided dolphins aren’t “performances”; they’re “demonstrations of natural mammalian behavior.”[59] Sea World of Florida has instructed its guides to call marine mammals’ cued stunts “behaviors,” not “tricks.”[60] “Behavior” sounds so scientific and natural. But whales and dolphins often don’t perform as ordered. As Sea World’s chief veterinarian has remarked, consistent obedience can be a sign that a whale or dolphin is underfed, “so hungry that they’ll do anything for food.”[61] “Sea World was created strictly as entertainment,” one of its founders has acknowledged. “We didn’t try to wear this false façade of educational significance.”[62] The entire aquaprison industry hides behind that façade.

“Conservation”

Aquaprisons claim to advance the preservation of species and their native habitats. Like their zoo counterparts, aquaprison professionals call themselves conservationists.

The aquaprison industry consistently has *opposed* restrictions on the capture and killing of free-living marine mammals. Through lobbying, U.S. institutions that display marine mammals quashed a federal law that would have empowered states to set tighter restrictions on marine mammal capture than those outlined in the Marine Mammal Protection Act (MMPA).[63] Industry lobbyists also prevented MMPA regulations that would have required display facilities to meet higher standards of care before obtaining permits to capture marine mammals.[64] A temporary federal ban on dolphin capture in the Gulf of Mexico? The industry said no.[65] International Whaling Commission (IWC) restrictions on the capture and killing of small cetaceans? No again.[66] The proposed IWC restrictions might have ended the Japanese fishing industry's annual mass murder of dolphins and small whales, who are herded into coves and slaughtered. Sea World and other exhibitors have paid the killers for Pacific black whales captured during the carnage.[67]

Aquaprisons also do their own capturing. A massive amount. The Florida Aquarium (Tampa), Monterey Bay Aquarium, NAIB, New England Aquarium, Steinhart Aquarium (San Francisco)—all continuously catch aquatic animals.[68] In a single capture expedition, a New England Aquarium team shipped some 350 tunas to Boston.[69] For its 1992 opening, the New Jersey State Aquarium (Camden) caught thousands of animals, including sharks, rays, frogs, and sea turtles.[70] Before the 1998 opening of the Maui Ocean Center (Wailuku, Hawaii), a newspaper article reported that 99 percent of the Center's captives would be "taken from Hawaiian waters."[71] Because great white sharks draw visitors, Sea World of California has repeatedly captured great whites, even though the species may be endangered and none apparently has survived in captivity longer than sixteen days.[72] Asked how long inmates at the Aquarium of the Americas live, a staff "naturalist" told Lundskow, "Most of the fish live three or four months at the most. Some of the larger species live a little longer, maybe six months to a year." Does the Aquarium buy animals from a breeder? "Oh no," the staff member answered. "It's much cheaper to capture replacements in the wild."[73]

Aquaprison captures aren't limited to invading the waters. Using nylon mist nets, baited box traps, and other means, the Tennessee Aquarium (Chattanooga) has captured U.S. birds, even as they roost in a nest box. "The capture of wild birds has proven to be the most successful and dependable means of species acquisition for our collection," a Tennessee Aquarium bird keeper has noted, while claiming that public display may assist the "conservation and preservation of our declining bird populations."[74]

Braker has called aquaprisons "environmental organizations." Murray Newman, former director of the Vancouver Aquarium, has called them "environmental institutions." Like high-tech zoos, aquaprisons consume massive amounts of energy and materials. To maintain its Floridian Wild Arctic, Sea World refrigerates a 100,000-gallon (379,000-liter) pool. The Shedd's Oceanarium relies on pumping machinery that continually salinates, cleans, and recirculates 3 million gallons (11 million liters) of water.[75]

Publicly the Shedd bemoans the "oil and hydroelectric development" and PCB (polychlorinated biphenyl) pollution that threaten marine animals.[76] Privately the Shedd has invested in such major polluters as Monsanto, Mobil, and Texaco.[77] Federal and Illinois agencies repeatedly have fined Chemical Waste Management for illegal practices such as failing to label poisonous wastes as toxic, storing hazardous materials in amounts that exceed state limits, and disconnecting pollution-monitoring equipment while incinerating PCBs.[78] Previously a Shedd trustee, Chemical Waste Management vice-president James Banks currently is a Shedd governing member.[79]

The Vancouver Aquarium was founded and expanded with money from the environmentally destructive fishing, mining, and timber industries.[80] In Newman's own words, its H. R. MacMillan Tropical Gallery honors a "timber baron."[81] Before serving as the aquaprison's president, Ralph Shaw headed MacMillan Bloedel, a primary destroyer of old-growth trees in British Columbian rainforest.[82]

A wetlands "developer" (Louisiana Land and Exploration) sponsored the Aquarium of the Americas' Wetlands Preservation Gallery, which has displayed photos celebrating corporate exploitation of wetlands. The Aquarium's central exhibit features a model of an offshore oil rig. At the exhibit, Lundskow has noted text touting offshore drilling's economic benefits while making no mention of its devastating environmental effects, as well as a large plaque paying homage to Amoco, Shell, Exxon, and other petrochemical giants.[83]

"Research"

Knowing that "Squid have long been considered too difficult and delicate to house," the New England Aquarium has been experimenting with displaying loliginid squids. The squids have abraded themselves against their tank's walls, developed bacterial infections and other pathologies, and died prematurely. The aquaprison also has been experimenting with bluefin tunas, with the goals of exhibiting bluefins and rearing them, in ocean cages, for human consumption. Capable of 50-mph (80-km/h) speed, bluefins swim about 100 miles (161 km) a day when migrating; they traverse waters ranging from sub-Arctic to tropical. Bluefins who survive capture refuse to eat for days or weeks. Their captors force-feed them by prying their jaws open and dropping a dead fish down their throat. Probably from vitamin, calcium, and fatty-acid deficiencies, the bluefins develop cranial deformities. Some go blind. Aquaprisons legitimize and dignify such abuse by calling it research.[84]

Most belugas born in captivity die shortly after birth.[85] However, because the presence of belugas means money and prestige, aquaprisons persist in trying to breed belugas. At the Point Defiance Zoo and Aquarium in 1992, the beluga Mauyak bore a calf who died at birth. In 1994 she bore a calf who survived only twenty minutes.[86] Days later, Mauyak still circled her small pool slowly and incessantly. Each time that she reached the poolside spot where her baby had been lifted from the water for attempted resuscitation, she poked her head above the surface and "took long, searching looks."[87] To Mauyak the death was a source of grief. To Point Defiance's director it was "a learning process," the ongoing experiment of captivity.[88]

When aquaprison staff assist free-living nonhumans—the stranded, injured, or ill—they acquire knowledge in the process of helping, not harming. Such rescue and rehabilitation can continue without exhibition or captive breeding.

Nonhumans deserve freedom from exploitive captivity. Abuse under the guise of education, conservation, or research remains abuse. "Aquariums" and "marine parks" deprive animals of their well-being, their rights, and often their lives. Verbal deception prevents much of the public from considering the captives' perspective and seeing the truth.

8

In the Name of Science

The Language of Vivisection

> [The vivisector] not only calls his method scientific: he contends that there are no other scientific methods. When you express your natural loathing for his cruelty and your natural contempt for his stupidity, he imagines that you are attacking science.
>
> —George Bernard Shaw

From the early eighteenth century to the early twentieth, experimenters who cut up living nonhuman animals termed their practice vivisection. Since then, *vivisection*'s meaning has broadened. Along with the older meaning, *Webster's* offers "any form of animal experimentation esp. if considered to cause distress to the subject." The *American Heritage Dictionary* defines vivisection as "the act or practice of cutting into *or otherwise injuring* living animals, especially for the purpose of scientific research" (emphasis added). Vivisection includes any harmful use of nonhuman animals in experimentation, product testing, or education. However, vivisectors and their supporters (vivisectionists) now shun the word *vivisection* because it bears images repugnant to the general public. Recommending the term's abandonment, bioethicist Andrew Rowan deplores its "vile" connotations of torture.[1] Vivisection commonly involves torture. Because it unjustly harms innocent beings, it always is vile.

At a minimum, vivisection restricts nonhumans to highly confining environments. Routinely it inflicts pain, physical injury, and extreme deprivation. Usually it entails death. Each year in the U.S., vivisection kills at least tens of millions of animals.[2] Like other forms of speciesist abuse, vivisection survives with the aid of language that falsifies.

"Biomedical Research" and "Science"

For PR purposes, supporters call vivisection "biomedical research." This misnomer erases vivisection's victims and rewrites suffering and death as healing (*medical*) and life (*bio*). Only some—not most—vivisection pursues medical goals. Also, biomedical research encompasses numerous research methods, such as epidemiology, use of cell and tissue cultures, and clinical studies of human and nonhuman patients. The National Association for Biomedical Research and Foundation for Biomedical Research (FBR) don't promote harmless biomedical research methods; they promote vivisection. Veteran vivisector Adrian Morrison knows that antivivisectionists aim to abolish only research that harms animals, yet he accuses them of plotting to "destroy biomedical research."[3]

Vivisectionists sometimes drop *biomedical* and refer to vivisection simply as "research"—a ploy that eliminates other research methods. Gregory Maas, head of the Incurably Ill for Animal Research, and Susan Paris, president of the Americans for Medical Progress Educational Foundation, have called their vivisection promotion groups "pro-research" organizations. (Doubling the deception, FBR's president has dubbed vivisectionists the "pro-research movement." Movements advocate change, not preservation of long-entrenched abuses such as vivisection.)[4]

Science too substitutes for *vivisection*, as when antivivisectionists are accused of being "anti-science." Vivisectionists, including most journalists, couch the vivisection controversy as "animal advocates" versus "scientists." As a means of learning about humans, vivisection is inherently unscientific. Because species differ in anatomy and physiology, observations in nonhuman animals can't provide a valid basis for conclusions about humans. To what extent do particular findings in mice, dogs, or other nonhumans apply to humans? No one can know without comparing the nonhuman-animal data to the corresponding human data. But if the human data are available, the nonhuman data are superfluous. In lieu of human data, nonhuman-animal data are dangerously unreliable. Eighty percent of drugs fail human trials *after* passing nonhuman-animal tests.[5] In humans the drugs prove ineffective or harmful.

Vivisection examines nonhuman conditions, usually artificially induced. At best, some features of these conditions seem analogous to some features of particular human conditions. Analogies can neither refute nor confirm hypotheses, so vivisection can neither disprove nor verify any theory about humans. Human autopsy, computer analysis based on human-derived data, and *in vitro* research on human cells or tissues possess more validity than vivisection because they focus on human phenomena. In general, epidemiology, noninvasive studies of healthy humans, and clinical research with human patients have still greater validity because they rely on actual observation of living humans. Far from being synonymous with science, vivisection is a fundamentally unscientific way of seeking insights into human health.

To sustain the myth that vivisection is indispensable, vivisectionists have attempted to vitiate the word *alternatives*, meaning research methods free of vivisection. By definition, an alternative to something doesn't include the thing itself. However, in vivisection doublespeak, "alternatives to animal research" include harmful animal research that uses fewer animals or causes less suffering than other cruel methods; "animal test alternatives" include harmful animal tests. Vivisection apologist Alan Goldberg has lamented that *alternative* often is "misunderstood" to exclude vivisection.[6] Goldberg's definition of *alternative* clashes with the name of the Johns Hopkins University center that he directs: the Center for Alternatives to Animal Testing. The center's name serves PR goals.

Vivisectionists also apply the word *alternatives* to vivisection on animals whose abuse arouses little public concern. At an American Association for Laboratory Animal Science conference, a speaker on "Alternatives" advised vivisectors to escape public scrutiny by experimenting on unpopular mammals, such as pigs and mice, rather than dogs and cats. The audience responded with warm approval.[7]

Morrison places *alternatives* inside nullifying quotation marks and contends that benign research methods such as the use of human-derived tissue cultures qualify only as vivisection "adjuncts." The

National Institute of Mental Health makes the same claim and warns that the word *alternatives* might suggest that vivisection can be eliminated. In reality, vivisection is the unnecessary adjunct, to human studies.[8]

Used to mean methods free of vivisection, *alternatives* misleads only in assigning vivisection an undeserved primacy. Historically, nonhuman vivisection arose as an alternative to harmful research on humans. Neither is necessary. For valid and useful results, harmless research on humans remains paramount.

In a nonspeciesist society, harmless research methods wouldn't be viewed as alternatives but as moral imperatives. The unjust treatment of nonhuman animals wouldn't be an option. It would be illegal.

"Minor Discomfort"

Concealing vivisection's cruelty requires many linguistic ploys. In the 1930s, as coeditor of the *Journal of Experimental Medicine*, F. Peyton Rous implemented an editorial policy of deliberate verbal deception.[9] The *Journal*'s in-house publication guidelines for vivisection reports proscribed candid accounts of nonhuman suffering and death. One "General Rule" instructed, "Avoid expressions such as 'acute,' 'intense,' 'severe,' where they imply suffering."[10]

As evidenced by his publications, vivisector Martin Seligman gradually adopted such a rule. In a 1967 report on "learned helplessness" experiments on dogs, Seligman rated an electric shock of 4.5 mA (milliamperes) "severe." Yet he subjected 24 dogs (each strapped in a hammock and yoked at the neck) to shocks of 6 mA. (Humans feel pain at electric shock lower than 1 mA and find more than 5 mA unbearable.) Sixteen of the dogs were shocked 64 times. The other eight suffered 640 shocks. Dogs used in two follow-up experiments (among them, 24 who remained fully conscious but paralyzed by the drug curare) suffered even "more intense" shocks, of 6.5 mA.[11] In Seligman's experiments dogs urinated, defecated, struggled, gasped, and howled.[12] At least one died while being repeatedly shocked.[13] By 1976 Seligman was fictionalizing history. Now he referred to five-second shocks of 6 mA as only "moderately painful."[14] Finally, according to his 1991 book *Learned Optimism*, the dogs he tortured experienced nothing worse than "minor pain."[15]

With reference to vivisected animals, vivisectors usually avoid the word *pain*, substituting weaker terms. As expressed by two vivisectors, humans with advanced cancer of the head and neck endure "pain and suffering" and potentially "agonizing" radiotherapy, but mice lethally irradiated in their head and neck experience mere "discomfort." In another vivisector's words, even vivisectors who study "pain" cause their victims only "some discomfort."[16]

For nearly three years (1985–87), sociologist Mary Phillips observed vivisection in 23 laboratories at two research facilities in the New York City area. In one laboratory, a rat placed on a small box had his head immobilized by a vise. When a postdoctoral vivisector started drilling into his skull, the rat began to struggle. Held by the head, he attempted to run. His lower body fell over the box's edge. The rat dangled there, struggling. The drilling continued. Some minutes later the rat kicked the box over, forcing the vivisector to stop and inject him with more anesthetic. Before the anesthetic took effect, the vivisector resumed drilling. Again the rat struggled. Finally, ten minutes into the vivisection, the rat quieted. Throughout the rat's ordeal the laboratory's senior vivisector sat a few feet away, vivisecting another rat. When Phillips interviewed him three months later, she described the incident and asked if he thought the rat had experienced pain. "In that kind of situation," he answered, "it's probably more uncomfort than anything else."[17]

The vivisection establishment avoids the word *suffering* even more studiously than *pain*. The original (1978) bylaws of the Scientists Center for Animal Welfare (SCAW) stated a goal of "reducing unnecessary suffering" in vivisected animals. In 1988 the organization's board of directors expunged every mention of "suffering." Bioethicist Barbara Orlans, who was SCAW's director, reports that members considered the word "too inflammatory and likely to dissuade scientists [vivisectors] from joining." While observing daily routine in twenty U.S. vivisection laboratories, sociologist Arnold Arluke noticed that vivisectors and their assistants avoid the word *suffering* by substituting *distress*. Strongly provivisection, the mainstream press too balks at applying the word *suffering* to vivisection's victims. "Researchers Said to Be Minimizing 'Suffering' of Laboratory Animals," a *Birmingham News* headline reads.[18]

To avoid acknowledging that vivisected animals suffer, many vivisectors deny their victims' very capacity to suffer. At a vivisection seminar attended by ethicist Bernard Rollin, some speakers emphasized that they were "talking in quotes" when they referred to nonhuman animals' mental states: "When are the animals quote happy end quote?" In a 1992 industry article, quotation marks negate any nonhuman "experiencing" or "consciousness."[19]

Written in the language of behaviorism, most contemporary vivisection reports contain no reference to nonhuman thoughts and feelings. They note only observed behaviors. Injected with a neurotoxin, guinea pigs don't cry out with pain; they "exhibit vocalization responses." Infant rhesus monkeys separated from their mothers don't suffer, or even feel stress; they demonstrate a "highly stressful response." Instead of experiencing grief or fear, they show "cognitive and affective responses to separation." Such jargon implies that nonhumans act without experiencing.[20]

Substitute "impersonal medical terms" for those that graphically convey suffering or debilitation, Rous instructed his staff. In keeping with this policy, a staff member edited a 1934 article so that Chinese hamsters' "convulsions" became "symptoms of meningeal irritation." Vivisection jargon obscures suffering, even at the expense of clarity and accuracy.[21]

"Stimulation"

Torture aptly describes much vivisection. But, as psychologist Alice Heim has remarked, vivisection reports "never" contain the word. When an editorial in the journal *Pain* compared vivisection's infliction of suffering to "torturing of prisoners," a reader protested that such "emotion-laden" language suggests "evil-doing." Only a speciesist could see the torture of humans as evil but the torture of nonhumans as morally acceptable. Language that condemns speciesist abuse frequently is dismissed as emotion-laden—by those with a vested interest in the abuse. The word *torture* does suggest evil-doing. That's why vivisectors (like sportfishers) don't want it applied to their practice. Discussing vivisection in strictly scientific or other nonmoralistic terms protects it from moral judgment.[22]

Before each test session of a City University of New York experiment, pigeons were denied water for two days. Throughout each session, they were individually restrained in a cloth bag and attached to an apparatus via a block cemented to their skull. As the apparatus recorded their jaw movements, the pigeons received water—drop by drop. In the language of vivisection, this isn't torture; it's "classical conditioning."[23]

In vivisection, to "stress" means to torture, terrify, or otherwise cause to suffer. As reported in 1994 from the University of Pennsylvania School of Medicine, vivisectors subjected rats to a three-week "schedule of different daily stressors." Among other experiences, the "stressors" included 24 hours without water, 40 hours without food, a forced swim in near-freezing water, 5 minutes in an oven at 104 °F (40 °C), 2 hours of immobilization in a tube 1.5 inches (3.8 cm) in diameter, and, over the space of 35 minutes, 210 1-mA foot-shocks (rats flinch at foot-shock as low as 0.06 mA and jump at shock of about 0.5 mA). This "stress schedule" was "effective in producing a stress response." Vivisectors at New Jersey Medical School "stressed" golden hamsters genetically susceptible to heart disease, some of them already "obviously sick" from congestive heart failure. The hamsters were immobilized on their backs—taped to a board, their four limbs extended—two hours each day for five consecutive days at near-freezing temperature. Most died during the "stress" period.[24]

"Stimulation" too includes any means of torture: electric pulses to the brain that cause rabbits to defecate, rear, and frantically try to escape; needle jabs to the face of rats already suffering chronic facial pain from a tied-off nerve in their cheek; caustic chemicals squirted into hens' ulcerated mouths. As described in a 1991 report from the Yerkes Regional Primate Research Center, squirrel monkeys confronted a "stimulus-termination schedule" in which onset of a light signaled an "impending electric stimulus." If they pressed a lever within three seconds of the cue, the monkeys "avoided the stimulus." Otherwise they received a 4-mA electric "stimulus." Not once do the vivisectors use the words *electric shock*. No negative word hints that the electrical "stimulation" was less than pleasant.[25]

Charged with regulating vivisection, the U.K.'s Home Office publishes annual vivisection statistics restricted to experimental methods that directly inflict suffering. Previously, the category referring to electric shock and other ways of inflicting pain bore this euphemistic heading: "Use of aversive stimuli, electrical or other." As of 1988 the language became even more euphemistic; *electrical* disappeared and the neutral word *training* replaced *aversive*, leaving "Use of training stimuli."[26]

In vivisection *treat* and *administer* refer to harming, not healing. Vivisectors at the Environmental Protection Agency "treated" (injected) mice with heavy metals and rated how "efficacious" these metals were in causing subnormal body temperatures. At Oregon Health Sciences University conscious mice had electric shock "administered" to their corneas. The vivisectors noted their seizure thresholds.[27]

Jargon softens myriad forms of abuse. Notorious for decapitating rhesus monkeys and keeping their severed heads conscious for hours, Robert White has admitted using the phrase *cephalic transplants* because people react to *head transplants* with revulsion.[28] Sounding scientific and benign, *bilateral lid suture* substitutes for *sewing both eyelids shut*. The plain English is more precise. *Thermally injured* stands in for *scalded*, which is more exact. Sometimes technical language does add precision; but morally detached, technical language always is out of place within a context of cruelty.

Jargon and euphemism overlap. A vivisector who immersed 40 unanesthetized newborn mice in ice water and cut out their eyes never says in his published report that he blinded the mice. Instead dozens of times he uses *enucleated* and *visually deprived*. When the words *blind* and *blindness* do appear (only three times), they refer to barn owls and guinea pigs blinded by *other* vivisectors.[29]

"Use the terms 'fast,' 'fasting,' and 'restricted diet' rather than 'starve' and 'starvation,'" Rous directed, "especially if animals are starved intentionally." As reported in 1994 from the University of Tennessee, fourteen pigs were "fasted" for nearly two weeks, until they lost one-fifth of their body weight. Vivisection also has other euphemisms for *starvation*. Two University of Kentucky vivisectors irradiated mice in their head and neck, destroying the mucous membrane lining their mouth. Unable to eat, the mice died in about ten days—from "nutritional insufficiency."[30]

Vivisectors verbally minimize tortuous restraint. Confining a rat to a tube 2.4 inches (6 cm) in diameter, so that he can move only 0.08–0.19 inches (2–5 mm) in any direction, imposes "significant" restraint, two vivisectors acknowledged in 1989.[31] By 1993 they contended that rats vertically suspended inside such a tube are "lightly" restrained.[32] Although mice restricted to tubes 1.2 inches

(3 cm) in diameter can make no "gross motor movement," National Institutes of Health (NIH) vivisectors term imprisoning mice in such tubes for three hours at 43 °F (6 °C) "partial" restraint, because the mice have room to shiver.[33]

Sometimes vivisectors go so far as to suggest that tortuously restrained animals feel right at home. At the University of Chicago three rats were kept awake 19, 20, and 21 days, until they nearly died. Throughout their ordeal the rats perched precariously on disks suspended over water. Whenever a rat fell asleep, his disk would tilt, forcing him to move in counterbalance or topple off. As expressed by the vivisectors, the rats "resided" on these platforms. Yellow baboons used in Johns Hopkins University drug addiction experiments were individually restrained in chairs for weeks. Held by a neck collar, a waist yoke, a bar across the top of their legs, and metal bands that kept their arms bent at right angles, each baboon sat on aluminum bars spaced an inch (25 mm) apart; another metal bar supported their feet. In their report the vivisectors refer to the restraint chairs as the baboons' "housing." On a poster distributed to elementary schools, the Alcohol, Drug Abuse, and Mental Health Administration states that such restraint chairs allow monkeys to "move about comfortably, but keep them from running around the room."[34]

In vivisection doublespeak, *humane* means cruel. How else could Pennsylvania State University vivisectors speak of a "humane" device for inflicting electric shocks or University of Southern California vivisectors discuss "humane" ways to burn animals?[35] With reference to vivisection, *humane treatment* is an oxymoron. Vivisection coerces and harms innocent individuals. It can't be humane.

"Sacrifice"

Vivisectors' verbal dishonesty extends through to their victims' deaths. In their experiments, vivisectors don't "kill" animals; they "produce lethality," for example, by irradiating beagles who then die from widespread bacterial infection or hemorrhaging.[36]

Nonhuman animals killed by vivisection technicians are *destroyed*, *put down*, *put to sleep*, *discarded*, *dispatched*, *disposed of*, and *terminated*. They also "go into data." Rooms of animals are "depopulated"—a process sometimes called "housecleaning." All these terms euphemize. *Destroy* equates nonhuman beings with inanimate things. Used matter-of-factly rather than in objection, *discard* and *dispose of* reduce animals to dirt or trash. So does *houseclean*. *Go into data* removes human agency, absolving the murderers of guilt.

Vivisectors and their assistants claim to perform "euthanasia," but they kill healthy animals or animals whose pathologies were vivisection-induced. The killings are acts of disposal, not mercy.

As a euphemism for *kill*, vivisectors especially favor *sacrifice*. This usage may have originated in 1825 with vivisector James Blundell: "When animals are sacrificed on the altar of science that Nature may reveal her secrets, the means are consecrated by the end."[37] *Sacrifice* drapes vivisectors in priestly robes and falsely suggests that no vivisected animal dies in vain. Because *kill* "may imply wasting life," one vivisector has urged others to use *sacrifice* instead.[38] In Phillips's presence, a veterinarian asked a vivisection technician if some monkeys would be "destroyed" following experimentation. "They'll be *sacrificed*," the technician responded.[39] At other times technicians drop the sanctimony, shortening *sacrifice* to *sac*. The reality of "sacrifice" is far from lofty. Killing becomes callous routine. Sometimes laboratory workers toss still-living animals into the trash.[40] However, the word *sacrifice* is apt insofar as it suggests vivisection's futility, primitive irrationality, and selfish desperation. Vivisection's victims literally are a blood sacrifice, killed for professional and financial gain and always-hypothetical public benefit. More a religion than a science, vivisection consists of ritual torture, animal sacrifice, and self-worship.

"Tools"

Vivisectors claim to *build*, *develop*, *produce*, *generate*, *fashion*, and *engineer* nonhuman animals, and the press echoes their inflated claims. "Nude mice did not exist in nature," a vivisectionist states. "We have created them for our use and are, therefore, justified in using them accordingly."[41] No human ever has created any nonhuman animal. While calling mice with a human cancer-promoting gene "man-made," an Industrial Biotechnology Association spokeswoman concedes that humans never have inserted more than a "handful" of genes into mice, who possess 50,000–100,000: "A mouse with a human growth hormone gene is still fundamentally a mouse."[42] Through gene insertion, vivisectors afflict nonhuman animals with abnormalities. They create pathologies, not animals. Even the much-publicized cloned sheep Dolly developed from an adult sheep's already-existing DNA inserted into another sheep's already-existing ovum. "Remove and insert" hardly qualifies as creation. What if vivisectors did create nonhuman animals? They still wouldn't be "justified in using them accordingly." All human and nonhuman beings are born as a consequence of others' actions. Nevertheless, we don't allow parents to kill or enslave their children. We don't allow physicians and technicians who perform *in vitro* fertilization to wield absolute power over the humans who result. Vivisection's "creation" myth simply justifies exploitation.

Like other exploiters, vivisectors categorize nonhuman animals by their use. They take organs from "donor pigs" and blood from "rabbit bleeders." "Acute animals" suffer in short-term studies, such as acute toxicity tests; "chronic animals" suffer in long-term ones. "Eye rabbits," "dermals," and "orals" undergo tests of eye irritancy, skin irritancy, or oral toxicity. Often, nonhumans who are no longer experimentally useful are designated "junk." *Laboratory animal*, *research animal*, and *test animal* label animals inherently, irreversibly victims. But animals can be freed from a laboratory and adopted into a human home. Many mice, rats, dogs, and other animals have gone from "laboratory animal" to pet. Like "game animal" and "zoo animal," "lab animal" is an artificial category.

Within institutions that perform vivisection, department names like Laboratory Animal Resources Division categorize nonhuman animals as exploitable things. Pennsylvania State University vivisectors Ralph Norgren and Thomas Pritchard have stated that the monkeys they use in taste-preference studies "are a valued resource, and are treated as such."[43] That's the problem. Among other ways in which they've abused monkeys, Norgren and Pritchard have caged them alone, given them electric shocks, deprived them of water 23 hours a day, and bolted their heads to an apparatus in which they've remained immobilized hours at a time.[44]

Vivisectors view mice and other animals inbred to have a particular disability as embodiments of that disability. WSP (withdrawal seizure-prone) mice are genetically susceptible to seizures from alcohol withdrawal. SCID™ mice have severe combined immunodeficiency. Identifying animals by their affliction prevents seeing them as suffering *from* the affliction. Mocking names, especially, preclude empathy. "Cone-head" mice suffer from the deformity indicated by their name and from cells that swell with waste material. Collectively called the Streaker, hairless ("nude") mice develop cancer of chest lymphatic tissue. Neurologically impaired, "wonky" (shaky) and "shiverer" mice start convulsing within weeks or months of birth and die prematurely.

Vivisectors call their victims "models" (supposedly of human behaviors and states). It's easier to dose rhesus monkeys with nerve gas and give them electric shocks if you see them as "an animal model (the rhesus monkey)." It's easier to inject mice with bacteria so that they lose limb function, bleed internally, and die of gangrene if—instead of mice suffering and dying—you view the result as "mortality in a mouse model." "What do you tell people you do for a living?" Arluke asked a vivisection technician, who answered, "I usually tell them that I'm a director of surgical research. When they say, 'What does that entail?' I say that I do experimentation on large animal models. And then if they say 'What does that mean?' I say 'Dogs, cats, pigs, sheep, cows.'" In this context the technician clearly uses the word *models* to evade and deny; *large animal models* simply substitutes for *large animals*. The conference title "The Well-being of Animal Research Models in Zoos and Aquaria" reveals hypocrisy; the word *Models* denies animals' very being, let alone their well-being.[45]

Showing a beagle, coonhound, and mixed-breed dog, an ad for Hazleton Research Products offers "Three Models to Choose From." An ad from Charles River Laboratories features two guinea pigs—one furry, one hairless—and announces, "Now available in standard. And stripped down model." In these ads, *model* suggests both a simulation device and a manufactured object.[46] Displaying other language that turns nonhumans into commodities, industry ads and catalogs sell animals as "items" and "products." "Ask for samples," they invite. Like zoo and aquaprison captives, laboratory captives are termed "inventory." On NIH grant applications, vivisectors list their anticipated victims under "Supplies." In vivisection parlance, dogs aren't hurt, just "modified," as if they were inanimate goods.[47] Wounded rhesus monkeys aren't healed, but "repaired."[48] Remembering a time when monkeys cost only $25, a vivisection veterinarian has remarked, "You'd use one once and you'd throw it away."[49] To vivisectors, nonhuman beings are disposable things.

Vivisected animals are "devices," "vehicles," and "tools." The words convey the speciesist's credo: Other animals exist for human use. A Stanford University vivisector has categorized cats and squirrel monkeys used in experiments as "wetware."[50] A vivisector who cuts rabbits open to inspect their ovaries, implants sex hormones through an incision in their neck, and kills them before reexamining their ovaries has said of her victims, "I find it's easier to think of them as test tubes, rather than animals—warm, furry test tubes."[51]

Vivisectors also see living nonhumans as data. Like digits on a computer screen, mice able to right themselves within three minutes of an alcohol dose are "deleted" from an experiment.[52] Poisoned rabbits who fail to respond as desired to 600 electric shocks are "deleted from further analysis."[53] Most vivisection reports refer to vivisected animals only within the context of experiments; they contain no information on other aspects of the animals' lives. Even the experimental "procedures" inflicted on nonhumans often remain vague; for details, readers must follow a reference trail back to earlier publications. Many vivisection reports fail to state the number of animals used and killed, specifying only the number from whom the vivisectors obtained useful data. Most vivisected animals are investigated in terms of type (such as strain) and group (especially, treatment group versus control group). The focus is on statistical averages.

Like other speciesists, vivisectors fail to perceive nonhumans as individuals. To a vivisector of rodents, rodents are "all the same."[54] To a vivisector of cats, cats don't have individual personalities.[55] The industry speaks of "standardized" nonhumans. That demeaning word misleads. However inbred for genetic uniformity, nonhuman animals are born with unique physical and mental characteristics. Unique life experiences further shape them as individuals. Cloned nonhuman animals are no less individual than human identical twins, who also develop from one split embryo.

Like hunters and fishers, vivisectors refer to plural nonhumans with singular nouns: "Similar findings have been noted in squirrel monkey, rabbit, and rat. It is unclear from previous reports whether this pattern occurs in cat."[56] This usage collapses all group members into a single entity, as if there were some substance called "rat" or one endlessly reproducible cat.

Rous enforced another way of denying vivisected animals' individuality: "Never use names."[57] With few exceptions (usually for nonhuman primates), journals that publish vivisection religiously adhere to this dictum. As related in the Prologue, I gave personal names to the ten rats I used in graduate school experiments. When I drafted a report for *Animal Learning and Behavior*, my advisor (who co-authored the report) told me to remove the rats' names because they wouldn't be published. He suggested that I substitute my own initials with numbers. I complied. The rats became JM1, JM2, and so on. I obliterated their individuality.[58] Even in private, most animals used in vivisection lack personal names.[59] Nonhuman anonymity helps vivisectors remain emotionally detached, they themselves admit.[60]

Contemptuous names, too, remove emotional obstacles to cruelty. At Biosearch, a Philadelphia product testing lab, technicians called a newly arrived dog Dead Meat. She was killed six days later. At Wright State University a dog experimentally infested with skin mites continually circled. Technicians named her Dizzy. At the University of California, Los Angeles, vivisectors severed kittens' spinal cords. Paralyzed in their legs, the kittens were given names such as Peg Leg, Speedy Gonzales, Snap, Crackle, and Pop. At England's Royal College of Surgeons, vivisectors named a monkey Crap and tattooed the epithet onto his forehead.[61]

Vivisectors and their assistants often address nonhuman animals by the name of their species or other animal group. In a video filmed undercover at a Gillette product testing lab, a technician applies deodorant concentrate to a rabbit's shaved skin. The rabbit struggles and the technician snaps, "Cut it out, rabbit." At the University of Pennsylvania's head-injury lab, vivisectors filmed themselves inflicting severe brain damage on unanesthetized baboons and mocking their victims. One vivisector derided a baboon who lay strapped to an operating table, "Oh, have some axonal [nerve-fiber] damage, monkey."[62]

In published reports and informal speech, vivisectors often refer to individual nonhumans more generically. Addressing a twitching, inadequately anesthetized rat, a vivisector observed by Phillips asked, "Are you light, animal?"[63] Vivisection's overuse of the general term *animal* helps sustain the myth that experimental results automatically transfer between species. It also erases a nonhuman's identity.

Through gene transfer, NIH vivisectors have afflicted mice with a disease unknown to occur naturally: cancer of the eye's lens. When the mouse pups first open their eyes, their lenses already are clouded. As the lens tumor develops, it breaks through a mouse's retina or cornea. For months, the mice suffer as the malignancy obliterates their eye and invades surrounding tissue, until they die. The vivisectors have perpetuated the cancer through multiple generations. They view their victims, collectively, as "the intact organism." Even more than *animal*, *organism* expunges an individual's unique consciousness, because the term encompasses living *things* as well as beings. By describing himself as someone who "experiments with living organisms," another vivisector hides among those who harmlessly experiment with insentient microorganisms or plants. In the words of two *Washington Post* writers who cheerlead vivisection, mice genetically manipulated to have a particular defective gene are "dispensable organism[s]." The word *organism* itself labels the mice dispensable and discourages sympathy. When an advocate of classroom vivisection claims to care about the "humane treatment" of "organisms" and professes "empathy" for "living systems," her contradictory language reveals the truth.[64]

Whereas *organism* at least acknowledges life, *specimen* can refer to the living or dead, organic or inorganic. Ratfishes refuse to eat in captivity. This doesn't stop vivisectors, who label the fishes "specimens" and experiment on them until they starve to death.[65]

Reducing nonhumans further, vivisectors term their victims "systems" and "preparations." In many journals, vivisectors specify their experimental subjects under the heading "Materials and Methods." A vivisector of hamsters and rats has remarked, "I don't see any difference between them, let's say, and a cell line."[66] Another vivisector has defined "an experimental animal" as "part instrument, part reagent" (test chemical). Verbal vivisection.[67]

In the video filmed inside the Gillette lab, a rabbit screams while undergoing a skin-irritancy test. Annoyed, the technician who has hurt the rabbit says to a co-worker, "Oh, make this *thing* shut up." Evasively using generic *you* instead of *I*, a vivisector of dogs told Arluke, "You have nothing against the things you're working with." The word *things* reveals that he has no empathy for them either.[68]

Often, instead of rendering the victims inanimate, vivisection reports altogether remove them. When we read that cocaine poisoning "produced episodes of wild running and ataxia," "convulsions generally occurred within 90 sec of injection," and "death generally occurred within the first 15 min following the injection," it is poisoned mice who ran about wildly, collapsed, suffered convulsions, and died. University of South Carolina vivisectors say that they delivered shock to "stainless steel wound clips" near "the margins of the upper and lower eyelids." The eyelids belonged to live rabbits. Ordinarily, vivisectors speak of burning body surfaces rather than animals: "A 30-second full-thickness scald burn over 20% total body surface area was inflicted." Each *rat* was scalded over 20 percent of *his* body.[69]

Injected with bacteria so that they developed gangrene, all mice in a control group died. The syntax of the preceding sentence highlights the mice and their fate. Subject: *all mice*. Verb: *died*. In contrast, vivisection's syntax de-emphasizes the victims: "Injection of [bacteria] was uniformly lethal in saline-treated control animals within 24 hours."[70] The sentences of vivisection reports abound with prepositional phrases that keep the focus off nonhuman suffering and death. Within, far removed from subject position, are the tortured and killed.

~~Guilt~~ "Feelings"

In their publications, vivisectors virtually never state that *they* inflicted the harm suffered by their victims. Instead they hide behind passive verbs. Avoiding first-person pronouns, vivisectors report that cardiac arrest "was produced" in puppies, rather than "We gave puppies cardiac arrest." Temple University vivisectors who inflicted brain damage on leopard frogs write, "After making the lesions, the patch of bone was replaced." Correction: no patch of bone made any lesions. The grammatically required subject is *we*.[71]

The wording of vivisection reports makes the victims' suffering sound inadvertent. Instead of being intentionally burned with a flame, rats "sustain" a burn that destroys every layer of skin over 30 percent of their body. "Contact" with corrosive chemicals burns guinea pigs. The agents, the vivisectors, remain safely out of sight.[72]

Or the victims volunteer. Crab-eating macaques "took part" in vivisection that involved depriving them of water and removing parts of their brain. At Massachusetts General Hospital twelve sheep "donated" 45 percent of their blood; six others "donated" at least 80 percent. At the University of Southern Colorado, golden hamsters dependent on morphine abruptly were denied the drug. During "abstinence" the hamsters writhed; their paws trembled, teeth chattered, and head and shoulders twisted in opposite directions.[73]

"They're co-workers of ours," a Ciba-Geigy vivisector has said of dogs subjected to chronic toxicity testing. In addition to suggesting that vivisected animals willingly participate, the word *co-worker* portrays vivisectors' stance toward nonhuman animals as egalitarian rather than abusive. Sharon Juliano has caused brain damage in squirrel monkeys and cats, amputated their toes, and kept them paralyzed but fully conscious for as long as 45 minutes. In a 1988 grant application, she rated the "level of pain or distress" that she expected to inflict as "three" on a scale of one to five. "We really aren't cruel to the animals," she has told the press. "They are our colleagues." When addressing her actual colleagues, she calls cats a "preparation."[74]

Blaming the victim transfers guilt. In multiple experiments, Harry Harlow and his collaborators kept female rhesus monkeys in solitary confinement for the first six to eighteen months of their lives. When these monkeys eventually gave birth, some of them—severely emotionally disturbed—attacked their infants. Harlow and his co-experimenters called these mothers *abusive*, *cruel*, *vicious*, *brutal*, *sadistic*, and *evil*, words that far better describe the vivisectors themselves.[75]

Naturally peaceable, rats sometimes "box" each other when subjected, as pairs, to electric shocks. Although vivisectors acknowledge that such boxing is a defensive reaction to pain (whose source the rats can't discern), they call this behavior shock-induced "aggression." At the New York State Psychiatric Institute, vivisectors gave paired rats 90 foot-shocks. In their published report they claim to have tallied "all aggressive behaviors." But while they diligently noted each time the rats stood upright on their back legs, faced each other, or pushed at each other with their paws, the vivisectors omitted their own infliction of electric shocks.[76]

At the Uniformed Services University of the Health Sciences, hungry pigeons pecked a key for food. Every thirtieth peck was "punished" with shock through electrodes implanted under their pelvis. As in elephant "training," in vivisection the word *punish* transforms the innocent victims into the wrongdoers.[77]

Although about 90 percent of the 130 vivisectors and vivisection assistants whom Arluke interviewed eventually "admitted to what most people would consider 'guilty' feelings," many did so reluctantly. Some objected to Arluke's use of the word *guilt* because it indicates culpability.[78] Industry representatives who invited Arluke to address a gathering of vivisectors rejected his proposed speech title, "The Experimenter's Guilt," as "too controversial." Following their recommendation, Arluke changed the title to "Stress among Researchers." Before publishing the speech, editors of the magazine *Lab Animal* replaced *Stress*, finding it, in Arluke's words, "extreme and inaccurate." The title became "Uneasiness among Laboratory Technicians." Soon after the article's appearance, a major pharmaceutical company asked Arluke to address its research staff but censored the supposedly inflammatory word *Uneasiness*. Arluke adopted the completely neutral title that the company suggested: "How Researchers Deal with Their Feelings."[79] From *Guilt* to *Stress* to *Uneasiness* to *Feelings*. Whatever is necessary to spare vivisectors any prick of conscience.

Although they certainly become desensitized, vivisectors shrink from describing themselves as callous. One vivisector has likened killing nonhuman animals to "recreational sex because you do it without much feeling." "There's not really a second thought for that animal as an individual," he has admitted while stating, "It doesn't mean that we're callous."[80] Then, what does *callous* mean?

While Home Office representative, vivisectionist Douglas Hogg commented that products free of nonhuman-animal ingredients and testing shouldn't be called "cruelty-free." The term is too "emotive," he claimed.[81] That is, *cruelty* is too candid and moralistic. Transforming cruelty into science, the U.K. has replaced its Cruelty to Animals Act 1876 with an Animals (Scientific Procedures) Act 1986.

Like other abusers, vivisectors profess strong affection and concern for their victims. Having paralyzed numerous cats by dropping a brass weight onto their spinal cord, a vivisector stated, "I like cats very much." For decades Charles Larson has vivisected pig-tailed macaques. Allegedly to learn about human speech, he has subjected the monkeys to food deprivation and solitary confinement; slit open their throat, chest, or abdomen to implant electrodes; fused their upper four neck vertebrae to their skull to limit head movement; forced them to vocalize for liquid; and killed them. By his own account, he "always" has "loved animals."[82]

According to Morrison and fellow vivisection promoter Frederick Goodwin, the "animal rights debate" ranges from the "extreme animal welfare" view that vivisected animals should be made as comfortable as possible to the view that their welfare doesn't matter. In Morrison and Goodwin's distorting terminology, the "animal rights debate" doesn't include animal rights; opinions about vivisection don't include antivivisection. Exclusion of the animal rights—true welfare—position enables Morrison and Goodwin to accord vivisectors "the middle ground" in the debate and call them "moderates." "Those concerned with animal welfare do not propose to ban the use of research animals," the American Medical Association has stated. To the contrary, those genuinely concerned about nonhuman welfare do advocate banning vivisection. Paris has defined *animal welfare* as experimenting on nonhuman animals while treating them "as humanely as possible." With *welfare* thus nullified, vivisectors can dub themselves animal welfarists.[83]

In numerous experiments conducted with and without his mentor Harlow, Stephen Suomi has tortured infant and juvenile rhesus monkeys. He has confined them in a small steel vertical chamber for as long as three months, subjected them to a "tunnel of terror" from which a mechanical "monster" emerges, and kept them in total isolation for the first six months of their lives.[84] Goodwin has declared Suomi "an animal protectionist of the first class."[85]

"Necessary" Evil

Proponents attempt to defend vivisection with the oxymoron *necessary evil*. By definition, evil entails unnecessary harm. And that's what vivisection inflicts. No one reasonably can claim that vivisection offers the only means of discovering some truth about humans. With sufficient desire and ingenuity, researchers always can employ harmless methods. "We have to use these animals," a vivisector has contended. "I don't think we have any choice." By pleading necessity, he avoids confronting the evil of his actions. "The paths to knowledge are countless," George Bernard Shaw remarked. "It is useless to assure us that there is no other key to knowledge except cruelty. When the vivisector offers us that assurance, we reply simply and contemptuously, 'You mean that you are not clever or humane or energetic enough to find one.' . . . No method of investigation is the only method."[86]

Seligman's "learned helplessness" experiments on dogs illustrate vivisection's false necessity. To test a hypothesis about humans, Seligman gave dogs painful, inescapable shocks. Why? He "needed" to use this method, he claims; at least, it "seemed" the only way.[87] In 1971, six years after Seligman began torturing dogs, graduate student Donald Hiroto obtained findings that paralleled Seligman's. Instead of dogs, Hiroto used human volunteers. Instead of painful electric shocks, he used annoying bouts of noise. By Seligman's own admission, Hiroto demonstrated that valid studies of "learned helplessness" could be harmlessly conducted with humans.[88] The dog experiments weren't necessary; Seligman just wasn't sufficiently inventive and compassionate to investigate by other means.

A society's time, money, and effort always are limited. Why should any of these go to vivisection? Other research methods are both more scientifically valid and more cost-effective. If the resources poured into vivisection went instead to supporting other research, educating people about healthy lifestyles, and increasing their access to medical treatment, public health would vastly improve.

However, fairness alone demands a ban on vivisection. We have no moral right to seek information by "sacrificing" others. As Shaw pointed out, the law restricts the pursuit of knowledge to methods that don't violate human rights, even though human vivisection would be far more scientifically valid (and therefore useful) than nonhuman vivisection.[89] Whatever their intellectual capacity, humans are spared vivisection because we consider it morally repugnant to inflict suffering or death on any innocent human. Nonhumans deserve equal justice.

By definition, any experiment has an uncertain outcome. At best, eventual benefit is possible, not definite. But the harm to vivisection's victims always is immediate and certain. Tragically and ironically, the only needs definitely affected by any particular act of vivisection are the needs that it violates: those of its nonhuman victims. They need—now—to be spared deprivation, pain, and death. They need—right now—to be freed.

Vivisection torments and kills innocent individuals. Evil is no less evil when its victims are nonhuman. Because vivisection is unjust, it is, and always has been, wrong. When society progresses beyond speciesism, this evil practice will end.

9

Feeding on Flesh, Milk, Eggs, and Lies

The Language of "Animal Agriculture"

Corpse eaters are people of the lie.

—Carol J. Adams

Divorced from the land, numerous "animal agriculture" operations have no farming component. Yet, the exploitation of captive nonhumans for food retains the name *agriculture*, evoking pastoral images of cows grazing, pigs rooting, and chickens pecking in the spacious outdoors. The National Cattlemen's Association (NCA) has urged those in the U.S. cow-flesh industry to use *animal agriculture* rather than *livestock industry*.[1] Whereas *industry* connotes environmental damage and profit motives, *agriculture* suggests an ecologically friendly enterprise based on need.

Say "family farm," not "factory farm," the NCA has cautioned.[2] *Factory* accurately conveys the flesh, egg, and milk production methods that now predominate in industrialized nations. *Farm* is largely an anachronism. But, however huge and corporate, operations that keep nonhuman animals in intensive, mechanized confinement are verbally disguised as small, rustic enterprises. Don Tyson's multibillion-dollar bird-flesh company—the world's largest—maintains the quaint façade of a "family farm" (a label that confers tax, as well as PR, benefits).[3]

Even before the automated mass production of animal-derived food, applying the words *agriculture* and *farming* to nonhuman exploitation misled. However primitive, "animal agriculture" doesn't necessarily entail land cultivation; it entails consumption, by nonhuman captives, of cultivated or naturally growing plants. Throughout its history the term *animal agriculture* has masked enslavement and murder. So has *aquaculture*. "Farmers" and "producers" who deal in flesh, milk, or eggs actually are slaveholders. Slaughterers are mass murderers. Assisted by words that falsify, consumers of products from nonhuman bodies pretend otherwise.

Deceptive language conceals the cruel conditions and treatment suffered by food-industry captives. Understatement, euphemism, positive description of negative realities, and outright lying hide the truth.

"Satisfied" Pigs

In the pig-flesh industry, most sows endure each pregnancy isolated in a stall with iron bars and a concrete floor. The stall is so narrow that a sow has room only to stand up and lie down. If the stall is open in the rear, she also is chained to the floor by a neck collar or body harness. The textbook *Intensive Pig Production* glamorizes sows' solitary confinement as "individual accommodation."[4] Typically, a sow reacts to tethering with violent escape attempts lasting up to several hours: repeatedly she yanks on her chain; screaming, she twists and thrashes; sometimes she crashes against the stall's bars before collapsing. After her futile struggle to break free, she lies motionless, groaning and whimpering, her snout reaching outward beneath the bars. Finally, she sits for long periods with her head drooping and her eyes vacant or closed.[5] According to the American Veterinary Medical Association (AVMA), which promotes "animal agriculture," chained sows generally seem "satisfied in their environment."[6]

Deprived of all exercise and bred to be overweight, sows and boars used in breeding become obese unless their food is severely restricted. To save money on feed and keep the pigs no heavier than necessary for successful reproduction, many pig enslavers feed them only once every two or three days. This regimen imposes perpetual hunger.[7] Starved sows and boars are "limit-fed," pig enslavers say, implying wholesome avoidance of excess.

The crate in which a sow gives birth and nurses her piglets is even more confining than the pregnancy stall. Metal bars directly above the sow restrict her to a lying position, or straps bind her to the floor. Often she develops sores from rubbing against the narrow crate or tears her nipples attempting to stand. While executive director of the Wisconsin Agri-Business Council, one enslaver termed the barbaric crate a "modern maternity unit."[8]

The "runts" among newborn piglets are killed. Pig enslavers commonly hold them by their back legs and swing them so that their head slams against the floor. Although many piglets still are conscious after the first assault, the industry calls this murder method "euthanasia."[9]

According to *Raising Pigs Successfully*, piglets don't find castration or tail amputation "particularly painful."[10] Unanesthetized, piglets scream as their scrotum is slit and their testicles are yanked out. They scream as their tail is severed with side-cutting pliers.

The mechanized facilities of pig enslavement bear comfy, homey names. Prematurely taken from their mothers, piglets go to the "nursery." Here they're confined to cages stacked in rows. Each cage standardly imprisons eight to ten piglets. Forced to stand on wire mesh, each piglet has less than 2 square feet (0.19 m^2) of floor space. At about two months of age, the pigs move to the "hog parlor," where thousands are crowded into pens with concrete floors. When they go to slaughter at five or six months of age, many pigs are crippled.

In the U.S. most pigs experience lifelong confinement, during which they breathe high levels of ammonia produced by accumulated waste. Most develop pneumonia—in a 1984 study, nearly three-fourths of those who survived until slaughter.[11] Having previously used the term *high-intensity confinement*, the *Pork Industry Handbook* now uses *environmentally controlled systems*.[12] Whereas the first phrase calls attention to pigs' plight, the second avoids even indirect reference to pigs. As illustrated by a statement from *Pork Production Systems*, substituting a positive term (*controlled environment*) for an appropriately negative one (*intensive confinement*) can yield incongruous results: "Situations of dust, odors, and noxious gases, which occur in most swine operations, can increase to become serious problems with controlled environment facilities."[13]

Chickens and Turkeys Who "Hardly Have to Move"

"In broiler and turkey growing, the housing density and litter condition often cannot be ideal," *Poultry Production* states.[14] Most turkeys and "broiler" chickens live amid thousands crowded across a floor. By slaughter time, each turkey has only about 3 square feet (0.28 m^2) of space; each chicken has less than a square foot (0.09 m^2). Throughout the birds' confinement, the same litter accumulates urine and feces. As the litter becomes wet, hard, and ammonia-saturated, the birds develop foot ulcers, ankle burns, breast blisters and ulcers, and respiratory and eye disease, including blindness. Such deplorable conditions never approach "ideal."

Of the 270 million U.S. hens currently laying eggs for human consumption, at least 98 percent live confined to wire cages.[15] Usually each cage holds at least four to six hens squeezed side to side on a sloping wire floor. As tall as their cage, the hens are crammed in too tightly to lift a wing. The Animal Industry Foundation has called cagemates "penmates."[16] One enslaver has said of the 100,000 hens caged in his egg factory, "They hardly have to move to get food or water."[17] Nor do human prisoners provided with rations while chained to a wall.

In 1993 I visited a "state-of-the-art" Maryland egg factory with the deceptive name Country Fair Farms. Four windowless warehouses imprisoned a total of half a million hens squeezed nine to a cage. Row after row, four tiers of cages extended into the distance, disappearing into the dimly lit haze. From manure pits directly below, huge mounds of excrement saturated the air with eye-stinging ammonia. Cagemates shared a single water nipple and were forced to climb over one another to reach the food trough in front of their cage. In bursts the birds gave frantic cries, worlds away from the soft clucking of contented hens. With a dazed look they stared outward, as if into empty darkness. However hellish, egg factories bear names, like Happy Hen Egg Ranch, that suggest chicken bliss.

Hens don't need to walk, flap their wings, perch, dustbathe, or scratch soil, an industry researcher contends. He terms such basic needs "amenities." The AVMA places chickens' "natural behavioral needs" in quotation marks and claims that they may not exist.[18]

Because increased egg laying generally follows a forced molt, many U.S. enslavers shock hens into molting after about ten months of laying. Suddenly left in total darkness, the hens are denied food and, in many cases, water. Usually the water deprivation lasts one to two days, the starvation at least ten. Forced molting should increase profits, *Commercial Chicken Production Manual* authors Mack North and Donald Bell note—provided that no more than 2 percent of the hens die.[19] In an egg factory with a million hens, 2 percent is 20,000 individuals. Euphemisms for the calculated starvation include *fasting*, *induced molting*, and *recycling*. *Fasting* falsely suggests that the hens' hunger is brief and voluntary. *Induced molting* conceals forced molting's violence and the birds' extreme deprivation. *Recycling* completely erases the birds, leaving only the additional laying cycle that follows forced molting. Exploiting the fact that forced molting temporarily halts laying, North and Bell state that the tactic gives hens "a good rest."[20]

To decrease the likelihood that intensely crowded chickens or turkeys will be injured if pecked by others, enslavers of turkeys, "broiler chickens," and "laying hens" debeak the birds, without anesthetic. A hot blade slices off about half of each bird's upper beak and less of the lower. The blade cuts through sensitive tissue, frequently burning a bird's nostrils or tongue, searing their eyes, or severing their tongue. Debeaking causes both immediate and chronic pain, but industry proponents downplay its effect as "minimum stress."[21]

After debeaking, birds eat less for days or weeks. Many stop eating altogether and starve to death. As expressed by a company that sells debeaking equipment, debeaking doesn't kill birds; it just "can damage bird livability." In addition to euphemizing and equivocating (*can* instead of *does*), that wording reduces *bird* to an adjective, thereby avoiding reference to multiple birds. The language communicates the industry's viewpoint: What matters is overall survival rate with its economic consequences, not the individuals who live or die. A statement by North and Bell leaves the birds completely absent: "Feed consumption is depressed following trimming [debeaking] and body weight is often reduced." In the bird-flesh industry, it's body weight that counts.[22]

Probably because *mutilation* describes debeaking so accurately, the word discomfits industry researcher James Craig, who finds it "emotion-laden." As used by defenders of speciesist abuse, *emotion-laden* translates to uncomfortably moralistic. Craig prefers the standard euphemism *beak trimming*. North and Bell state that hens who undergo a second debeaking have their beaks "touched up." Mutilation becomes beautification, the equivalent of manicure.[23]

Densely crowded birds easily can scratch each other, so chickens and turkeys also undergo what the industry calls "toe clipping." Unanesthetized, many chicks and most newborn turkeys have their three front toes hacked off at the outer joints. As if *toe clipping* weren't mincing enough, an industry textbook terms this amputation "toe nail clipping." Craig calls it "removing" the "toe nails." Honest language—*amputation without anesthesia*—would amount to a confession of cruelty.[24]

Goats Who Feel "Little Pain"

Because nonhuman pain counts for so little in "animal agriculture," goats usually are castrated without anesthetic. Often a male goat has a rubber ring snapped tightly around the base of his scrotum. He feels pain until the area numbs. Because the constriction blocks circulation, within several weeks the scrotum and testicles wither and fall off. The procedure "causes pain for only about an hour," a goat enslaver says.[25] Placed in the goat's situation, he wouldn't use the word *only*.

Raising Milk Goats the Modern Way describes burning away a newborn goat's horn buds—without anesthetic—as "relatively quick, easy, and painless." The goat enslaver presses a red-hot iron against a kid's head for approximately fifteen seconds while the kid reacts with "violent struggling" and "maybe some screaming."[26] Some goats die from the shock. Many develop brain inflammation accompanied by symptoms that include foaming at the mouth and nose, blindness, and convulsions. Horn-bud removal is "quick, easy, and painless" only for an abuser incapable of cross-species empathy.

"Comfortable" Cattle

Cattle have such sensitive skin that they feel a fly alight. Yet, at least once in their lives most cattle enslaved by the flesh industry are burned with a red-hot iron without receiving any anesthetic. While admitting that branding leaves a thick scar, the textbook *Beef Cattle Production* minimizes a cow's pain as "some discomfort" (a euphemism popular with vivisectors as well).[27]

The industry claims that dehorning and castration cause only "stress" (another vivisection favorite).[28] Cattle are fully conscious when blades gouge out their horns, slicing through arteries, veins, and nerves. During castration a calf or bull feels the knife slit his scrotum and sever his testicles.

Don't say that branding, dehorning, and castration cause "pain," the NCA has instructed members; say "short-term discomfort." And don't use *castrate* or *cut* when addressing the public; use *neuter*.[29] As the cow-flesh industry knows, people associate the word *neuter* with surgery performed by a veterinarian, under sterile conditions and anesthesia, on a beloved dog or cat. Such surgery bears no resemblance to throwing a terrified calf to the ground, pinning him there, and abruptly cutting off his testicles with a sometimes-rusty pocket knife.

The NCA has recommended calling cattle enslavement operations "ranches" or "farms."[30] Having evolved as forest animals, cattle naturally seek out trees and streams. Most U.S. cattle spend the first six months of their lives on open range, vulnerable to all weather extremes. Then they're shipped to a shelterless dirt feedlot, usually in the Southwest, for feeding to slaughter weight. Feedlots hold tens of thousands of cattle, often more than 100,000. Crowded together, beset by flies, the cattle stand in mud and manure. In winter they endure sleet and snow, in summer relentless sun and dust. Ranches and farms.

The cow-flesh industry doesn't admit to cruelty. To an industry veterinarian, *cruel* is only a "buzz word."[31] That is, morality doesn't apply where cattle are concerned.

In the cow-milk industry, tie-stall operations keep each cow chained by the neck, for months at a time, in a stall so narrow that she can't turn around or groom herself. Many cows confined to tie stalls become lame. Such stalls deny cows the physical comfort of free movement and the emotional comfort of social contact, but the industry sometimes calls them "comfort stalls."

Free-stall systems confine cows to a crowded barn and adjacent dirt or concrete yard, frequently throughout the year. The largest feedlot cow-milk operations hold thousands of cows, year round, in crowded dirt lots; fed from troughs, these cows never see pasture. In free-stall and feedlot systems, cows file in and out of large, automated milking facilities, where suction cups hurriedly attached to their teats rapidly drain them of milk. The industry terms these buildings "milking parlors."

When calves discarded by the cow-milk industry are exploited as "white veal," they receive no food except an iron-deficient formula primarily of water, powdered milk, and fat. Deprived of roughage because its iron would darken their flesh, the calves become anemic. Their unnatural diet commonly causes heat stress, bloat, ulcers, and chronic diarrhea (which often is fatal). Without roughage a calf's digestive system can't develop normally, but two industry researchers put quotation marks around calves' "need" for roughage.[32] Disguising what is artificial as natural, the industry describes formula-fed calves as "milk-fed." Equally popular, the terms *special-fed* and *fancy-fed* depict the calves' extreme deprivation as pampering.

Because movement slows fattening and toughens muscles (flesh), each calf is chained inside a crate so narrow that they can't turn around or lie with their legs outstretched. As expressed by one calf enslaver, this severe restraint prevents the calves from "running around a little bit too much." (Vivisection restraint chairs, you'll recall, keep monkeys from "running around the room.") Partitions between adjacent calves thwart their efforts to nuzzle and lick each other. Avoiding moralistic words like *cruel* and *inhumane*, an industry apologist terms the crate confinement of calves "unaesthetic." Depicting cruelty as generosity, the American Veal Association has touted the crate system as offering each calf "his own private stall" that "features" partitions for "privacy."[33]

Fishes Who "Benefit"

According to *Meat & Poultry* editor Steve Bjerklie, catfishes, trouts, and other fishes "benefit" from "aquaculture."[34]

More than 2 billion catfishes (mostly channel catfishes) and hundreds of millions of trouts (primarily rainbow trouts) currently live on intensely crowded U.S. "farms."[35] One cubic foot (0.03 m^3)—that's how much space a typical pond allows a channel catfish 15 inches (381 mm) long. That's also how much water a standard shallow concrete trough allots five or more foot-long (0.3-m) rainbow trouts. Because crowding and pollution reduce water's oxygen content, enslaved fishes frequently mass, gasping, at inlet pipes or the water's surface, where oxygen levels are highest.

Rare among free-living fishes, parasite infestation is rampant among captives, such as salmons crowded into cages that sit in water fouled with waste. Fifty or more skin lice may beset a caged salmon, latching on from head to tail and eating into their flesh. Afflicted fishes scrape themselves against their cage in a futile effort to relieve the intense irritation.

Bacterial, viral, and fungal infections plague intensively reared fishes, whose symptoms include scattered hemorrhages; red, swollen, and oozing gills; eroded skin, tails, and fins; and degeneration of internal organs. In the U.S. in 1990 (the last year for which the National Agricultural Statistics Service provided catfish disease figures), approximately one in six "farmed" catfishes died from disease.[36] In nature, channel catfishes can live 40 years; in the flesh industry they're slaughtered before they're two.

Such are the "benefits" to fishes imprisoned and killed for their flesh.

"Food-Animal Welfare"

Rarely do "animal agriculture" apologists admit that slavery doesn't benefit the slaves. At most, they venture that "some" production practices "do not fully consider animal welfare." In the words of a pig-flesh researcher, confinement practices are "not always of immediate benefit to the confined animal." Are they of eventual benefit, such as when the pig becomes crippled, develops chronic pneumonia, or loses all hope of escape?[37]

Disingenuously, promoters of animal-derived food equate nonhuman "productivity" with nonhuman welfare. "Hens stop laying eggs if they are subject to any form of adversity," an industry researcher claims.[38] The truth? Hens with deep, infected wounds or broken bones lay eggs at a normal rate, as do hens who have lost the ability to stand or even sit upright.[39] Cows with foot disease produce abundant milk.[40] Sows and ewes "crippled by lameness" reproduce.[41] Pigs with pneumonia grow as desired.[42] On a pig enslavement operation with a high rate of piglet birth and survival, *Successful Farming* livestock editor Betsy Freese found sows "in gestation crates so narrow that when they laid down, their legs rested on their neighbor. In the crowded nursery, pigs had bleeding tail stumps and ulcered holes in place of ears." She admits, "We've held up herd production figures and stated that abused animals wouldn't produce like this."[43]

Food-industry enslavers concern themselves with overall profit, not individual nonhumans. Captives who die at the production site are "deadstock." Their deaths constitute "production mortality," a phrase that fails to acknowledge individuals. Omitting any reference to death, the industry also uses *inventory shrinkage*. Words like *stock*, *production*, and *inventory* show that enslavers care about their economic losses, not their victims' loss of life.

Like vivisectors, food-industry enslavers call themselves animal welfarists, feigning deep affection and concern for their victims. While claiming that she "loved" ewes whose udder infections she left untreated, a sheep enslaver states that providing treatment would have amounted to "sentiment" and "pampering." It wasn't worth her time, energy, or money. She sent the ewes to slaughter. According to an American National CattleWomen spokeswoman, cattle enslavers "nurture" and "protect" cattle as they do family members. Since when does protecting family members include enslaving them, subjecting them to pain and hardship, and selling them to slaughter?[44]

Bjerklie places "animal exploitation on one far side, animal welfare in the middle, and animal rights on the other far side." At the same time he states, "No one in the animal welfare movement is calling for an end to the meat industry."[45] The flesh industry oppresses and kills animals, so it certainly constitutes animal exploitation. For the flesh industry and animal welfare to be compatible, animal exploitation and animal welfare must be compatible. But Bjerklie himself differentiates exploitation from welfare. More importantly, the flesh industry and animal welfare truly conflict. Animals who are enslaved and murdered certainly lack well-being. Even under the best of circumstances, *food-animal welfare* is an oxymoron. In contrast, animal rights and genuine animal welfare are causally related. Adequate legal rights would protect nonhuman animals from institutionalized abuses like "animal agriculture."

"Humane" Slaughter

Although *cull* means to sell or otherwise discard a nonhuman no longer deemed useful, the term usually substitutes for *kill* or *send to slaughter*. *Cull* sends the speciesist message that other animals deserve to live only if their existence serves human ends. Comfortably abstract, *depopulation-repopulation* denotes sending all of a site's captives to slaughter and bringing in a new group. The industry uses the jaunty abbreviation *depop-repop*. In the synonymous phrase *farm renewal*, the victims and their slaughter completely disappear.

For their trip to slaughter, cattle, pigs, and other mammals are crowded onto trailers and trucks that leave them exposed to any weather extremes. Although transport may last for days, the animals receive no food or water. En route many die from heat, cold, or stress-induced pneumonia. In winter, numerous pigs arrive frozen to the vehicle but still alive. Routinely they're yanked, pried, or hacked loose with a violence that rips muscles, breaks bones, or tears off limbs.[46]

However weak, injured, or ill, animals are "unloaded" at the "stock" yard with haste. Those who fail to keep pace may be whipped, kicked, clubbed, caned, jabbed with a pitchfork, electrically shocked with a cattle prod applied anywhere from face to genitals, or hit with a board, a piece of concrete, or anything else available.[47]

Cows too disabled to walk are pulled or hoisted by a chain around one leg—which often tears their skin or muscles and dislocates or breaks their chained leg. Or they're dragged by a chain around their neck. Many choke to death. Smaller disabled animals, such as calves, goats, and young pigs, commonly are thrown from the vehicle. Grabbed by the leg, tail, ear, or nostrils, they're dragged to the slaughter area. Crippled or collapsed animals also are beaten to death with metal pipes or left to die without shelter, food, or water.[48]

The word *stockyard* evokes harsh images, so the NCA has advised members to use *livestock market* instead. In an effort to disguise assault as assistance, the American Farm Bureau has recommended ousting the vivid words *whips* and *sticks* and replacing them with *guides*.[49]

Annually, U.S. slaughterers kill more than 9 billion individuals. In 1999 those slaughtered included, among others, approximately 4 million sheep, 23 million ducks, 38 million cattle, 48 million trouts, 102 million pigs, 265 million turkeys, 414 million catfishes, and 8.274 billion chickens.[50] The flesh industry wants the public to believe that this ongoing mass murder is "humane." Contributing to the charade, the Humane Methods of Slaughter Act supposedly mandates the "humane" slaughter of nonhuman mammals. The slaughter of mammals, fishes, and birds all entail extreme cruelty.

As cattle approach the killing area, they smell blood and bellow in terror. Electric shocks, often in the anus, drive them forward. Those who balk may be whipped; stabbed; or bashed with shovels, hoes, chains, or boards, including in the face. In the restraining chutes, cattle thrash and rear, struggling to escape. If their head gets caught, they may be decapitated. If their leg gets stuck, it may be hacked or sawed off.[51]

Killed proficiently, cattle die when a slaughterer holds a captive-bolt pistol to their forehead and shoots a steel rod into their brain—once. But the pistol often lacks adequate air pressure, and slaughterers frequently aim poorly. Numerous cattle feel repeated slams of the rod. Many are conscious when shackled by one rear leg and hoisted into the air. Often, a cow's shackled leg dislocates or breaks under the strain. To end a hoisted cow's frantic kicking, slaughterhouse employees sometimes cut off the lower part of their front legs. Cattle commonly are knifed in a way that fails to slit their throat. In any case, the line moves too quickly for blood loss to render cattle unconscious. Within seconds—conscious or not—they're being skinned. Even when the lower third of each leg is cut off, many cattle are conscious.[52]

As pigs scream in fear and pain, electric shocks (in the anus, the throat, the eye) force them to the slaughter chutes. Commonly they're whipped, kicked, and beaten with boards or pipes. Often pigs who escape restraint are stabbed with a hook in the anus, face, or roof of the mouth and dragged back to the kill area.[53]

Electrodes held to the head and back supposedly stun pigs and cause cardiac arrest. The electrodes often are placed incorrectly, if applied at all. Also, slaughterhouses routinely keep the current too low; instead of being stunned, pigs feel electric shock, often accompanied by the type of pain suffered during a heart attack. Even after three or more shocks, many pigs are conscious. Some pigs are beaten on the head with a metal pipe until they're dazed or dead. Paralyzed or flailing, others remain conscious while shackled and hoisted by one rear leg; they feel excruciating pain as the slaughterer slashes their jugular vein or cuts them elsewhere. Rushed along to the scalding tank, many pigs are conscious when they enter the boiling water.[54]

Sadism is common in slaughterhouses. Slaughterhouse workers have tortured cows by shoving a broomstick up their anus or shooting out their eyes. They've tortured pigs by slicing off their nose and rubbing brine into the wound, cutting out their eyes, or chasing them into the scalding tank.[55] Some of the cruelest workers discount their victims as "just" or "only" animals.[56]

By pairing *humane* with *slaughter*, legislators have sanctioned horrific cruelty and mass murder. What if slaughter were freed (miraculously) of all terror and pain? Like any other unnecessary killing of innocent beings, it still wouldn't be humane.

Euphemisms conceal slaughter's violence. Replace *slaughterhouse* with *meat plant* or *meat factory*, the U.K.'s *Meat Trades Journal* has told readers.[57] The slaughterhouse also hides behind *processing plant* and *packing plant*.

Those who slaughter pigs are "processors who convert the live animal into pork products." A designer of highly automated killing systems has credited automation with transforming slaughterers into "food technologists."[58]

According to slaughter expert Temple Grandin, slaughterhouse managers euphemize *kill* as *process* and *dispatch* to deny "the reality of killing." She herself calls technically proficient slaughter "euthanasia," as if murdering nonhumans for their flesh and other body parts were an act of mercy.[59]

"People react negatively to the word slaughtering," *Meat Processing* has warned; best to avoid the term, which hurts "the industry's image."[60] Purge *slaughter* from your public vocabulary, the NCA has instructed members; substitute *process* or *harvest*, or say that animals "go to market."[61] The flesh industry's servant, the U.S. Department of Agriculture (USDA) now uses *harvest* in lieu of *slaughter*.

As expressed by a trout-flesh industry spokesman, calling fish slaughter "harvesting" keeps the public "happy."[62] At slaughter, most trouts are dumped into a mix of water and ice. Struggling to breathe, they suffer until, after about ten minutes, lack of oxygen renders them unconscious. At about this time, the mix is drained of water, leaving the trouts to suffocate.[63] Most salmons are dumped into water infused with carbon dioxide, which is painful to breathe. The carbon dioxide paralyzes them, but most still are conscious when their gill arches are slit for bleeding.[64] Standardly, catfishes are paralyzed when electricity surges through the water of their holding tanks. Because the current isn't directed through their brain, they feel a shock. If the current is too weak, they're conscious when a band saw or other blade cuts off their head.[65]

Gainsaying the very notion of slaughter, a newspaper article refers to "'slaughtering' chickens for human consumption."[66] In U.S. slaughterhouses, chickens and turkeys are foot-shackled to a conveyor line from which they hang upside down—flapping, urinating, defecating, and crying out. Usually the conveyor carries them to a so-called stun bath of electrified saline. Heads submerged, the birds pass through. The charged liquid shocks and paralyzes them but leaves them conscious. They feel the mechanized or human-wielded blade that slits their throat. Except for those who miss the blade. These birds, and the many allowed too little time for blood loss, enter the scalding tank still conscious.[67] Humans murder millions of chickens and other birds each day. In what way is the endless killing not slaughter?

"Meat," "Chevon," and "Drumsticks"

Flesh consumers deny nonhuman death. Avoiding direct reference to the bodies of murdered nonhumans, they say "meat" rather than "flesh," "muscle," "remains," or "corpse portion."

Because so many English-speakers eat the flesh of cattle, pigs, and sheep, the words *beef*, *pork*, and *mutton* identify species only indirectly. In contrast, an aversion to flesh from horses and dogs permits those species to be named in *horse meat* and *dog meat*; "rabbit meat" and "goat meat" too are unpopular. To increase goat flesh's popularity, in 1922 the Texas Sheep and Goat Raisers' Association proposed that "goat meat" be called chevon. "People don't eat ground cow, pig chops, or leg of sheep," a goat enslaver explains by way of comparison. "Beef, pork and mutton sound much more appetizing."[68] Recalling how she would bring kids to slaughter and later return for their packaged flesh (which she would eat), another goat enslaver relates, "Once I got all my packages back stamped 'GOAT MEAT.' This has a sort of 'turn off' ring to it. It angered me a little too because goat meat is a perfectly respectable meat. It is called chevon, like PIG MEAT is called pork—like COW MEAT is called beef. A simple request next time brought back beautifully stamped packages of CHEVON CHOPS, CHEVON STEAKS, GROUND CHEVON, etc."[69] How would she have reacted to *goat muscle* or *goat flesh*?

Among terms for mammalian flesh consumed by many English-speakers, *lamb* is exceptionally explicit. So a lamb enslaver suggests finding a new word: "The beef people have the right idea; they call the meat from young calves veal—not calf."[70] Birds, fishes, and other nonmammals apparently elicit so little sympathy that humans who eat their remains are willing to evoke the slain animals with words like *chicken*, *salmon*, and *lobster*.

Such terms as *bacon* and *chuck* allude to particular species and body parts but, once again, without direct naming. How many people know that "bacon" comes from a pig's back and sides? When they hear the word *chuck*, how many picture a cow from neck to ribs?

Metaphors, too, obscure species and body part. A "drumstick" may come from a chicken, turkey, or other bird; "sweetbread" may come from a calf, lamb, or other young mammal. *Drumstick* avoids any reference to animals. *Sweetbread* transforms a thymus or pancreas into plant-derived food.

Words like *burger*, *steak*, and *sausage* retreat from the idea of remains by focussing on manner of preparation and final form. The words matter. Lorri Bauston, cofounder of Farm Sanctuary, a refuge for nonhumans abused by the food industry, remembers a telling incident. When a group of children visited the sanctuary, one boy informed a younger girl that "pepperoni" comes from pigs. Upset, the girl asked Bauston if this is true. "Yes, that's why we don't eat pepperoni," Bauston answered. The girl declared, "I'm not going to eat pepperoni either!"[71]

If humans were being enslaved, murdered, and eaten, our language would broadcast that fact (no doubt in strongly moralistic terms), not trivialize and conceal it with terms that specify cut of flesh or manner of preparation while omitting direct mention of those slain. Words like *giblets*, *cutlets*, and *pastrami* are morally irresponsible because they obliterate the victims and their murder. In contrast, terms like *chicken organs*, *cow flesh*, and *pig feet* acknowledge the victims (*chicken*, *cow*, *pig*) and their dismemberment (*organs*, *flesh*, *feet*).

Much popular usage fails to differentiate corpse parts from living nonhumans. As if there never existed a thinking, feeling individual—

only, from the beginning, a slab of flesh—*milk-fed* is applied to "veal" and *grain-fed* to "beef." Instead of acknowledging death and dismemberment, consumers call a turkey's headless remains "a turkey" or "a whole bird." The turkey is gone; they were killed. Only body parts remain.

Each year, "food animals" suffer and die by the billions, but they do so one by one. To rest easy, those who buy or sell products from nonhuman bodies must forget that each victim suffered personal loss of freedom, well-being, and life.

"Animal Units" and "Meat Machines"

Autonomy attests to individuality, so the autonomy of food-industry captives is denied. "We don't regard the hen as a bird," an egg factory's assistant manager has stated. "It's a production unit."[72] Month after month, the USDA's *Feed Situation and Outlook Report* refers to grain- and roughage-consuming "animal units." The industry commonly calls cows or goats exploited for their milk "udders." An industry researcher has described cows as "nothing but cells on the hoof."[73] Units, udders, cells. Mere parts.

Verbally subsumed into the flock or herd, nonhumans disappear as individuals. Flocks, not individual chickens, gasp and wheeze: "A flock with a respiratory disease shows signs of respiratory distress, such as gasping, wheezing, nasal discharge, and coughing."[74] If "welfare pressures" increase, "it may be more important in the future to consider birds as individuals rather than flocks," *Poultry Production Systems* warns.[75] Industry veterinarians concern themselves with "herd health," not the health of individual cattle or sheep. All salmons in a cage merge to form its "contents." (Would anyone say, "The room's contents consisted of one sofa, three chairs, and four people"?)

Reference to captives' location replaces reference to the captives themselves, removing them from consideration. "Aquaculture" insiders speak of feeding, vaccinating, and dosing a "pond" rather than its fish inhabitants. Polluted "sites," not caged salmons, "suffer oxygen stress."[76] Industry veterinarians monitor "the health status of the feedlot." "Hog farms," not pigs, "experience" reproductive and respiratory disease.[77]

Like hunters and fishers, food-industry enslavers apply amount (rather than number) words to nonhuman animals: "part of his calves," "a great deal of ducks," "a hundred pounds of fish swimming around." In the food industry, as elsewhere, speciesist language reduces living nonhumans to mere substance. Calves and pigs are "raw materials" used to make flesh products. Of no use to the egg industry, male chicks are hatchery "material" and "waste." They're ground up alive or tossed one after another into a trash bag, where they suffocate. (The industry calls these murder methods "euthanasia.")

Along with other speciesists, food-industry enslavers speak of nonhuman animals as interchangeable: "replacement boars," "replacement calves." Turkey breeders may "keep a few spare toms [adult male turkeys] to replace those that die." A sheep enslaver expresses the pervasive callous attitude: "If one of my sheep can't cut it living under our system, . . . I don't waste time and money on her. There are a great many sheep in our world and I figure I can find another to take her place, as well as a better one."[78]

Empathy requires perceiving another being as an individual. Because a personal name acknowledges individuality, naming a nonhuman victim poses the same emotional threat to food-industry enslavers as to vivisectors. "Do not give names to meat kids for obvious reasons!" a small-scale goat enslaver cautions. Recalling a goat "earmarked for dinner," another relates, "To keep things in perspective, we named him 'T-bone.'" "Resist the temptation to become too attached," two pig enslavers warn. "If you're going to eat it, don't give it a pet name. Try something like 'Porky' or 'Chops' or 'Spareribs' if the urge to name is too strong." "If you must name your future meal, call it Colonel Sanders or Cacciatore," two chicken enslavers advise. The size of the largest enslavement operations precludes naming the captives, whose anonymity helps enslavers remain detached as they cause suffering.[79]

To their exploiters, food-industry captives *are* milk, eggs, or flesh. In the cow-milk industry, bulls who father daughters "sire milk." A food-industry veterinarian refers to the "health needs" of the "meat and egg supply."[80] Would any of us seek medical treatment from a physician who viewed humans as cadavers? Enslavers call cattle "veals" and "beeves." Slaughterers utter oxymorons like "kill beef" and "slaughter pork." "It's probably wrong to call them hogs at all," a pig-flesh researcher has said of piglets artificially conceived and reared. "What they are, when you get right down to it, is pork."[81] The *live* in *livestock* is merely an inconvenience.

Like hunters and fishers, food-industry enslavers equate nonhuman animals with plants. In "aquaculture," mollusk and crustacean growing cycles begin with the "seed"; fishes and other aquatic "crops" are "planted" and "cultivated," resulting in a "yield per acre." Birds and mammals used for breeding are "seedstock"; their offspring, such as the chick or pig "crop," are "watered" and "grown" by the pound. When gathered for transport to slaughter, catfishes, chickens, and other small animals are "harvested." As previously mentioned, *harvest* also substitutes for *slaughter*.

In *The Forbidden Zone* Michael Lesy recounts visits to two slaughterhouses. At one he interviewed a pious shochet (kosher slaughterer), at the other an operations director with a penchant for obscenity and lurid description. Although opposite in manner, the two men gave similar answers when asked how they came to kill with equanimity. "I didn't think any more of it than if I went out to the garden and pulled up a carrot," the operations director told Lesy, adding that a cow is "like a crop, like corn or cabbage or wheat. We harvest them." "A steer has more life in it than an apple," the shochet said, "but if I went to a tree and picked an apple, it would be no sin. The same with an animal." From a nonspeciesist perspective, needlessly killing a nonhuman is evil for the same reason that killing an innocent human is evil: death ends the capacity to experience. Killing a conscious being (as opposed to destroying a plant) obliterates a mental world. Also, whereas destroying a plant causes no suffering, slaughtering an animal inflicts terror and pain. Morally the two actions vastly differ.[82]

Industry wide, machine metaphors rob nonhuman animals of life as well as sentience. Hens enslaved for their eggs are "egg machines," sheep "meat machines," and cattle "recycling machines" that convert plant foods into flesh. *Vealer USA* has counseled calf enslavers to discard a calf suffering from bloat and "find a replacement that has all the proper working parts." Using typical industry lingo, two historians of the pig-flesh industry have written that pigs are "assembled on the farm, disassembled at the packing plant." In its treatment of nonhuman animals, the industry acts as if the machine metaphor were literal truth. "The breeding sow should be thought of, and treated as, a valuable piece of machinery whose function is to pump out baby pigs like a sausage machine," a flesh-industry export manager has advised. "Forget the pig is an animal," pig enslaver John Byrnes instructs. "Treat him just like a machine in a factory."[83]

"Instead of shiny new cars or a newfangled widget your product is feeder pigs," Byrnes comments.[84] Those who exploit nonhuman animals for profit view them as commodities. Under current law, that's what they are. The U.S. Internal Revenue Service teams up with food-industry enslavers in designating nonhuman animals "inventory": "items" that are *financed*, *capitalized*, *depreciated*, *invoiced*, *leased*, and *liquidated*. Like other "tangible personal property," food-industry captives have a certain number of years of "useful life." One goat enslaver includes goats among feed pans, milking equipment, and other "things that aren't used up all at once."[85] Classifying nonhuman animals with inanimate things averts concerns about causing suffering or destroying life. Questioned about cruelty to cattle, the owner of a "livestock" auction responded, "Our job is to sell merchandise at a profit. It's no different from selling paper-clips, or refrigerators."[86] A man willing to design systems to kill pigs, but not cattle, has given this explanation: "Hogs are just a commodity."[87]

In the end, "food animals" represent money. Flavomycin controls bacteria that "prey on your profits," an industry ad tells turkey enslavers. Use it to "protect poultry profits." When she sends calves to slaughter, an enslaver has said, she follows the truck so that she knows "what is happening to our $40,000+ from the time they leave our property."[88]

The language of "animal agriculture" is primarily economic, increasingly that of factory production. To speak of enslavement and mass murder in economic terms is to discard morality.

"Employees"

A common industry metaphor depicts nonhuman slaves as human employees. The cow-milk industry advertises bulls used for breeding as "udder specialists." After being used, these bulls are "laid off" until their daughters' milk production records can be assessed. A cow's milk production is her "livelihood." She can accumulate "impressive credentials" before she "retires."[89] The worker metaphor suggests some ugly truths to which the industry is either oblivious or indifferent. It *is* nonhuman animals, not their enslavers, who "produce" eggs, milk, and flesh. Like human assembly-line workers, enslaved nonhumans are exploited as steps in a production process and seen as replaceable parts rather than individuals.

Otherwise the metaphor misleads. Human factory workers comprehend their situation. Nonhumans on factory "farms" must be bewildered and frightened by their mechanized, human-created environment. Severed from nature, kept nearly immobilized, denied normal contact with others of their species, and subjected to a monotonous regimen and suffocating filth, they experience a completely hostile world. Above all, "food animals" aren't free to walk out. Unlike human workers, they remain imprisoned and exploited every hour of every day, until they die.[90] Like vivisection's "colleague" metaphor, "animal agriculture's" employee metaphor belies coercion. The slaves "perform as they are asked to."[91] They "supply" their eggs, milk, and flesh instead of having these forcibly taken. The media share the pretense that nonhumans consent to work and die for humans. According to a *National Geographic* writer, pigs' "contribution" to humans includes the "hams, roasts, and chops they surrender."[92] As expressed by two other journalists, chickens "give" their lives and "let" humans eat them.[93]

The worker metaphor also provides a way of blaming the victim. Captives who show inadequate "performance" in "producing" offspring, milk, eggs, or flesh are despised as "poor specimens," "inferior," and "junk." "A low producer certainly shouldn't be allowed to take up space," a *Hoard's Dairyman* article says of cows. A *National Hog Farmer* piece compares sows who are neither pregnant nor nursing to employees who fail to do their job but still receive room, board, and pay. Sows who accumulate too many "non-productive" days are "culled."[94]

"Lazy" Turkeys and "Stubborn" Pigs

As in other forms of speciesist abuse, blaming the victim is common in "animal agriculture." Like zoo, aquaprison, and vivisection captives, food-industry captives react to severe deprivation with pathological behaviors, such as feather pecking and tail biting. The industry calls these behaviors "vices." Chickens have an aggressive nature that necessitates debeaking, their enslavers claim.[95] Free-living chickens rarely fight. Normally they peck the ground, not each other. A natural component of foraging and dustbathing, pecking lacks an appropriate outlet in intensive confinement.

By her own account, enslaver Cathryn Baskin confined chickens to a windowless building that soon filled with stench and choking, eye-stinging ammonia. She fed the chickens moldy grain, allowed them so little space at maturity that they barely could move, and "didn't always treat the birds with the greatest of gentleness." Many of the chickens became so crippled that they couldn't reach food or water. Many died from bacterial infection or heart attack. Workers who gathered the survivors for slaughter grabbed six or seven at a time, by their legs. Chickens were kicked, thrown, and trampled underfoot. Rejecting any pity for chickens as "incompatible with commercial poultry raising," Baskin reviles them as *fat*, *lumpish*, *lethargic*, *mindless*, *dumb*, *stupid*, *filthy*, *detestable*, and *loathsome*.[96]

In addition to being chained by the neck, many "veal" calves are kept in dim light or total darkness all the time except for two brief feeding periods each day.[97] According to their exploiters, calves who fight against their chain or react to light with nervous sensitivity show "hyper-irritability."[98] Calves jumpy from severe confinement are "flakey."[99] Those too upset or ill to eat are "duds."[100] Lightweight calves are "knotheads" and "pukes."[101]

Having abused a sow, Freese blames her for resisting incarceration: "One time, I gouged a *stubborn* old sow in the eye when she wouldn't go in[to] a farrowing [birthing] crate" (emphasis added). Slaughterhouse workers give the same excuse for beating pigs on the head with metal bars: "Hogs are stubborn."[102]

Severely inbred by the flesh industry, turkeys grow so quickly and become so top-heavy with breast flesh that their skeletons can't keep pace. Because their legs can't support their unnatural weight, turkeys have difficulty standing. Painful deformity, illness, and dense crowding prevent them from moving about, so they spend most of their time sitting on wet, filthy litter. An industry writer blames the turkeys themselves for the blisters and skin ulcers that result. The number and severity of sores depend on a turkey's "degree of laziness," she says.[103]

Flesh consumers share the industry's penchant for blaming the victim. Why not kill and eat turkeys? a *Washington Post* columnist has mused, offering this supposedly humorous justification: "A turkey is too mentally unendowed to even stand upright." Showing genuine ugliness, eaters of turkey flesh call turkeys ugly and stupid. Do they also consider it acceptable to enslave and kill humans whom they regard as ugly and stupid? A *Chicago Tribune* writer has declared chickens "stupid and despicable creatures," "worthless" except for their eggs and flesh, which—no surprise—he likes to eat.[104]

"Food Animals" and "Meat Eaters"

"It is the purpose of food animals to serve mankind," the NCA has stated.[105] The designation *food animal* already declares an animal's "purpose" to be consumption by humans. Like *game animal* or *lab animal*, the terms *food animal*, *farm animal*, and *agricultural animal* label nonhumans for human use. Each food-industry captive also bears more-specific exploitive labels, such as *veal calf*, *dairy cow*, or *beef cow*; *feeder pig* or *breeder pig*; *layer* or *broiler*. "Dual-purpose" chickens can be exploited for both eggs and flesh, "dual-purpose" cows for milk and flesh. As Carol Adams points out, "There is nothing inherent in a cow's existence that necessitates her future fate as hamburger or her current fate as milk machine."[106] A cow produces milk for her calf, not us.

The false inevitability of categories like "poultry," "food fish," and "livestock" becomes evident when an individual escapes their grasp. If a hen is rescued from an egg factory and adopted by someone who never would exploit her, she's no longer "poultry." In 1989, after two Cambodians killed and ate a dog in California, the state enacted legislation making it a misdemeanor to kill for food any animal "commonly kept as a pet or companion." Animals viewed as edible—"livestock, poultry, fish, shell fish," and "game animals"—were excluded from this protection. A proponent of the legislation summed up its rationale: "In our society we don't eat pets."[107] Just who is a pet, as opposed to a "food animal," depends on who does the labeling. As reported by Nick Fiddes in *Meat: A Natural Symbol*, the newspaper ad "Rabbits for sale: as pets, or for the freezer" provoked a public outcry. Apparently the ad upset readers because it placed rabbits in two conflicting categories: pet and "food animal." The clash showed that such categories are artificially imposed.[108]

While labeling pigs "livestock" and turkeys "poultry," humans label themselves "meat eaters." "I am human. I eat meat," a restaurateur has stated, as if being human automatically entailed eating flesh.[109] Meanwhile, vegans throughout the world demonstrate the health benefits of avoiding animal-derived foods.

Complicit in enslavement and mass murder, consumers who eat products from the bodies of nonhuman animals feed on lies. When more humans confront the truth, "animal agriculture's" demise will begin.

10

Pronoun Politics

> I was generally introduced as a "*chattel*"—a "*thing*"—a piece of southern "*property*"—the chairman assuring the audience that *it* could speak.
>
> —Frederick Douglass

Having escaped from slavery three years before, in 1841 Frederick Douglass began a lecture tour for the Massachusetts Anti-Slavery Society. Invited to speak of his experiences during enslavement, Douglass addressed Massachusetts audiences who were predominantly white. Although these audiences supported the abolition of human slavery, Douglass found his guest appearances humiliating. Often he was introduced as a "thing," an "it," he later would write.[1] *Webster's* primary definition of *it* is "a lifeless thing." Most likely, those who introduced Douglass as "it" intended no insult; their worldview was so racist that they failed to perceive *it*'s falsehood and effrontery. Whereas slaveholders regarded Douglass as an object of use, many white abolitionists regarded him as an object of curiosity. Seen as either a slave or a former slave, he represented some*thing* other than a man.

Today terming a human "it" still exhibits lack of empathy or respect. Parents who refer to their newborn as "it" have failed to form a loving attachment, a book on parenting warns.[2] Calling an adult "it" deliberately demeans. "Just listen to it talk," *Webster's* illustrates. Applied to any individual, *it* signals and helps maintain emotional distance and feelings of superiority.

Our pronoun choices reflect and influence our attitudes toward others. Standard English pronoun use perpetuates disregard of nonhuman beings by characterizing them as genderless, insentient things. Politically loaded, English pronouns have special power to promote or undermine speciesism.

Males, Females, and Hermaphrodites

According to current knowledge, all animals are male, female, or hermaphroditic. (Biologists don't classify viruses, bacteria, or protoctists such as amoebas and paramecia as animals.) Yet, humans routinely term other animals "it." Referring to a white rhino killed after she escaped from a zoo, a *Washington Post* article states, "It was believed to be pregnant."[3] Such gender disagreement has no rationale but speciesism. Accuracy and fairness require *he*, *she*, and *she/he* (or *he/she*) for nonhuman animals.

Along with conditions like pregnancy, sex-specific behaviors and traits may announce a nonhuman's gender. Soldier ants, worker ants and bees, mosquitoes who bite, wasps and bees who sting—all are "she." Like a lion with a mane, an elk, moose, or deer with antlers is male. So is a red cardinal or a mallard whose head and neck are green. Only female "black widows" are black; the males are brown. Sex-specific animal terms and personal names also indicate gender. A rooster, or a dog named Prince, obviously is "he."

What if an animal has been "neutered"? The word *neutered* misleads. A dog, cat, or other nonhuman whose ovaries and uterus have been removed still is female; one whose testicles have been removed still is male. I once objected when a woman called a steer "it" rather than "he." "A steer has been castrated," she responded. "Would you refer to a castrated *man* as 'it'?" I asked. She wouldn't.

When a nonhuman group comprises individuals all of the same sex, one sex-specific pronoun accurately describes any member of the group. If four female cats ate their supper, "Everyone ate *her* supper." When a nonhuman group possibly or definitely includes individuals of different sexes, a plural pronoun avoids the speciesism of *it*, sexism of pseudogeneric *he*, and clumsiness of *he or she*: "Everyone [two male and two female cats] ate *their* supper."

Similarly, reference to a hypothetical animal of a particular sex warrants a gender-specific pronoun: "When another buck approaches, warn *him* away from the hunters." Reference to a hypothetical animal of unknown gender calls for a plural pronoun: "When another deer approaches, warn *them* away from the hunters."

Convention categorizes indefinite terms like *everyone* and *another deer* as grammatically singular. But they're conceptually plural. When we say "each crow" or "every crow," we mean all crows in some group. Even "either crow" and "some crow" don't specify which crow among two or more. Despite academic objections, common practice long has paired grammatically singular indefinite terms such as *someone* and *any crow* with plural pronouns. A sentence like "Somebody left their umbrella" sounds natural and familiar. A plural pronoun serves equally well with reference to nonhumans.

Those unwilling to combine a plural pronoun with a grammatically singular indefinite term (such as *any deer*) can reword: "Warn away any deer who approaches." Or they can use some variant of *he or she*, as they would for humans: "Everyone ate *her/his* supper"; "When another deer approaches, warn *him or her* away from the hunters." (While greatly preferable to sexist pseudogeneric *he*, the terms *he/she* and *he or she* still give males precedence. To avoid sexual bias when using dual-sex terms, I alternate between feminine first and masculine first.) Failure to apply the same linguistic rules to nonhuman and human animals represents a speciesist double standard.

An actual nonhuman individual of unknown gender poses the only genuine pronoun problem. Does their appearance, behavior, or situation suggest their sex? Nearly always, tortoise-shell and calico cats are "she"; predominantly, orange tabbies are "he." Most rats used in vivisection, most large mammals targeted by hunters, and the vast majority of calves slaughtered for their flesh are male. Most elephants exploited by circuses and zoos and most "trophy-size" fishes are female. Some species of insects, fishes, reptiles, and other animals are primarily or exclusively female. Provided with such a clue as to a particular animal's sex, I choose *she* or *he* in keeping with the odds. Otherwise I choose arbitrarily (except to assign *he* and *she* equally often within any given communication).

Of course, guessing a particular animal's sex or arbitrarily calling them "she" (or "he") brings some chance of error. That chance is 50 percent when we randomly assign gender to an animal whose species has a 1:1 ratio of females to males. But using *they*, *he/she*, or *it* would have worse consequences.

They would turn an individual into a plurality. Humans urgently need to regard nonhumans as individuals. It's harder to feel for a "they" than a "she" or "he."

He/she perfectly describes a hermaphrodite such as an earthworm or barnacle, but not a single-sex animal. Besides, the awkwardness of *he/she* or *he or she* distracts. More importantly, gender alternation interferes with empathy. A "she or he" has no real identity. As observed by Mary Phillips, vivisectors and their assistants often refer to the same nonhuman animal as "he," "she," and "it" on different occasions. Such inconsistent pronoun use reinforces a failure to see nonhumans as individuals, who have enduring traits.[4]

Convenience doesn't justify using *it* for any individual of unknown gender, whether they're human or nonhuman. Unlike gendered or plural pronouns, neuter *it* is both speciesist and inaccurate when applied to an animal—always. Animals have gender. *It* perpetuates speciesist abuse by classifying nonhuman beings with insentient things.

The education director of Waikiki Aquarium (Honolulu) recommends that zoo and aquaprison personnel use *it* for a nonhuman animal of unknown gender. Some Denver Zoo staff consider *he* and *she* "too human" for zoo captives. An "it" doesn't need or desire freedom, but imprisoning an innocent "he" or "she" diminishes someone's well-being and violates their rights.[5]

F. Peyton Rous's editorial guidelines for the *Journal of Experimental Medicine* included this instruction, aimed at reducing sympathy for vivisected animals: "Never use 'he,' 'she,' 'his,' or 'hers' in reference to an animal. Use 'it,' 'its.'" Generally, editors of journals that publish vivisection insist on *it* for nonhuman animals. Throughout, a 1969 report in the *Journal of the Experimental Analysis of Behavior* refers to a female rough-toothed porpoise, Hou, as "it": "Hou ran through its repertoire." According to the report's first author, the journal "believes in saving 'he' and 'she' for human beings." No doubt the same editors who demanded a neuter pronoun for a female porpoise prided themselves on scientific accuracy. When Jane Goodall submitted a paper on chimpanzees to *Annals of the New York Academy of Sciences*, the editors initially substituted *it* for every chimpanzee *she* or *he*. Angered, Goodall restored her original pronouns. She prevailed. The published article "did confer upon the chimpanzees the dignity of their appropriate genders and properly upgraded them from the status of mere 'things'" to beings.[6]

With speciesist illogic, many journals that publish vivisection accept gendered pronouns for some nonhuman animals (especially nonhuman primates) but not others. The ten male rats whom I used in graduate school research lost their gender identity along with their personal names when I prepared my report for *Animal Learning and Behavior*. As instructed by my advisor, I changed each rat from "he" to "it." At the same time, I continued to refer to monkeys used by another vivisector as "he or she."[7] No one remarked on this inconsistency. Because monkeys are more human-like than rats, speciesists more readily think of them as gendered individuals.

Using *it* for an entire animal group isn't speciesist: "The flock altered *its* course"; "Unless the species receives endangered status, *it* may soon be extinct." However, even when speaking of an entire group, I usually prefer plurals: "The geese altered their course," "Unless Atlantic salmons receive endangered status, they may soon be extinct." The plural serves as a reminder that any group of nonhumans comprises individuals.

Most importantly, though, avoid using *it* for any individual animal.

Sentient Whos

Pure speciesism leads people to call a brain-dead human "who" but a conscious guppy "that" or "which." The *who/that* divide belongs between beings (sentient) and things (insentient), not between humans and all other animals.

All vertebrates and most bilaterally symmetrical invertebrates possess a brain (primary nerve center in the head). Because the presence of a brain indicates consciousness, these animals—including such "lowly" creatures as flatworms, dust mites, oysters, and slugs—deserve the moral consideration signaled by *who*.

Radially symmetrical, comb jellies, cnidarians (such as jellyfishes and corals), and echinoderms (among them, sea stars and sea urchins) have no brain but do possess a nervous system. Their probable sentience warrants *who*.

That and *which* appropriately apply to sponges, placozoans (which resemble amoebas but are multicellular), and two types of tiny worm-shaped parasites: rhombozoans and orthonectids. Of all creatures currently classified by biologists as animals, only these lack a nervous system. Because of their insentience, I don't include them in "animal" (eventually, taxonomists too may exclude them, because of their biologically anomalous nature). I consider it too important that the word *animal* remain unequivocally linked to sentience and its claim on moral consideration. Whereas excluding humans from "animal" is speciesist, excluding insentient things is logically consistent and fair, based on the morally crucial capacity to experience.

Using *who* for every creature with a nervous system avoids dismissing any sentient being. Overly generous inclusion? Perhaps. But I'd rather accord an insentient thing undue respect than slight any being who feels. I'd rather extend moral consideration to something that can't suffer than fail to extend it to someone who can.

Because speciesism involves logical and linguistic contradictions, pronoun references to nonhuman animals often show inconsistency. In a book on honeybees, within one sentence the same honeybee is "that" and then "who."[8] A nervous-system criterion for *who* eliminates such confusion. Honeybees certainly qualify.

Standard writing manuals limit *who* to animals with personal names. They recommend "Rover, *who* leaped the fence" but "The dog, *which* leaped the fence." This pronoun disparity reflects the speciesist view that nonhumans matter only insofar as they matter to some human. Marked by bestowal of a personal name, a relationship with a human elevates a nonhuman from "that" to "who." In reality, an unnamed animal is no less an individual than a named one.

Speciesists cherish nonhuman *that* and *which*. Along with each chimpanzee *she* and *he*, the editors of Goodall's journal article initially expunged every *who*.[9] A human monopoly on *who* flatters and privileges humans. Rous's editorial guidelines directed, "Never say 'who' of an animal."[10] Nonhuman *who* would acknowledge nonhuman victimization.

Although *whose* can refer to things as well as beings, Rous's guidelines warned against this word as well: "permissible" in reference to nonhuman animals but "not desirable."[11] Apparently, the *who* in *whose* might suffice to remind readers that vivisected animals think and feel.

Speaking carelessly, people often use *that* or *which* for humans. While objectionable, this usage isn't meant to offend. In contrast, calling a human "what" conveys scorn. "Look what I've caught," someone might say in apprehending a thief. *What* routinely denigrates nonhuman animals. Even more than *that* or *which*, *what* negates sentience; it suggests some nonindividuated substance. Trappers, fishers, and hunters boast about "what I caught" and "what I shot." "Whom I caught" and "whom I shot" would amount to confessions of murder.

Someone, Not Something

Native Americans and blacks haven't always qualified as "somebody" in the minds of whites. In the early nineteenth century, a white trapper remarked that he was hundreds of miles from "any body" while in Native American territory.[12] After a steamboat accident in *The Adventures of Huckleberry Finn*, Aunt Sally asks Huck, "Anybody hurt?" "No'm," he answers. "Killed a nigger."[13] In 1994 a U.S. airliner collided with a bird, reportedly a heron or goose. No humans were harmed, but the bird was killed. "Nobody was injured," the evening news reported. (Anybody hurt? No'm. Killed a bird.) Having formerly excluded many humans from "somebody," common usage continues to exclude nonhumans.

Standard linguistic practice restricts *-one* and *-body* to humans, relegating nonhumans to *-thing*. "Catch anything?" fishers or trappers ask each other. "Catch anyone?" might jolt them into awareness of their cruelty. As expressed by a man who sells exotic birds and nonhuman mammals, "Auctions are a good place to get rid of something."[14] "Get rid of someone" would expose his dealings as slave trafficking. Any sentient being is an individual, not some *thing* like a toaster or rock. Classifying nonhuman animals with inanimate objects fosters their abuse.

In defense of pelt wearing, a woman in a raccoon-pelt coat told *New York* magazine, "Everybody has a right to do what they want. You're not hurting anybody."[15] In her view, "everybody" and "anybody" don't include animals with coveted fur. Most raccoons killed for their fur are caught in the steel-jaw leghold trap, which snaps shut on their leg, foot, or hand. The trap severs toes, dislocates joints, rips tendons and ligaments, and breaks bones. Because many trappers don't return to their traps for a week, the victim may suffer prolonged hunger, thirst, fear, and pain. Many trapped animals die from dehydration or exposure. Others bite or wring off a limb to escape; these animals often die slowly from blood poisoning or gangrene.[16] Routinely, a raccoon still alive when the trapper returns is clubbed or stomped to death.[17] As witnessed by a *Washington Post* reporter, one raccoon remained conscious after "repeated whackings and stompings" by a veteran trapper. Finally, the trapper killed the raccoon with a rifle blast.[18] You're not hurting anybody?

Pronoun use that robs nonhuman animals of sentience and individuality may be the most widespread linguistic ploy by which English-speakers legitimize speciesist abuse. No sentient being is an "it," "that," or "-thing." Each is equally someone.

11

"Bitches," "Monkeys," and "Guinea Pigs"

"Animal" Metaphors

> [One dog to another:]
>
> "That bitch that Rover took out last night was a real human, wasn't she?"
>
> —a Ray Smith cartoon

Most nonhuman-animal metaphors perpetuate a contemptuous view of nonhuman beings that fosters their oppression. When such metaphors denigrate all members of a human group—say, women or blacks—they also promote human political inequality. As Haig Bosmajian notes in *The Language of Oppression*, "Defining people as non-human or sub-human" commonly precedes and accompanies "their subjugation or annihilation."[1] Derogatory nonhuman-animal metaphors rely on speciesism for their pejorative effect.

Chicks, Vixens, and Women

Female-specific "animal" metaphors communicate varying degrees of insult: *old crow*, *catty*, *shrew*, *dumb bunny*, *queen bee*, *sow*. Viewed through speciesism, a nonhuman animal acquires a negative image. When metaphor imposes that image on women, they share its negativity.

Because *dog* refers to physical appearance when applied to women but not men, it implies that women have a special obligation to be attractive. More directly, the metaphor denigrates all dogs as ugly. Reserved for women, *dumb bunny* links femaleness to mindlessness. The expression rests on the speciesist assumption that rabbits are stupid.

In addition to speciesist attitudes, speciesist practices underlie nonhuman-animal metaphors that disparage women. Apparently inured to human abuse of "domestic animals," French poet Charles Baudelaire described women as "domestic animals which ought to be kept locked up in captivity; they should be well fed and cared for and beaten regularly." As philosopher Robert Baker notes, most female-specific "animal" metaphors refer to "domesticated" nonhumans, those bred to serve human interests.[2]

Commonly used by dog breeders and other dog exploiters, *bitch* denotes a female dog. Why should calling a woman a "bitch" impute malice and selfishness? Given that so many English-speakers find dogs lovable and sweet-natured, the metaphor's contempt seems puzzling. Breeders, however, always have treated female dogs with contempt, requiring them to deliver puppies who will bring money or prestige. As a method of force-breeding bulldogs, an article in the American Kennel Club's magazine recommends "holding the bitch in the proper position," with straps or by her legs, and "assist[ing]" the male in "penetration." Breeders subject female bulldogs to this ordeal because they've afflicted bulldogs with a low front and high rear, characteristics that preclude natural mating. Also bred to be flat-faced, bulldogs suffer chronic breathing difficulty from pathologically short and twisted air passages; often an overlong soft palate further obstructs breathing. As reported in a veterinary newsletter, a bulldog was "placed on her back" for artificial insemination even though she was having trouble breathing. Her breathing remained labored. When she started to struggle, she was restrained. Her breathing worsened. Still the forced insemination continued. Struggling to breathe, she died. Familiarity with the numerous ways in which breeders have disabled dogs and treated them like commodities dispels any mystery as to why *bitch* carries contempt.[3]

Cow characterizes a woman as fat and dull. Kept perpetually pregnant or lactating, with swollen belly or swollen udder, cows enslaved for their milk are seen as fat. Confined to a stall, denied the active role of nurturing and protecting a calf (so that milking becomes something done *to* them rather than *by* them), they're seen as passive and dull. "Milk cows" then become emblematic of these traits. Their image easily transfers to women because their exploitation focuses on uniquely female capacities to produce milk and "replacement" offspring. When these capacities decline, a cow is slaughtered.

Comparison to chickens spans a woman's life, linguist Alleen Pace Nilsen observes: "A young girl is a *chick*. When she gets old enough she marries and soon begins feeling *cooped up*. To relieve the boredom she goes to *hen parties* and *cackles* with her friends. Eventually she has her *brood*, begins to *henpeck* her husband, and finally turns into an *old biddy*."[4] Nilsen doesn't delve beneath the metaphors' sexist use, to their origins in hens' exploitation. Comparing women to hens communicates scorn because hens are exploited as mere bodies, for their egg-laying capacity or flesh. In viewing an actual female chick, egg or flesh purveyors anticipate her exploitation as a hen. Analogously, sexist men desire to exploit a human "chick" as a female body, for sexual pleasure. A hen's exploiter values only her physical servitude, dismissing her experiential world as unimportant or nonexistent. Similarly, *hen party* empties women's experiences of all substance or significance; like hens, women have no worth apart from their function within the exploiter's world. A hen ("biddy") whose flesh is considered undesirable and who no longer lays eggs at a profitable rate is regarded as "spent" and discarded. No longer sexually attractive or able to reproduce, a human "old biddy" too has outlived her usefulness. Hens' lives supply symbols for the lives of stifled and physically exploited women because hens are enslaved.

Comparisons between women and "domesticated" nonhumans are offensive because they "reflect a conception of women as mindless servants," Baker concludes.[5] But the metaphors' offending components derive from speciesist attitudes and practices. Without speciesism, "domesticated" nonhumans wouldn't be regarded as mindless. Without speciesism they wouldn't be forced into servitude.

The exploitation of "domesticated" nonhumans also has led to negative images of predators who may interfere with that exploitation. A woman termed a "vixen" is resented and somewhat feared as scolding, malicious, or domineering, especially toward a man. In the days when most "poultry" were kept in coops or yards, actual vixens were widely resented and feared as intruders. Being predators, they crossed human-drawn boundaries to kill chickens or other "fowl" whom humans considered their property. Quick-witted and fleet, they frequently evaded capture, "outfoxing" the human oppressor. Pejorative use of *vixen* derives from speciesist hostility toward foxes as predators.

Foxes as quarry or "furbearers" conjure a different image, which forms the basis for *foxy lady*. Hunters and trappers view foxes as objects of pursuit: future trophies or pelts. To the extent that a vixen eludes capture, she arouses their admiration and piques their desire to possess her. A man who labels a woman "foxy" admires her as stylish and attractive yet sees her largely as a sex object worth possessing. Overwhelmingly, hunters and trappers are male. Their skin-deep view of those they pursue easily extends from nonhuman animals to women. Each year in the U.S., at least hundreds of thousands of foxes are killed for their fur.[6] Most trapped foxes are caught in the excruciating steel-jaw leghold trap. When the trapper returns, the fox is bashed on the head, then stomped to death.[7] On "fur farms," foxes live confined to small wire cages and usually die from anal electrocution, which inflicts severe pain.[8] Any woman who wears a fox-pelt coat wraps herself in the skin of one-to-two dozen foxes who suffered intensely. She also invites continued sexist comparisons between women and nonhuman victims.[9]

Few women have considered how closely they resemble patriarchal oppressors when they denigrate nonhuman animals or participate in their abuse. The expression *male chauvinist pig* displays the same speciesism as *stupid cow*. Particularly amiable and sensitive, pigs possess none of the sexist's ugly character traits. Affection, cooperation, and protection of others characterize natural pig society, which is matriarchal. Boars rarely show aggression, even toward other boars, and are especially gentle with the young. A boar mates with a sow only if she is sexually receptive, after much mutual nuzzling, rubbing, and affable grunting. Intended to castigate men for their assumption of superiority to women, *male chauvinist pig* conveys the speaker's own assumption of superiority, to pigs. Referring to sexism, feminist philosopher Stephanie Ross notes that "many women adopt the very attitudes which are oppressing them."[10] Those attitudes include speciesism.

Many speciesist pejoratives are specific to male rather than female humans: *buzzard*, *skunk*, *lap dog*, *toad*, *weasel*, *snake*, *jackass*, *worm*, *cock of the walk*, *dumb ox*, *old goat*, *shark*, *wolf*, *cur*. Almost exclusively, the quintessential nonhuman-animal epithets—*animal*, *beast*, and *brute*—are aimed at men. "Animal" metaphors can find any target. But they're especially harmful to human equality when directed at members of vulnerable groups.

Monkeys, Cattle, and Blacks

Nonhuman-animal terms commonly serve as racist epithets. For centuries, whites figuratively and literally have identified blacks with supposedly inferior nonhuman animals. Belief in a natural hierarchy comprising higher and lower beings underlies all notions of black inferiority, historian Winthrop Jordan observes in *White over Black*.[11] Yet he doesn't address speciesism, on which the entire hierarchy is based.

Speciesists require a psychological buffer zone between humans and other primates. White racists have populated that zone with blacks. In seventeenth-century mainland America and the West Indies, slaveholders and plantation overseers frequently named enslaved blacks Monkey, Ape, or Baboon. Announcing a black man's flight from slavery, a 1734 notice in a South Carolina newspaper quipped that a "stately baboon," having "learned to walk very erect on his two hind legs," had "slipped his collar and run away."[12]

In 1788 a British historian categorized blacks as more similar to orangutans than to whites. Eighty years later another white writer contended, "The negro is more like the chimpanzee than like the Englishman." Such judgments' racist effect depends on speciesism: the smug assumption that any orangutan or chimpanzee, however astute and sensitive, automatically is less worthy and important than any white, however stupid and cruel. Also in the nineteenth century, an Englishman who designated blacks a "lower species of man" explained his reluctance to accept them as "brothers": "The gorilla would then also have to be admitted into the family." This speciesist would be unhappy to learn that biologists now place gorillas and humans in the same taxonomic family.[13]

In *The Negro a Beast* (1900) and *The Tempter of Eve* (1902), American Charles Carroll expressed contempt for blacks *as* nonhuman animals. Speaking literally, he declared them "monkeys" and (nonhuman) "apes."[14] For several weeks in 1906, the Bronx Zoo delivered the visual equivalent of Carroll's words. Exhibiting racism alongside speciesism, the zoo displayed the African pygmy Ota Benga caged with the orangutan Dohong.

More recently, neo-Nazi flyers have railed against "grinning Black monkeys" and "subhuman blacks" who act like "antisocial chimpanzees."[15] In the late 1980s, two black college students found this anonymous message on their dormitory door: "African monkeys, why don't you go back to the jungle?"[16] *Ape*, *monkey*, and *gorilla* remain common racist epithets.

While the speciesist concept of inferior beings gave whites an excuse for enslaving blacks, the speciesist practice of "animal agriculture" supplied a how-to model. When black slavery began in America, nonhuman slavery had existed for thousands of years. Black slavery in America was patterned after the forced breeding and labor of nonhuman animals, especially cattle.

Like cattle, enslaved blacks legally were movable property: chattel. (The words *cattle* and *chattel* share the Latin root *capitale*.) Along with cattle and horses, enslaved blacks were examined (naked) for age and physical condition and sold at auction. Cattle and blacks were shipped in the same way, sometimes together. Also like cattle, some blacks were hot-iron branded with their owner's mark. Recaptured after running away, some were forced to wear an iron yoke, which impeded any future escape attempts. To "punish" and demoralize black men or prevent them from reproducing, slaveholders frequently had them castrated. This practice showed "the ease with which white men slipped over into treating their Negroes like their bulls and stallions," Jordan notes.[17]

To slaveholders a black was a "white man's tool like another beast of burden," historian George Fredrickson comments.[18] He fails to question why nonhumans themselves should be regarded as tools. The very notion "beast of burden" is speciesist. Like *work animal*, *beast of burden* falsely connects forced labor to a nonhuman's own nature rather than to coercion. *Burdened beast* is more accurate.

"The whole vocabulary of slaveholders" shows that they regard their slaves as "working animals," an abolitionist observed in 1839.[19] "Drivers" compelled cattle and blacks to toil. *Breeder* signified a cow or black woman who reproduced. Rebellious blacks were "broken" like horses, by a "nigger breaker." When no longer useful, black slaves were "culled" (sold).

Such slaveholder terminology extended beyond the South. During the Civil War a Massachusetts clergyman described blacks as grateful for their "domestication." Even after black enslavement ended, the language of "animal agriculture" adhered to blacks. At South Carolina's 1895 Constitutional Convention, a state senator scorned blacks as "cattle." In 1900 another speciesist praised slaveholders for having applied to blacks "the laws of breeding obtained through centuries of experience with the lower animals." In 1905 another remarked that slave "stock" had been "strengthened by artificial selection." Today slang for a black includes *Black Angus*, the name of a cattle breed.[20]

Just before a Wednesday midnight in 1993, a noisy outdoor celebration by five black women attending the University of Pennsylvania prompted a white student, Eden Jacobowitz, to shout from his dormitory window. By his own account he yelled, "Shut up, you water buffalo! If you want to party, there's a zoo a mile from here."[21] According to the women, Jacobowitz yelled, "Shut up, you black water buffaloes! Go back to the zoo where you belong."[22] Under Penn's code of conduct, the women charged Jacobowitz with racial harassment. Jacobowitz insisted that he had intended no racial slur. Born in Israel, he explained that the Hebrew word for water buffalo also means fool. After nationwide press coverage overwhelmingly supported Jacobowitz, the women withdrew their charge. However, they protested that his words "likened us to beasts."[23] The women's faculty advisor, anthropologist Peggy Reeves Sanday, stated that identifying black women with Asia's primary "beast of burden" (water buffaloes) "reduces them to work animals." The zoo remark, too, associated the women with "animality," she said; and notions of black "animality" had served to justify black enslavement.[24] Whether or not Jacobowitz's words were racist, they definitely were speciesist, equating nonhuman with stupid and coarse. A Tony Auth cartoon captured the essence of the "water buffalo" insult: two water buffaloes angrily face off, and one fumes, "You... You... You Human Being!"[25]

Comfortable with the idea of subjugated nonhuman animals such as enslaved cattle, speciesists tend to resent nonhumans who live free, resist human control, and pose some competition or threat. Speciesists have caricatured "wild animals," especially carnivores like lions and wolves, as destructive, rapacious, and fierce. Following black emancipation, racist whites attached the "wild animal" stereotype to black men, depicting them as dangerous creatures escaped from their cage.[26] White Southerners described black men as "monstrous beasts" who lurk in the dark, "African tigers" who leave their "lairs" to "devour" white women, "brutes" with "the savage nature and murderous instincts of the wild beast."[27] The Ku Klux Klan denounced "black beasts."[28] Later, neo-Nazis would excoriate "Black animals."[29] A popular image of blacks as violent "animals" continues to hinder their social, economic, and political equality.

Wolves, Lice, and Native Americans

Like blacks, Native Americans have suffered from the racist use of speciesist language. Most often that usage has identified them with "wild animals."

Labeling Native Americans predators, especially wolves, marked them for displacement and massacre. In the seventeenth century, American colonists passed bounty laws on wolves and then Native Americans, offering rewards for scalps from either group. A 1638 Massachusetts law mandated a fine for firing a gun within town limits "at any game except an Indian or a wolf." Terming Native Americans "wild beasts" and "rabid wolves," Puritan minister Cotton Mather urged their extermination. In 1783, four days after the American Revolution ended, George Washington pondered how white settlers might best acquire the land of Native American "beasts of prey." Several decades later General Andrew Jackson initiated U.S. Army attacks on Florida's Mikasukis, to strike "the Wolf" in "his den."[30]

Whites targeted Native Americans in "trophy hunting" as well as "predator control." By the eighteenth century, "Indian-shooting" was "a recognized sport," a historian notes.[31] In the same way that they flaunted bear claws and deer antlers, white hunters displayed the body parts of Native American "game." They made jewelry from Native Americans' teeth and trophies from their scalps. "I've fought bear and panther and cougar," one killer boasted, "but there ain't no game like Injins."[32] Tracking "Injin sign" as they did deer spoor, nineteenth-century whites called Native American men "bucks."

Veteran hunters and trappers of nonhuman animals also killed Native American "critters" and "varmints." Transferring speciesist habits, they sometimes flayed their Native American victims and fashioned leggings, pouches, or other clothing and accessories from their skin.

Even more contemptuous than the "varmint" metaphor, references to Native American "vermin" legitimized genocide. In 1763 Sir Jeffrey Amherst, commander-in-chief of the American colonies' British forces, described Native Americans as "more allied to the brute than the human creation" and instructed Colonel Henry Bouquet to infect them with smallpox.[33] Bouquet, in turn, was eager to "extirpate" Native American "vermin."[34]

After shooting a Sauk infant in an 1832 massacre, a U.S. soldier offered this explanation: "Kill the nits, and you'll have no lice." The expression caught on. In 1864 at Sand Creek, Colorado, U.S. soldiers massacred Cheyennes after their colonel ordered, "Kill and scalp all, big and little; nits make lice."[35]

Speciesist language is a weapon that any human group can wield against any other, but an especially deadly one when used by the politically powerful against the weak.

Scapegoats and Sacrificial Lambs

Comparing humans to other animals often displays no bigotry except speciesism: *sheepish*, *birdbrain*, *crazy as a loon*. Whether or not a human is avaricious, labeling them a "vulture" exhibits prejudice against no group except vultures.

Some nonhuman-animal metaphors express praise: *busy as a bee*, *eagle-eyed*, *brave as a lion*. Sports team names like the Detroit Tigers, Chicago Bears, and St. Louis Rams suggest courage and strength. Car names like Skylark, Mustang, and Jaguar evoke grace, power, and speed. But the vast majority of nonhuman-animal metaphors disparage. In the *American Heritage Dictionary* more than a hundred nonhuman-animal names bear some derogatory meaning: *jellyfish*, *swine*, *ostrich*, *hog*, *turkey*, *louse*, *crab*, *leech*. "You're a _______." Fill in the blank with any nonhuman-animal name used as a metaphor for humans. Positive or negative? Apart from *lovebird*, *dove*, *pussycat*, and *lamb*, how many complimentary ones come to mind? (Not surprisingly, most English-speaking parents avoid giving their children names that refer to nonhuman animals. Only three such names appear among more than 10,000 entries in two books of suggested infant names: Jay, Robin, and Wolf.)[36] Nonhuman-animal adjectives and verbs also serve to criticize: *waspish*, *cocky*, *harebrained*; to *parrot*, *hound*, *ape*. For each favorable nonhuman-animal simile, dozens convey disapproval: *cross as a bear*, *drunk as a skunk*, *mean as a junkyard dog*.

Every negative image of another species helps keep that species oppressed. Most such images are gross distortions; in reality the imputed traits are human ones. Wolves don't philander like the human "wolf." They're sexually active only a few days each year. Most mate for life and show monogamous devotion. Chickens aren't "chicken." Hens fiercely protect their chicks, as roosters do their flock. Pigs don't "make pigs of themselves." Unlike many other animals (including humans), they show no tendency to overeat. Pigs aren't filthy. Whenever possible, they avoid fouling their living area. If unable to bathe in water, they may wallow in mud to cool themselves. Lacking functional sweat glands, they can't "sweat like a pig."

Why the lies, then? Why the contempt? Humans like to feel superior to other beings, especially those they abuse. Physically unable to fly, lacking any experience of predators (which would have taught them fear), dodos were massacred by humans. And *dodo* became synonymous with *fool*. *Stubborn as a mule* blames mules for their reluctance to haul human loads. *Trained seal* implies that mindless obedience, not bribery and coercion, prompts captive seals to perform unnatural and demeaning acts. *Pig* accuses pigs, who are forced to live in filth and bred to be fat, of being filthy and fat.

Some human–nonhuman comparisons convey disrespect *only* toward other species. *Work like a horse* expresses concern, even admiration, for a human worker but suggests that horses rightly toil for humans. *Human guinea pigs* voices sympathy for humans unwittingly used as experimental subjects, and indignation over their unjust treatment, but implies that actual guinea pigs are appropriate victims.

Numerous hackneyed expressions originated in speciesist abuse. Their use as metaphors obscures the reality from which they arose.

Hunters tied the first "stool pigeons" to a stool as a way of luring other pigeons to their death. People who "lived high on the hog" ate the most expensive parts of pigs' bodies. During eighteenth-century riverside picnics, a "fine kettle of fish" consisted of salmons boiled alive.

Clichés like *beat a dead horse*, *bleed like a stuck pig*, and *run around like a chicken with its head cut off* trivialize violence toward nonhuman animals. All too many such clichés sound a positive note: *have other fish to fry*, *kill two birds with one stone*, *There's more than one way to skin a cat.*

In contrast to most nonhuman-animal metaphors, *scapegoat* and *sacrificial lamb* accurately identify other animals as humans' innocent victims. But even these metaphors trivialize the murder of nonhuman animals except when applied to humans actually killed or otherwise grievously harmed.[37]

Nonhuman animals occupy oppression's deepest level. Worldwide their status is much lower than any human group's. For this reason, comparisons between humans and other animals usually denigrate humans. "Animal" metaphors encourage injustice toward humans, especially those who belong to vulnerable groups, because "animals" themselves lack justice. If our treatment and view of nonhuman beings became caring, respectful, and just, nonhuman-animal metaphors quickly would lose all power to harm.

12

Persons of Other Species

Toward Legal Redefinition

> The more you look at animal eyes, the more you begin to perceive them not as animal eyes but as the eyes of other people. So we call animals "people."
>
> —Oren Lyons, a chief of the Onondaga Nation

Less than three years old, Floyd was in excellent health when he entered the American Airlines jet. A golden retriever, he would travel as "excess baggage"—in the cargo hold, not in the passenger cabin with his human companion, Andrew Gluckman. After the plane was loaded and boarded, mechanical problems delayed takeoff. For more than an hour, the plane sat at an Arizona airport in 115 °F (46 °C) heat. Neither air-conditioned nor ventilated, the baggage compartment where Floyd was confined reached a temperature of 140 °F (60 °C). Gluckman got off the plane and had Floyd removed. In his crate, which was covered with blood, Floyd lay on his side panting. Bleeding from his face and paws, he had struggled to escape. Forty-five minutes later Floyd was taken to a veterinarian and placed in overnight intensive care. But he had suffered heat stroke and brain damage. The next morning Floyd was euthanized. Gluckman sued the airline. Among other grievances, he cited Floyd's "pain and suffering." The judge summarily dismissed this grievance, noting that New York State law doesn't recognize "the pain and suffering of an animal" as grounds for legal action.[1]

"Property"

In the U.S., as elsewhere, only humans possess legal rights. People seeking legal redress for wrongs committed against nonhuman animals must sue in their *own* behalf; to prevail, they must demonstrate that *they* have been harmed. If a human abuses a nonhuman owned by someone else, the human owner—not the nonhuman victim—is "the aggrieved party."

Legally, nonhuman animals are human property. In the U.S. a free-living deer or trout is public property. A cat or dog living with a human family is personal property. A cow commercially exploited for her milk is business property. When a Virginia woman took a neglected, roaming cat named Goober to a veterinarian for medical treatment and an ovariohysterectomy, Goober's owners complained to the authorities, and the state charged the good Samaritan with "defacing or injury of personal property." (Fortunately, she was acquitted.) As reported in *The New York Times*, an arsonist "burned $1 million worth of barns and livestock." The "livestock" included horses, pigs, and cows. Imagine someone writing, "The blaze destroyed valuable houses and people."[2]

By defining nonhuman animals as property, the law sanctions their enslavement and murder. Like other countries' "animal" laws, U.S. laws that ostensibly protect nonhumans largely perpetuate their abuse. The Animal Welfare Act doesn't promote animal welfare. It endorses the vivisection, exhibition, and sale of nonhuman beings. The Humane Methods of Slaughter Act doesn't guarantee a humane death. It legitimizes unnecessary and cruel slaughter. State "anti-cruelty" statutes aren't anticruelty. They allow all of the standard practices, from rodeo to commercial fishing, that terrorize, hurt, and kill billions of nonhuman animals each year.

In 1995 two friendly Yorkshire terriers, Guinevere and Lancelot, were kidnapped from the yard of their Virginia home and killed. As reported on the evening news, police conducted a "so-called murder investigation." Had a suspect been arrested, the charge would have been theft. Currently, U.S. criminal codes define first-degree murder as unjustifiably killing an "individual" or "person." A dog certainly is an individual. The law, however, falsely defines *individual* as human individual. It also restricts "persons" to humans (individual humans as well as entities, such as corporations and governmental bodies, that represent some group of humans).

Under the law, "persons" are rights-holders whereas "animals" are not. (Legally, *animal* always excludes humans. After all, we never would consent to be "treated like animals.") The boundary for rights belongs between beings and things, not between human and nonhuman animals. In all ways relevant to moral consideration, gorillas and shrimps resemble humans rather than trees or cars. A chicken or honeybee needs and deserves legal rights. Equitable laws would redefine *person* and *individual* to include nonhuman animals or replace those terms with *animal* or *sentient being*.

Pleading for Personhood

In both legal and everyday language, *person*'s meaning has changed over time.

An 1858 case exemplified enslaved blacks' property status, their lack of legal personhood. In his will, a Virginia slaveholder granted his slaves the choice between freedom and public sale. Virginia's supreme court ruled this provision void because property can't choose its fate. "The slave is not a person, but a thing," the court declared. To regard (human) slaves, dogs, horses, cattle, or "wild animals" as more than property would be "bad law," the court noted, even though "it might be good logic." As Mark Twain illustrated in *The Adventures of Huckleberry Finn*, everyday speech in the antebellum South conveyed the view that blacks weren't persons. When Huck tells Aunt Sally that a steamboat accident killed a black but injured no white, she remarks, "Well, it's lucky because sometimes people do get hurt."[3]

Whether American women qualified as legal persons remained an issue into the twentieth century. In 1931 the Massachusetts Supreme Court barred women from jury duty, for which only "persons" were eligible. *Person* lacks a "fixed and rigid signification," the (male) judges stated; in the present context the legislature surely intended to "confine its meaning to men."[4] Psychologically, much sexist language continues to exclude women from full personhood. Referring to all humans with a pseudogeneric masculine pronoun, as in "Every able and eligible person should exercise *his* right to vote," limits *person* to males.

Standard English usage doesn't recognize nonhuman "persons." Legal definition, too, reflects speciesist precedent rather than "good logic." To date, no U.S. judge has advocated full legal personhood for any nonhuman animals.

In a 1972 Supreme Court dissenting opinion, Justice William O. Douglas urged legal personhood for rivers, meadows, and other ecosystems. Citizens then could file suit to preserve ecosystems from pollution, "development," or other harm. But Douglas's vision was deeply speciesist. He sought to preserve environments and species for humans. An ecosystem's individual nonhuman inhabitants still would lack legal rights. Humans still could kill them for sport. In fact, Douglas named hunters and fishers among ecosystems' suitable "spokesmen."[5] If we applied Douglas's concept to humans, we would ensure a city's continued existence and protect its population as a whole while allowing the torture and murder of individual residents.

Douglas's Supreme Court opinion was strongly influenced by Christopher Stone's essay "Should Trees Have Standing?—Toward Legal Rights for Natural Objects."[6] To Stone's title question I would respond, "No, trees shouldn't have legal standing. Human and nonhuman beings should have standing. Humans should be able to sue in behalf of any nonhuman or human animal adversely affected by a tree's destruction." Legal rights for nonhuman animals (rather than natural objects) would protect natural objects (such as trees), entire ecosystems, *and* their inhabitants. No natural environment could legally be destroyed because its nonhuman inhabitants would be entitled to their home territory, intact. Preserving natural objects makes sense only because they have value to animals, both human and nonhuman. The rationale for legal rights is to minimize injustice and compensate its victims. Since a tree can't experience injustice (or anything else), *trees' rights* amounts to doublespeak. Proposing legal "rights" for insentient things trivializes the notion of rights and increases the conceptual distance between moral rights and legal ones. Ideally, moral and legal rights would fully correspond.

To serve justice, the law must recognize every sentient being, individually, as a person with rights. Taught to uphold speciesist law, most U.S. judges have resisted any move in that direction.

In 1975 Kenneth LeVasseur became a research assistant at the University of Hawaii's Marine Vertebrate Laboratory of Comparative Psychology. The lab's captives included two free-born Atlantic bottlenose dolphins, Kea and Puka. LeVasseur fed them, swam with them, and maintained their tanks. Shortly before dawn of a spring day in 1977, LeVasseur and several other people transferred Kea and Puka to a van, drove an hour's distance, and released the dolphins into the Pacific Ocean. LeVasseur was charged with first-degree theft. He pleaded necessity on the grounds that his unlawful act had prevented imminent harm to "another," each of the dolphins. Forced to perform repetitive experimental tasks, subjected to reduced food rations, confined alone in small concrete tanks, Kea and Puka had been in danger of dying, LeVasseur said. Puka, especially, had shown signs of physical and mental deterioration: a chronic cough, habitual jaw snapping and tail slapping, and self-destructive behavior such as beating her head against the experimental apparatus until she bled. Hawaiian law defines *another* as "any other person." A dolphin isn't a person, but property, the judge ruled. LeVasseur was convicted of theft. On appeal the court again ruled, "A dolphin is not 'another.'"[7]

However, in 1979, while the case against LeVasseur was underway, a New York City judge took an unprecedented step toward recognizing individual nonhumans as persons. Elderly and ailing, Kay Corso's beloved poodle companion had been euthanized by a veterinarian. Although the veterinarian had agreed to give Corso the poodle's body, Corso had received a cat's remains instead. Seeking damages for consequent psychological distress, Corso filed suit. New York State law doesn't recognize mental suffering resulting from loss of personal property as a valid cause for legal action. But wrongfully withholding the body of a "person" *is* actionable. The appropriateness of damages, then, depended on whether the poodle had been a "person" or "personal property." Overruling prior opinion, Judge Seymour Friedman awarded Corso damages for mental suffering. "A pet is not just a thing," he stated, "but occupies a special place somewhere in between a person and a piece of personal property."[8] Among U.S. opinions, Friedman's remains the most progressive to date regarding nonhuman personhood; it stands in virtual isolation.

In a 1993 case, three animal protection organizations named a bottlenose dolphin, Kama, among the plaintiffs. The organizations challenged the legality of Kama's transfer from the New England Aquarium to a Navy research facility. A federal judge dismissed the suit on the grounds that all plaintiffs lacked legal standing: the organizations because they couldn't demonstrate imminent or actual harm to their own interests, Kama because he didn't qualify as a "person."[9]

In 1994 the judge in *Gluckman v. American Airlines* dismissed Friedman's opinion as an "aberration." "Categorizing pets as more than property" flouts "overwhelming authority to the contrary," he noted.[10]

However, another 1994 ruling included commentary akin to Friedman's. A Texas hunter intentionally shot and killed a Dalmatian named Freckles and an Australian shepherd named Muffin, who were chasing two deer. The dogs' human companions sued the hunter, who was ordered to pay them thousands of dollars. "Animals are not *merely* property," Judge Eric Andell stated. As "sentient and emotive beings," they belong to "a unique category of 'property' that neither statutory nor case law has yet recognized."[11]

So far, then, only dogs have inspired U.S. judges to question nonhuman animals' property status. Having known dogs as individuals and companions, Americans are primed to see them as persons. Of course, there's no rational basis for viewing bottlenose dolphins as less deserving of legal personhood. All nonhuman animals need, but currently lack, legal rights. Andell took a small judicial step toward recognizing nonhuman beings as persons. Friedman took a relative stride. We need a legislative leap.

Justice

The law should protect the innocent and punish the guilty, most humans would agree. Inbreeding, confinement, beatings, and other human abuses can make nonhumans aggressive. Otherwise, few nonhumans seriously injure or kill except out of immediate necessity. Unless abused, most nonhuman animals cause serious harm only to preserve themselves or others. Nonhuman animals who do inflict apparently gratuitous harm may have no sense of wrongdoing. As with young children and "mentally incompetent" adults, we shouldn't hold them accountable. By the legal standards of human democratic societies, nonhumans are innocent. Yet, the law fails to protect them. We too are innocent when we hurt or kill someone (human or nonhuman) who threatens our lives. We're innocent when we sustain ourselves by growing crops, causing no more harm than we must to survive. But we're guilty if we wear cow skin and sheep hair, eat flesh and eggs, or visit aquaprisons and zoos. We're guilty if we participate in needless, unjust practices that cause suffering or death. Most humans are guilty. Yet, the law fails to punish them.

Currently the law serves speciesism rather than justice. The owner of a single egg factory causes millions of hens to live in misery and die from deprivation, disease, or slaughter. Instead of charging such a person with atrocities, society rewards them with money and respectability. From trappers to vivisectors, humans guilty of torturing, enslaving, and murdering nonhuman beings retain freedom and life; their innocent victims do not.

No "person" shall be deprived of "life, liberty, or property, without due process of law" or be denied "the equal protection of the laws," the Fourteenth Amendment to the U.S. Constitution states. Justice requires that *person* include all sentient beings. According to the Thirteenth Amendment, "Neither slavery nor involuntary servitude, except as a punishment for crime whereof the party shall have been duly convicted, shall exist within the United States." That promise awaits fulfillment.

"Animal" law is slave law. It must be abolished. The same body of law that protects humans must protect nonhumans, extending to them all applicable rights currently reserved for humans. When justice finally prevails, the law will not permit any human to

> buy, sell, breed, exhibit, imprison, deprive, or torture any nonhuman animal;
>
> use any nonhuman animal in an experiment not undertaken for that individual's own potential benefit;
>
> compel any nonhuman animal to labor, perform, compete, or provide any service to humans;
>
> intentionally kill any nonhuman animal except to end their apparently incurable suffering; prevent them from parasi-

> tizing, injuring, or killing someone; or prevent someone's imminent starvation;
>
> intentionally injure any nonhuman animal except in someone's defense;
>
> interfere with normal predation or other natural activities among free-living nonhumans;
>
> destroy or dramatically alter any natural habitat.

Envision nonhuman emancipation. With hunting, fishing, and trapping outlawed, free-living nonhumans adjust to their ecosystems in ways guided by natural selection; human interference no longer harms individuals, populations, or environments. Humans stop "producing" dogs to be merchandise, mice to be tools, and turkeys to be flesh. A ban on "selective breeding" ends centuries of inflicting deformity and genetic disease. The number of "domesticated" nonhumans rapidly declines. All captive nonhumans are liberated from exploitation and cruel confinement. Those incurably suffering from deformity, injury, or illness are euthanized; all others receive any needed veterinary care. Liberated non-"domesticated" nonhumans are set free if they can thrive without human assistance (after any necessary rehabilitation) and if appropriate habitat exists. If not, they're permanently cared for at sanctuaries. As much as possible, these sanctuaries provide natural, fulfilling environments. Hens liberated from egg factories, cats liberated from "shelters," and other homeless "domesticated" nonhumans are fostered at sanctuaries and private homes until adopted. A screening process helps to safeguard each adoptee's well-being. Under the law, nonhumans in human care have essentially the same rights as young children.

Like *human equality*, *animal equality* doesn't mean equal abilities; it means equal moral and legal rights. In a just society, comparable human and nonhuman interests, such as the desire to live and be spared suffering, would carry equal weight.

Currently our language conceals the truth about nonhuman animals and the way that we treat them. Nonhuman emancipation requires legal redefinition and other linguistic change. “A noun is a person, place, or thing.” The old chant is true after all, if we hear “person” in a new way.

Whether nonhuman or human, all animals are persons. In our need for protection and our right to justice, we all are the same.

Style Guidelines

Countering Speciesism

Manner of Presentation

Use . . .

narration (nonhuman biography and slices of life) to convey a sense of individual nonhuman lives

vivid description of particular nonhumans and their experiences to help readers or listeners visualize their situation and empathize

actual examples of mistreatment to illustrate general facts about nonhuman oppression

Avoid . . .

strictly theoretical discussion of nonhuman-animal abuse

exclusively generic or abstract reference to nonhuman animals (all members of some category or the "average" member)

Sentence Structure

Use . . .

syntax that makes nonhuman animals the grammatical subject, especially if they're the primary actors or victims

word order that gives nonhuman animals a sentence's most emphatic position: beginning or end

word order that frequently places nonhumans before humans (*nonhuman and human animals*; *the cat Jessie and her human companion Steve*)

SENTENCE STRUCTURE (*cont.*)

Avoid . . .

syntax that buries nonhuman animals inside a list, dependent clause, or prepositional phrase

syntax that equates nonhuman beings with inanimate things (The tornado *destroyed a barn and ten cows*)

WORD CHOICES

Animalkind

Use . . .

animals to include all creatures (human and nonhuman) with a nervous system

mammals, *primates*, and *apes* to include humans

persons, *individuals*, *others*, and *people* to include nonhumans

the same vocabulary for nonhumans and humans (pigs and humans *eat* rather than *feed*; the bodies of dead sheep or humans are *corpses*, not *carcasses*; like women, female dogs and cats *have ovariohysterectomies* rather than *are spayed*)

parallel forms for humans and nonhumans (*nonhuman and human animals*; *humans and dogs* instead of *human beings and dogs*, *mankind and dogs*, or *man and dogs*)

Avoid . . .

expressions that elevate humans above other animals (*human kindness*; *the rational species*; *the sanctity of human life*)

human–nonhuman comparisons that patronize nonhumans (*almost human*; Chimpanzees have many *human characteristics*) hierarchical references to animals (*lower animals*; *subhuman*; *inferior*)

dismissive *just*, *mere*, *only*, and *even* before animal terms (a *mere* beetle; They're *just* animals)

pejorative nonhuman-animal metaphors and similes (*bitch*; to *parrot*; *eat like a pig*)

the imprecise, demeaning terms *beast*, *brute*, and *dumb animal*

terms that portray nonhumans relatively free of human control and genetic manipulation as dangerous or inferior (*wild animals*; *mongrel*; *mutt*)

category labels that vilify nonhumans (*vermin*; *pests*; *trash fish*)

category labels that depict nonhuman animals in a particular *situation* as animals of a particular *type* (*lab animal*; *poultry*; *companion animal*)

Nonhuman Thought and Feeling

Use . . .

words that directly attribute thought and feeling to nonhuman animals (*understand*; *joy*; *eager*)

verbs that imply nonhuman emotion and intention (*romped* instead of *leaped about*; *fled* instead of *ran*)

connecting words that invest nonhuman action with purpose (bounded in *for* his supper; jumps onto the windowsill *so that* she can look outside; barked *because* someone rang the doorbell)

strong words for intense nonhuman feelings (*severe suffering*; *love* rather than *affection*; *pain* rather than *discomfort*)

Avoid . . .

overqualified reference to nonhuman thought and feeling (*seemed* to recognize; *as if* she felt pain; This behavior *might* indicate loneliness)

WORD CHOICES (*cont.*)

Nonhuman Individuals

Use . . .

he for a male animal, *she* for a female, and *she/he* or *he/she* for a hermaphrodite—not *it*

she or *he* for a particular individual of unknown gender (*She* [a chipmunk] lives under the porch; *He* [a roaming cat] ran off before I could get near)

they for an unspecified individual of unknown gender (Whenever I see a turtle on the road, I move *them* to safety; If another hawk comes, let's watch *them* through binoculars; One of the puppies [among males and females] already had *their* vaccinations)

a singular sex-specific pronoun when a singular indefinite term, such as *any* or *each*, refers to group members of the same sex (Every cow stayed close to *her* calf; Any cock who tried to escape had *his* neck wrung; Each earthworm struggled when *she/he* was pierced by the hook)

they when a singular indefinite term refers to members of a group that includes individuals of different sexes or unknown sex (Neither deer [a buck and a doe] recovered from *their* wounds; Each alligator had so little space that *they* barely could move)

who (not *that*, *which*, or *what*) for any sentient beings

anybody/anyone, *everybody/everyone*, *nobody/no one*, and *somebody/someone* (not *anything*, *everything*, *nothing*, or *something*) for any sentient beings

relational references to nonhuman animals after possessive pronouns (*my cat companion*, not *my cat*; *our canary friends*, not *our canaries*)

personal names for nonhuman animals (*Sally*; *Max*)

the most specific nontechnical way of referring to a particular nonhuman (*Toby the horned toad* rather than *a horned toad*; *a beagle* rather than *a dog*; *an albino rat* rather than *a Sprague-Dawley rat*) language that correctly distinguishes nonhuman individuals from their groups (*killed a member of an endangered species*, not *killed an endangered species*; *captured birds of 22 species*, not *captured 22 species of birds*)

inflected animal plurals in preference to uninflected (*many fishes* rather than *many fish*; *five trouts* rather than *five trout*; *three quails* rather than *three quail*)

plural forms of words for individual animals in preference to collective nouns (*the chickens* instead of *the flock*; *free-living nonhumans* instead of *wildlife*; *the ants* instead of *the colony*)

number (not amount) references to living animals (*how many geese*, not *how much geese*; *catch three catfishes*, not *catch eight pounds of catfish*; *some of the cows*, not *part of the herd*)

Avoid . . .

language that replaces nonhuman animals with a site (poisoned *the fish tank*; *pig farms* that experience disease)

reference to living animals as if they were remains (raise *beef*; *trophy* hunter; *fur* trapper)

reference to remains as if they were living animals (*milk-fed* veal; *grain-fed* beef; *a turkey* in reference to turkey remains)

terms that equate nonhuman animals with insentient things (the oyster *crop*; reference to mice as *research tools*; reference to sharks as *killing machines*)

commodity references to nonhuman animals (*livestock*; *surplus* dogs and cats; reference to male chicks as egg-industry *byproducts*)

language that conveys a proprietary view of nonhuman animals (*fisheries*; wildlife *conservation*; *Vandals* killed *the zoo's* falcon)

reference to nonhumans as human-created (*build* a better cow; genetically *engineered* mice; trout *production*)

terms that negate any animal's uniqueness (*replacement* lambs; *standardized* dogs; reference to nonhumans as *renewable resources*)

WORD CHOICES (*cont.*)

Nonhuman Individuals

Avoid . . .

reference to all members of a group as if they were a single animal (*the woodpecker* for all woodpeckers; *the silverfish* for silverfishes in general)

Speciesist Abuse

Use . . .

everyday language free of jargon (*stab with a large hook*, not *gaff*; *breaking the neck*, not *cervical dislocation*)

moralistic language (*murder*, *cruelty*, *speciesism*), not morally detached language such as that of economics, experimentation, or recreation

political terms with legal implications (*animal rights*; *justice*; *personhood*)

equally strong words for human and nonhuman suffering or death (*extreme*; *tragic*; *terrible*)

wording that keeps nonhuman animals in view (*Many pigs died*, not *Mortality was high*; *The trapped fox struggled*, not *Struggling occurred*)

Avoid . . .

expressions that trivialize violence toward nonhuman animals (*kill two birds with one stone*; *have other fish to fry*)

euphemisms for abuse (*fur farming*; *animal agriculture*; *biomedical research* for vivisection)

euphemisms for animal-derived products (*leather*; *sausage*; *veal*)

understatements about nonhuman suffering and death (Zoos *may* not be *ideal* homes; Hunters don't *always* aim *perfectly*) positive words in reference to abuse (farm-animal *welfare*; *humane treatment* in reference to vivisection; *educational* in reference to aquaprisons or zoos)

oxymorons (*humane slaughter*; *necessary evil*; *shooting preserve*; *responsible breeding*)

terms that naturalize the unnatural (*habitat* for a cage; *wildlife center* for a zoo; *naturalist* for someone who studies imprisoned nonhumans)

terms that disguise killing as protection (*shelter* for a facility where healthy nonhumans are killed; *wildlife refuge* for a place where hunting or fishing is allowed)

words that glamorize inbreeding (*thoroughbreds*; *purebred* dogs; *improved* turkeys)

language that blames nonhuman victims (an orangutan who escapes from a zoo and *stubbornly* resists recapture; elephants *punished* for rebelling against circus enslavement)

expressions that imply nonhuman victimization is natural and acceptable (*work like a horse*; *human guinea pig*; *treated us like animals*)

wording that portrays nonhumans as willing victims (monkeys who *participate* in experiments and *give their lives*; a captured octopus who *took up residence* in an aquaprison)

over- terms that implicitly sanction less-rampant killing and less-extreme coercion (*overhunt*; *overfish*; *overwork* a horse)

language that depicts choice as necessity (*necessary evil* in reference to vivisection; *carnivores* or *predators* in reference to humans)

reference to abusers as protectors (*animal lover* in reference to a vivisector; *animal welfarist* in reference to a cattle enslaver)

punning or other wordplay that invites people to smirk at atrocities (the title *They Eat Horses, Don't They?* or *You Can Lead a Horse to Slaughter* for an article on horse slaughter; the slogan *Don't Gobble Me* or *Thanksgiving Is Murder on Turkeys* intended to protest turkeys' mass murder)

PUNCTUATION

Use . . .

quotation marks around euphemisms (predator *"control"* for the killing of predators; *"discipline"* for beatings; *"collection"* for capture)

quotation marks around language that reduces animals to things (the crab *"harvest"*; *"depleted"* fish *"stocks"*; the use of mouse *"models"*)

quotation marks around terms that indirectly denigrate nonhuman animals (*"brutal"*; *"animal instinct"*; *"bestiality"*)

Avoid . . .

scare-quotes around accurate terms for speciesist abuse (*"torture"*; *"enslavement"*; *"genocide"*)

scare-quotes around words that acknowledge nonhuman thought and feeling (*"grief"*; *"happiness"*; *"realized"*)

quotation marks around a nonhuman animal's personal name (*"Billie"* the golden hamster) unless the name is contemptuous

Thesaurus

Alternatives to Speciesist Terms

Terms to Avoid	Alternatives
Pronouns for Nonhuman Animals	
anything	anyone, anybody
everything	everyone, everybody
it	she (female); he (male); he/she, she/he (hermaphrodite); she, he (particular individual of unknown gender); they (unspecified individual of unknown gender)*
nothing	no one, nobody
something	someone, somebody
that, what, which	who
Nonhuman/Human Terms	
animal instinct	instinct
animals (excluding humans), dumb animals, lower animals, subhuman animals	nonhuman animals, other animals, nonhumans, nonhuman beings, nonhuman persons

* Within any multiple-term Thesaurus entry, a parenthetical comment applies to all preceding terms not separated from the comment by a semicolon. For example, within the entry "she (female); he (male); . . . ," the comment "(hermaphrodite)" applies to *he/she* and *she/he*.

TERMS TO AVOID	ALTERNATIVES
Nonhuman/Human Terms (*cont.*)	
apes (excluding humans)	nonhuman apes, other apes
beast, brute	nonhuman animal, nonhuman mammal
bestial	barbaric, depraved
bestiality	rape, cross-species rape, human rape of a nonhuman
bond *n.* (between two nonhumans or a human and nonhuman)	friendship, love
brutal	cruel, violent, harsh, severe
brutish	coarse, crude, insensitive
calf, foal, whelp (etc.) *v.*	give birth
dam *n.*	mother
endangered animal, endangered species (in reference to an individual not personally endangered)	member of an endangered species
even (as in "Even insects feel")	also, too, including, as well (as in "Insects, too, feel")
feed on	eat
gestation	pregnancy
higher animals	mammals, birds and mammals, vertebrates
human kindness	kindness

humane	kind, compassionate
humans' animal nature	human carnality, human physicality
inhumane	cruel
just animals (as in "They're just animals"), mere flies, only rodents (etc.)	nonhuman animals, flies, rodents (etc.)
living things, organisms (excluding humans)	other living beings and things, other organisms
man, mankind, people (meaning all humans)	humans, human animals, human people
many bird species, various species of ants (etc., in reference to individuals)	birds of many species, ants of various species (etc.)
necropsy	autopsy, postmortem
person (meaning any human)	human, human person
primates (excluding humans)	nonhuman primates, other primates
sire	father
species of lizard, spider species (etc., meaning an individual)	lizard, spider (etc.)
specimen, thing (in reference to an individual, as in "this thing")	garter snake, centipede (etc.); individual
water *v.* (a nonhuman animal)	give water to
the wild	nature, native habitat, a natural environment
wild animals, wildlife	free-living nonhumans, non-"domesticated" nonhumans

TERMS TO AVOID	ALTERNATIVES
Hunting Terms	
bag, collect, cull, harvest, remove (etc.)	kill, murder
fowl, gamebirds, wildfowl	sport-hunted birds, targeted birds
game, game animals, trophy animals	sport-hunted animals, sport-hunted mammals, targeted nonhumans
game farm, game ranch, hunting ranch	bird-shooting operation, mammal-shooting operation, animal-shooting operation, shooting operation
game management	promoting hunting, regulated hunting, manipulating populations for hunting
game preserve, game refuge, shooting preserve; wildlife refuge (that allows hunting)	hunting area
overhunting	hunting, genocide by hunting, decimating a nonhuman population
sportsman, trophy hunter	hunter, sport hunter, trophy-seeking hunter, nonhuman-animal killer
waterfowl (pl.)	sport-hunted water birds, targeted water birds
Sportfishing Terms	
bait	animal used as bait
baitfish	fish used as bait

catch *n.*	caught fishes, killed fishes
fight a fish, play a fish	abuse a fish, torture a fish
fisheries management	promoting fishing, regulated fishing, manipulating populations for fishing
fisherman, sportsman	fisher, sportfisher, fish killer
gamefish, sportfish (pl.)	fishes caught for sport, fishes killed for sport
overfishing	fishing, genocide by fishing, decimating a fish population
overplay a fish	torture a fish to death
trash fish	despised fish, resented fish
trophy fish	large fish, targeted fish

Zoo and Aquaprison Terms

aquarium, marine park	aquaprison, aquatic-animal prison
aquarium animal, aquarium resident	aquaprison inmate, aquaprison captive
caretaker	captor, keeper
collection	inmates, prisoners, captives
curator	captor, principal keeper
display animal, exhibit	aquaprison inmate, aquaprison captive, zoo inmate, zoo prisoner, zoo captive
enclosure (in reference to a cage)	cage

TERMS TO AVOID	ALTERNATIVES

Zoo and Aquaprison Terms (*cont.*)

habitat, home (in reference to a confinement area)	confinement area, enclosure, cage, cell, tank, pool
handler (as in "elephant handler")	keeper, oppressor, abuser
pool (in reference to a tank)	tank
trainer (as in "dolphin trainer")	exploiter, oppressor, abuser
zoo animal, zoo resident	zoo inmate, zoo prisoner, zoo captive

Vivisection Terms

animal experimentation, animal research, animal testing, biomedical research, research, science (that harms animals)	vivisection
donor animal, experimental animal, laboratory animal, research animal, test animal	vivisected animal, animal used in vivisection
euthanize, put down, sacrifice (etc.)	kill, murder
experimenter, researcher, scientist (who harms animals)	vivisector
genetic engineering (of nonhuman animals)	gene insertion, vivisection
necessary evil	evil

Food-Industry Terms

abattoir; meat plant, packing plant, processing plant (in reference to a killing facility)	slaughterhouse
agricultural animal, farm animal, farmed animal, food animal	enslaved nonhuman, food-industry captive, animal enslaved for food, animal exploited for food
animal agriculture; farming (of nonhuman animals); ranching	food-industry enslavement and slaughter, food-industry captivity, enslaving animals for food, exploiting animals for food
aquaculture	fish enslavement, crustacean enslavement, mollusk enslavement, aquatic-animal enslavement; fish (etc.) captivity; fish (etc.) enslavement and slaughter; enslaving fishes (etc.) for food; exploiting fishes (etc.) for food
aquaculturist	fish enslaver, crustacean enslaver, mollusk enslaver, aquatic-animal enslaver; fish (etc.) exploiter
bacon, ham, pork (etc.)	pig flesh
beef, hamburger, steak (etc.)	cow flesh
beef cow	enslaved cow, captive cow, exploited cow, cow reared for slaughter
beef industry, pork industry, poultry industry, veal industry (etc.)	cow-flesh industry, pig-flesh industry, bird-flesh industry, calf-flesh industry (etc.)

TERMS TO AVOID	ALTERNATIVES
Food-Industry Terms (*cont.*)	
beef producer, dairy farmer, egg producer, pork producer, poultry producer, veal farmer (etc.)	cattle enslaver, cow enslaver, hen enslaver, pig enslaver, bird enslaver, calf enslaver (etc.); cattle (etc.) exploiter
broiler, roaster (meaning a chicken)	enslaved chicken, captive chicken, exploited chicken, chicken reared for slaughter
catfish farm, cattle ranch, sheep farm, turkey farm (etc.)	catfish confinement facility, cattle confinement facility (etc.); catfish (etc.) enslavement facility; catfish (etc.) enslavement operation
catfish farming, cattle ranching, sheep farming, turkey farming (etc.)	catfish enslavement, cattle enslavement (etc.); catfish (etc.) captivity; enslaving catfishes (etc.) for food; exploiting catfishes (etc.) for food
chevon	goat flesh
chicken, lamb, tuna (etc., meaning the food)	chicken flesh, lamb flesh, tuna flesh (etc.)
a chicken, a turkey, a whole bird, a whole fish (etc., in reference to remains)	chicken remains, turkey remains, bird remains, fish remains (etc.)
cowboy	cattle abuser, cow abuser
cull *v.*	kill, murder, send to slaughter, sell
cutlet, fillet, meat (etc.)	flesh, muscle

dairy cow, milk cow	enslaved cow, captive cow, exploited cow, cow enslaved for her milk, cow exploited for her milk
dairy goat, milk goat	enslaved goat, captive goat, exploited goat, goat enslaved for her milk, goat exploited for her milk
dairy industry	cow-milk industry, goat-milk industry, milk industry
drumstick	chicken's leg, turkey's leg (etc.); bird's leg
egg farm	hen confinement facility, hen enslavement facility, hen enslavement operation, egg factory
farm (with enslaved nonhumans), ranch	confinement facility, enslavement facility, enslavement operation
farmer, producer (who enslaves nonhumans); rancher	enslaver, food-industry enslaver, nonhuman-animal exploiter
foie gras	goose liver, duck liver (etc.); bird liver
food fish	enslaved fish, captive fish, fish enslaved for food, fish reared for slaughter, fish exploited for food
giblets	chicken organs, turkey organs (etc.); bird organs
grow (a nonhuman animal)	rear for slaughter
harvest, process (etc., meaning kill)	slaughter
head of cattle	cattle, cows

TERMS TO AVOID	ALTERNATIVES
Food-Industry Terms (*cont.*)	
hog, swine	pig
humane slaughter	slaughter
lacto-ovo vegetarian, vegetarian (who eats egg or milk products but not flesh)	non-flesheater
layer, laying hen	enslaved hen, captive hen, exploited hen, hen enslaved for her eggs, hen exploited for her eggs
livestock	enslaved nonhuman mammals, captive nonhuman mammals, exploited nonhuman mammals, mammals enslaved for food, mammals exploited for food
livestock market	mammal auction, mammal market
meat animal	animal reared for slaughter
meat-packer	slaughterer, butcher, nonhuman-animal killer, flesh purveyor
milk (from cows)	cow milk
mutton	sheep flesh
poultry (in reference to living birds)	enslaved chickens, enslaved turkeys (etc.); captive chickens (etc.); exploited chickens (etc.); enslaved (etc.) birds; birds enslaved for food; birds exploited for food

spareribs	pig ribs
stockyard	mammal pens, slaughterhouse pens
sweetbread	calf thymus, lamb thymus (etc.); calf (etc.) pancreas; calf (etc.) thymus or pancreas; thymus; pancreas; thymus or pancreas
veal	calf flesh
veal calf	enslaved calf, captive calf, exploited calf, calf reared for slaughter
vegetarian (who eats the flesh of mollusks, fishes, or other nonmammals)	flesheater

Pet-Related Terms

aquarium	small tank
companion animal	nonhuman companion, nonhuman friend; pet (with reference to possibly or definitely disrespected nonhumans, as in "the pet trade")
destroy, euthanize, put to sleep (a healthy animal)	kill, murder
discipline, punishment, training (in reference to beatings, deprivation, or other abuse)	abuse
her cat, my dog, your parakeet (etc.)	her cat companion, my dog friend, your parakeet companion (etc.)

TERMS TO AVOID	ALTERNATIVES
Pet-Related Terms (*cont.*)	
master, mistress	human companion, human friend, adopter, guardian, provider, caregiver; owner (in legal contexts and in reference to someone who may not love or adequately care for a nonhuman they legally own)
mongrel, mutt	mixed-breed dog
be neutered	have an orchiectomy, have his testicles removed, have an ovariohysterectomy, have her ovaries and uterus removed
pedigreed, purebred	inbred
shelter (that kills healthy nonhumans)	adoption-and-killing facility
be spayed	have an ovariohysterectomy, have her ovaries and uterus removed
terrarium	glass case, small tank
Pelt-Industry Terms	
fox coat, mink coat (etc.)	fox-pelt coat, mink-pelt coat (etc.)
fox farm, mink ranch (etc.)	fox confinement facility, mink confinement facility (etc.); fox (etc.) enslavement facility; fox (etc.) killing facility

fox farmer, mink rancher (etc.)	fox enslaver, mink enslaver (etc.); fox (etc.) killer; fox (etc.) exploiter
fur (meaning part of a pelt); fur collar, fur trim (etc.)	pelt portion
fur coat	pelt coat
fur farm, fur ranch	furred-animal confinement facility, furred-animal enslavement facility, furred-animal killing facility
fur farmer, fur rancher	furred-animal enslaver, furred-animal killer, furred-animal exploiter
fur industry	pelt industry
fur trapper	trapper, furred-animal killer
furbearer	furred animal, animal targeted for their fur, animal killed for their fur
furrier	pelt purveyor

Other Terms of Speciesist Abuse

animal dealer	nonhuman-animal dealer, nonhuman-animal trafficker
animal husbandry	nonhuman enslavement, nonhuman exploitation
animal welfare, humane treatment (in reference to nonhuman exploitation)	exploitation, abuse, less-cruel treatment

TERMS TO AVOID	ALTERNATIVES
Other Terms of Speciesist Abuse *(cont.)*	
beast of burden, pack animal, work animal	enslaved nonhuman, nonhuman slave, nonhuman forced to labor
build, create, engineer (etc., a nonhuman animal)	inbreed, genetically manipulate, genetically harm, insert genes into
bullfight	bull torture, bull murder
carcass	body, corpse, remains
cashmere	goat hair
circus animal	circus captive
crop *n.* (in reference to nonhuman animals)	new group
domestic animal, domesticated animal	enslaved nonhuman, exploited nonhuman, bred nonhuman
domestication	nonhuman enslavement, nonhuman subjugation, forced breeding, manipulated breeding
gamecock	enslaved cock, captive cock, cock forced to fight
hide *n.*	skin
leather	cow skin
mohair	goat hair
nuisance animal, pest, varmint, vermin	resented nonhuman, persecuted nonhuman, targeted nonhuman

pest control	murdering nonhumans, extermination, nonhuman genocide, mass murder of nonhumans
predator control, predator removal	killing predators, murdering predators
produce *v.* (a nonhuman animal)	breed, breed for exploitation, breed for killing
racehorse	enslaved horse, exploited horse, horse forced to race
renewable, surplus (in reference to a nonhuman animal)	viewed as disposable
resource (in reference to a nonhuman animal)	exploited nonhuman, targeted nonhuman
stock *n.* (in reference to nonhuman animals)	nonhuman captives, enslaved nonhumans
tame *v.* (a nonhuman animal)	subjugate, oppress
thoroughbred *adj.*	inbred
venison	deer flesh
wildlife conservation, wildlife management	regulated killing of nonhumans, restricted killing of nonhumans, manipulating nonhuman populations
wool	sheep hair
wool producer	sheep enslaver, sheep exploiter

Notes

Portions of Chapters 1, 2, 3, 9, and 11 are reprinted, by permission, from Joan Dunayer, "Sexist Words, Speciesist Roots," in *Animals and Women: Feminist Theoretical Explorations*, ed. Carol J. Adams and Josephine Donovan (Durham, N.C.: Duke University Press, 1995), 11–31.

Prologue: From Vivisection to Animal Rights

1. Throughout *Animal Equality*, in keeping with popular (loose) usage, "rats" are Norway rats, members of the western hemisphere's predominant rat species. (Most "domesticated" rats, such as the albinos routinely used in vivisection, are Norway rats. Free-living Norway rats often are called brown, common, or "sewer" rats.) Similarly, with reference to vivisection or "animal agriculture," "cattle" and "cows" are European cows (except that a small percentage of cattle enslaved by the flesh industry are zebus or European–zebu crosses), "ducks" primarily are white Pekins descended from mallards, "mice" belong to albino and other strains bred from house (common) mice, "pigs" are descendants of European wild boars, "pigeons" are rock pigeons (especially white Carneaus), and "rabbits" are European rabbits such as New Zealand-breed albinos.

2. For nonhumans as well as humans, I use *persons* in legal contexts and to emphasize individuality, *people* when otherwise referring to multiple individuals, and *peoples* for entire communities and cultures (as in "Different chimpanzee peoples have developed different methods of tool use").

3. Richard Ryder coined the word *speciesism* in 1970.

4. I use *animal* as a synonym for *sentient being*. Biologists, too, include all sentient beings in "animal." Currently, however, they also include some biologically anomalous creatures that lack a nervous system. I exclude these creatures from "animal" because I consider the difference between sentience and insentience to be of overriding importance.

1 Speciesism and Language

Epigraph: Adrienne Rich, "The Burning of Paper Instead of Children," in *The Will to Change: Poems 1968–1970* (New York: W. W. Norton, 1971), 15–18, at 16, 18.

1. See *Mink* (National Agricultural Statistics Service [NASS]), July 1999, 1; Peter Singer, *Animal Liberation*, 2d ed. (New York: New York Review of Books, 1990), 36–37; *Fisheries of the United States, 1997* (Silver Spring, Md.: National Marine Fisheries Service, 1998), 32; *Poultry Slaughter* (NASS), Feb. 2000, 2–3; *Fisheries of the United States*, 4.

2. Kevin McManus, "Orangutans Take Plunge into Zoo's Abstract 'Think Tank,'" *Washington Post*, 16 Oct. 1995, A3.

3. Quoted and analyzed in Deborah Cameron, "Introduction: Why Is Language a Feminist Issue?" in *The Feminist Critique of Language: A Reader*, ed. Deborah Cameron (London: Routledge, 1990), 1–28, at 17.

4. Katharine Webster, "Lobster Stew," Associated Press, 13 June 1994.

5. Photo caption in Jack Rosenberger, "Whose Life Is It, Anyway?" *New York*, 15 Jan. 1990, 30–31, at 31.

6. Henry T. Dunbar, "A Haunting Tail," *Washington Post*, 11 Dec. 1994, F1, F5; Paul Farhi, "The Story of BAM-bi," *Washington Post*, 1 Sept. 1996, F1, F5; John Painter Jr., "How Did the Chickens Cross the Road? Well-Scrambled," *Oregonian* (Portland), 19 Jan. 1993, A1, A14.

7. Robert Reinhold, "Cat Mutilations Spread Fear of Cults in Suburb," *New York Times*, 13 Aug. 1989, 16.

8. *Companion animal* is doubly speciesist. First, it turns "companion" into a trait, something inseparable from a nonhuman's being; the term obliges certain nonhumans to be (and remain) some human's companion. Second, it restricts *animal* to nonhumans. *Nonhuman companion*, *nonhuman friend*, and *pet* avoid these problems. Meaning "an animal kept for amusement or companionship" (*American Heritage Dictionary*), *pet* indicates a nonhuman's situation without labeling them of a certain type. Whereas *nonhuman companion* and *nonhuman friend* declare a nonhuman animal an active, equal partner in a loving relationship with a human, *pet* suggests a less egalitarian, possibly exploitive relationship. *Pet*, in fact, bears longstanding associations of breeding, buying, selling, and discarding nonhuman animals. Unfortunately, *pet*'s negative connotations are in keeping with the plight of many dogs, cats, and other nonhumans who never receive the respect implied by *nonhuman companion* or *nonhuman friend*. For these reasons, I use *nonhuman companion* and *nonhuman friend* with reference to nonhumans treated with full respect; I use *pet* with reference to nonhumans who are sold, discarded, or otherwise disrespected (as in *pet store*); and I always avoid *companion animal*.

2 False Categories: How We Define "Us" and "Them"

Epigraph: Ambrose Bierce, *The Devil's Dictionary* (1911; reprint, New York: Dell, 1991), under *Man*.

1. *American Heritage Dictionary*, 3d ed., under *animal*.

2. Annie Groer and Ann Gerhart, "The Reliable Source," *Washington Post*, 16 Nov. 1995, D3.

3. Darwin to J. D. Hooker, 30 Dec. 1858, *More Letters of Charles Darwin: A Record of His Work in a Series of Hitherto Unpublished Letters*, vol. 1, ed. Francis Darwin and A. C. Seward (London: John Murray, 1903), 114; see *More Letters*, 114 n. 2; Euan M. Macphail, *Brain and Intelligence in Vertebrates* (Oxford: Clarendon, 1982), 331; William Hodos, "Evolutionary Interpretation of Neural and Behavioral Studies of Living Vertebrates," in *The Neurosciences: Second Study Program*, ed. Francis O. Schmitt (New York: Rockefeller University Press, 1970), 26–39, at 27.

4. Terrence W. Deacon, "Rethinking Mammalian Brain Evolution," *American Zoologist* 30, no. 3 (1990): 629–705, at 657.

5. Deacon, 656.

6. Ann B. Butler and William Hodos, *Comparative Vertebrate Neuroanatomy: Evolution and Adaptation* (New York: Wiley-Liss, 1996), 293, 73.

7. Sven O. E. Ebbesson, "On the Organization of the Telencephalon in Elasmobranchs," in *Comparative Neurology of the Telencephalon*, ed. Sven O. E. Ebbesson (New York: Plenum, 1980), 1–16, at 1.

8. John E. Dowling, *Neurons and Networks: An Introduction to Neuroscience* (Cambridge, Mass.: Harvard University Press, 1992), 214; Heinrich Reichert, *Introduction to Neurobiology*, trans. G. S. Boyan (Stuttgart: Georg Thieme, 1992), 4.

9. See Irene M. Pepperberg, "Numerical Competence in an African Gray Parrot (*Psittacus erithacus*)," *Journal of Comparative Psychology* 108, no. 1 (1994): 36–44.

10. Quoted in Irene M. Pepperberg, "Referential Mapping: A Technique for Attaching Functional Significance to the Innovative Utterances of an African Grey Parrot (*Psittacus erithacus*)," *Applied Psycholinguistics* 11, no. 1 (1990): 23–44, at 38.

11. Quoted in Irene M. Pepperberg, "Evidence for Conceptual Quantitative Abilities in the African Grey Parrot: Labeling of Cardinal Sets," *Ethology* 75, no. 1 (1987): 37–61, at 49.

12. Quoted in Eugene Linden, "Can Animals Think?" *Time*, 22 Mar. 1993, 54–61, at 59.

13. Quoted in Duane M. Rumbaugh and Timothy V. Gill, "Language and the Acquisition of Language-Type Skills by a Chimpanzee (*Pan*)," *Annals of the New York Academy of Sciences* 270 (1976): 90–123, at 104, 110.

14. See Francine Patterson and Eugene Linden, *The Education of Koko* (New York: Holt, Rinehart & Winston, 1981), 109–10.

15. See Roger Lewin, "Look Who's Talking Now," *New Scientist*, 27 Apr. 1991, 48–52; Linden.

16. Quoted in Roger Fouts with Stephen Tukel Mills, *Next of Kin: What Chimpanzees Have Taught Me about Who We Are* (New York: William Morrow, 1997), 157; quoted in H. Lyn White Miles, "Language and the Orang-utan: The Old 'Person' of the Forest," in *The Great Ape Project: Equality beyond Humanity*, ed. Paola Cavalieri and Peter Singer (New York: St. Martin's, 1993), 42–57, at 50; quoted in Patterson and Linden, 146.

17. See Fouts with Mills, 242–45.

18. Quoted in Roger S. Fouts and Deborah H. Fouts, "Chimpanzees' Use of Sign Language," in *Great Ape Project*, 28–41, at 36.

19. See Patterson and Linden, 182, 80–81.

20. See Francine Patterson and Wendy Gordon, "The Case for the Personhood of Gorillas," in *Great Ape Project*, 58–77, at 67, 68.

21. See Lewin.

22. Mark Twain, "What Is Man?" in *The Works of Mark Twain*, vol. 19, ed. Paul Baender (Berkeley: University of California Press, 1973), 124–214, at 194, 195.

23. See Dorothy L. Cheney and Robert M. Seyfarth, *How Monkeys See the World: Inside the Mind of Another Species* (Chicago: University of Chicago Press, 1990), 102–3, 110–11.

24. See C. N. Slobodchikoff, C. Fischer, and J. Shapiro, "Predator-Specific Words in Prairie Dog Alarm Calls," Abstract 557, *American Zoologist* 26 (1986):

105A; C. N. Slobodchikoff et al., "Semantic Information Distinguishing Individual Predators in the Alarm Calls of Gunnison's Prairie Dogs," *Animal Behaviour* 42, no. 5 (1991): 713–19.

25. *Webster's Third New International Dictionary*, under *man*.

26. *American Heritage* and *Webster's*, under *man*.

27. See Ronald J. Schusterman and Robert Gisiner, "Artificial Language Comprehension in Dolphins and Sea Lions: The Essential Cognitive Skills," *Psychological Record* 38, no. 3 (1988): 311–48; Louis M. Herman, Douglas G. Richards, and James P. Wolz, "Comprehension of Sentences by Bottlenosed Dolphins," *Cognition* 16, no. 2 (1984): 129–219.

28. See Pepperberg, "Quantitative Abilities."

29. See Sarah T. Boysen, "Counting as the Chimpanzee Views It," in *Cognitive Aspects of Stimulus Control*, ed. Werner K. Honig and J. Gregor Fetterman (Hillsdale, N.J.: Lawrence Erlbaum, 1992), 367–83; Sarah T. Boysen and Gary G. Berntson, "Numerical Competence in a Chimpanzee (*Pan troglodytes*)," *Journal of Comparative Psychology* 103, no. 1 (1989): 23–31.

30. See Hank Davis and Rachelle Pérusse, "Numerical Competence in Animals: Definitional Issues, Current Evidence, and a New Research Agenda," *Behavioral and Brain Sciences* 11, no. 4 (1988): 561–79, 611–15.

31. See Ronald J. Schusterman and Kathy Krieger, "Artificial Language Comprehension and Size Transposition by a California Sea Lion (*Zalophus californianus*)," *Journal of Comparative Psychology* 100, no. 4 (1986): 348–55; Irene M. Pepperberg and Michael V. Brezinsky, "Acquisition of a Relative Class Concept by an African Gray Parrot (*Psittacus erithacus*): Discriminations Based on Relative Size," *Journal of Comparative Psychology* 105, no. 3 (1991): 286–94, quotations at 291.

32. See Patterson and Linden, 199–200.

33. See Irene M. Pepperberg, "Comprehension of 'Absence' by an African Grey Parrot: Learning with Respect to Questions of Same/Different," *Journal of the Experimental Analysis of Behavior* 50, no. 3 (1988): 553–64.

34. See David Premack and Ann J. Premack, *The Mind of an Ape* (New York: W. W. Norton, 1983), 24–26, 40–47.

35. Quoted in Patterson and Linden, 76.

36. Quoted in Jeffrey M. Masson and Susan McCarthy, *When Elephants Weep: The Emotional Lives of Animals* (New York: Delacorte, 1995), 35.

37. See Kenn Kaufman, "The Subject Is Alex," *Audubon*, Sept./Oct. 1991, 52–58.

3 Animal Attributes: The Verbal Dichotomy

Epigraph: Will Cuppy quoted in Jon Wynne-Tyson, *The Extended Circle: A Dictionary of Humane Thought* (Fontwell, England: Centaur, 1985), 61.

1. P. B. Dews, "Some Observations on an Operant in the Octopus," *Journal of the Experimental Analysis of Behavior* 2, no. 1 (1959): 57–63, at 62.

2. Dews, 62.

3. Alex Kerstitch, "Primates of the Sea," *Discover*, Feb. 1992, 34–37, at 36.

4. C. Lloyd Morgan, *An Introduction to Comparative Psychology* (London: Walter Scott, 1894), 53.

5. See Jennifer A. Mather and Roland C. Anderson, "Personalities of Octopuses (*Octopus rubescens*)," *Journal of Comparative Psychology* 107, no. 3 (1993): 336–40.

6. Jane Goodall, "Chimpanzees—Bridging the Gap," in *The Great Ape Project: Equality beyond Humanity*, ed. Paola Cavalieri and Peter Singer (New York: St. Martin's, 1993), 10–18, at 12.

7. Hope Ryden, *Lily Pond: Four Years with a Family of Beavers* (New York: William Morrow, 1989), 177.

8. Ryden, 20.

9. Ryden, 182.

10. Ryden, 138–39.

11. Ryden, 20.

12. Ryden, 185, 185, 186.

13. Ryden, 186.

14. Quoted in Ryden, 186.

15. Sterling North, *Raccoons Are the Brightest People* (New York: E. P. Dutton, 1966), 151–52.

16. Len Howard, *Birds as Individuals* (New York: Doubleday, 1953), 26.

17. Howard, 26.

18. Erasmus Darwin, *Zoonomia; or, The Laws of Organic Life*, vol. 1 (1794–96; reprint, New York: AMS, 1974), 183; "Habits and Intelligence of *Vespa maculata*," *Proceedings of the Academy of Natural Sciences of Philadelphia*, 22 Jan. 1878, 15; R. S. Newall, "Carnivorous Wasps," *Nature*, 25 Mar. 1880, 494.

19. John S. Watson, *The Reasoning Power in Animals* (London: L. Reeve, 1867), 455; John Topham, "Ingenuity in a Spider," *Nature*, 5 Nov. 1874, 8.

20. *American Heritage Dictionary*, 3d ed., under *intelligence* and *intelligent.*

21. Susan Kohn Green, *Gentle Gorilla: The Story of Patty Cake* (New York: Richard Marek, 1978), 206.

22. Green, 289.

23. Green, 37.

24. William Youatt, *Cattle: Their Breeds, Management, and Diseases* (Philadelphia: Grigg & Elliot, 1836), 285.

25. Donald L. Bath et al., *Dairy Cattle: Principles, Practices, Problems, Profits*, 3d ed. (Philadelphia: Lea & Febiger, 1985), 326.

26. Elizabeth Marshall Thomas, *The Hidden Life of Dogs* (Boston: Houghton Mifflin, 1993), 55, 57.

27. Thomas, 106.

28. Patricia Holt, "Puppy Love Isn't Just for People," review of *The Hidden Life of Dogs*, by Elizabeth Marshall Thomas, *San Francisco Chronicle*, 9 Dec. 1993, E1, E4, at E4.

29. See Holt.

30. Mary Macdonald, "Max's Trouble," *Rat Report: The Rat Fan Club Monthly Newsletter*, Feb. 1993, 1.

31. Quoted in Theodore X. Barber, *The Human Nature of Birds: A Scientific Discovery with Startling Implications* (New York: St. Martin's, 1993), 82.

32. Barber, 84.

33. Loren Eiseley, "The Bird and the Machine," in *The Immense Journey* (New York: Vintage, 1959), 179–93, at 191–92.

34. Eiseley, 181, 193.

35. Eiseley, back cover.
36. Green, 127.
37. Sherry Hansen Steiger and Brad Steiger, *Mysteries of Animal Intelligence* (New York: Tor, 1995), 130.
38. Maurice Burton, *Just Like an Animal* (New York: Charles Scribner's Sons, 1978), 72.
39. Geza Teleki, "They Are Us," in *Great Ape Project*, 296–302, at 297.
40. North, 93.
41. Quoted in Karl von Frisch, *Animal Architecture*, trans. Lisbeth Gombrich (New York: Harcourt Brace Jovanovich, 1974), 243–44.
42. Heinz Sielmann, *Ins Reich der Drachen und Zaubervögel* (Gütersloh, Germany: Bertelsmann Sachbuchverlag, 1970), 152.
43. Howard, 183, 184.
44. Howard, 187.
45. *American Heritage*, under *brute*.
46. *American Heritage*, under *human*.
47. Virginia C. Holmgren, *Raccoons: In Folklore, History and Today's Backyards* (Santa Barbara, Calif.: Capra, 1990), 95.
48. E. M. Menmuir, "Strange Reasoning among Wild Animals—III," *African Wild Life* (Johannesburg), Mar. 1952, 67.
49. Burton, 27.
50. Burton, 26.
51. Trevor Berry quoted in Robin Brown, "Blackie Was (Fin)ished until Big Red Swam In," *Weekend Argus* (Cape Town), 18 Aug. 1984, 15.

4 Victims Mistaken for Game: The Language of Hunting

Epigraph: Ralph Waldo Emerson, "Forbearance" (1847), line 1.
1. See Glen Sherwood, "Carnage at Sand Lake," *Audubon*, Nov. 1970, 66–73, quotation at 68.
2. Estimate provided by Norm Phelps of The Fund for Animals, 29 Mar. 2000, and based primarily on 1996–97 data from state "wildlife" agencies and 1998–99 data from the U.S. Fish and Wildlife Service (FWS). See *Body Count: The Death Toll in America's War on Wildlife* (booklet) (New York: Fund for Animals, 2000).
3. Jim Posewitz, *Beyond Fair Chase: The Ethic and Tradition of Hunting* (Helena, Mont.: Falcon, 1994), 73.
4. See Carlos Vinson, "When You Tackle Wild Boars," in *Hunting Secrets of the Experts*, ed. Vlad Evanoff (Garden City, N.Y.: Doubleday, 1964), 229–37.
5. Posewitz, 73.
6. Stewart Edward White, "A Chapter of Encouragement," in Saxton Pope, *Hunting with the Bow and Arrow* (New York: G. P. Putnam's Sons, 1925), 242–53, at 243.
7. See Glenn Helgeland, *Complete Bowhunting* (Minneapolis: North American Hunting Club, 1987), 203.
8. See Adrian Benke, *The Bowhunting Alternative* (San Antonio: B. Todd, 1989), 39–40, 88.
9. Quoted in David E. Samuel et al., "Animal Rights Challenges to Bowhunt-

ing," *Transactions of the Fifty-sixth North American Wildlife and Natural Resources Conference* (1991): 377–86, at 384.

10. See Benke, 88, 85.

11. Clare Conley, "Butchers with Bows and Arrows," *True: The Man's Magazine*, Nov. 1959, 36+, at 88.

12. Helgeland, 198.

13. Helgeland, 198; Michael Fedora quoted in Cleveland Amory, *Man Kind? Our Incredible War on Wildlife* (New York: Dell, 1974), 179; see Conley.

14. Linne' Hansen, "Shooting Lessons for Young Hunters," *Fur–Fish–Game*, Mar. 1993, 26–29, at 26.

15. See Edward E. Langenau Jr., "Factors Associated with Hunter Retrieval of Deer Hit by Arrows and Shotgun Slugs," *Leisure Sciences* 8, no. 4 (1986): 417–38.

16. See Jim Harrison, "A Sporting Life," in *Silent Seasons: 21 Fishing Adventures by 7 American Experts*, ed. Russell Chatham (New York: E. P. Dutton, 1978), 148–61.

17. John Leahy, "Hunter Harassment: Case Histories," *Outdoor Life*, Oct. 1990, 88–89, at 88.

18. See Jack O'Connor, *The Art of Hunting Big Game in North America*, 2d ed. (New York: Outdoor Life and Alfred A. Knopf, 1977), 102; Ray Bentzen, "Pronghorn Antelope," in *Hunting Secrets*, 169–78.

19. See O'Connor, 102.

20. See Ted Nugent, *Blood Trails: The Truth about Bowhunting* (Jackson, Mich.: Ted Nugent, 1991), 64.

21. Nugent, 64; Helgeland, 203.

22. See Michael Winikoff, "Inside a Canned Hunt," *HSUS News* (Humane Society of the United States), summer 1994, 42–43.

23. White, 242.

24. Vance Bourjaily, "Hunting Is Humane," *Saturday Evening Post*, 15 Feb. 1964, 6, 10.

25. See George H. Haas, "Unretrieved Shooting Loss of Mourning Doves in North-Central South Carolina," *Wildlife Society Bulletin* 5, no. 3 (1977): 123–25; Charles Frederick Robinette, "The Influence of Hunting on Mortality and Movements of Northern Bobwhite Quail in the North Carolina Sandhills" (master's thesis, North Carolina State University, 1990), 70; George S. Hochbaum and Carl J. Walters, *Components of Hunting Mortality in Ducks: A Management Analysis* (Winnipeg, Manitoba: Canadian Wildlife Service, 1984), 17.

26. See Reginald T. Paget, "Introduction: Cruelty in Sport," in *In Praise of Hunting: A Symposium*, ed. David James and Wilson Stephens (London: Hollis & Carter, 1960), 1–7.

27. *Hunting—The Facts* (booklet) (London: British Field Sports Society Campaign for Hunting, [1997]), 13.

28. Quoted in *Deadline 2000: The Campaign to End Hunting with Dogs* (booklet) (Horsham, England: Campaign for the Protection of Hunted Animals, [1998]), 19.

29. See Paul Brown, "Fox's Terror 'Proof Hunting Is Cruel,'" *Guardian* (London), 17 Feb. 1999, 12.

30. See *Hunting—The Facts*, 4.

31. Posewitz, 58.

32. Confinement-reared pheasants are crowded into pens. A plastic blinder, attached to their upper beak by means of a plastic nail stuck through their nostrils, prevents forward vision. (Able to see in front of them, the pheasants would be more likely to peck each other, from frustration.) One day the pheasants are yanked from their pens, their blinder is removed, and they're deposited on hunting grounds to be shot.

33. David E. Petzal, "Hunting as War," *Field & Stream*, Nov. 1991, 16–17, at 17.

34. *Webster's Third New International Dictionary*, under *sportsmanship*.

35. Anonymous hunter quoted in Stuart A. Marks, *Southern Hunting in Black and White: Nature, History, and Ritual in a Carolina Community* (Princeton: Princeton University Press, 1991), 100.

36. Steve Smith, *More and Better Pheasant Hunting* (Piscataway, N.J.: Winchester, 1986), 123.

37. Nelson Bryant, "Wood, Field and Stream: Pleasure of Hunting Not in the Killing," *New York Times*, 10 Dec. 1972, sec. 5, p. 9.

38. Richard K. Nelson, "The Gifts," in *On Nature: Nature, Landscape, and Natural History*, ed. Daniel Halpern (San Francisco: North Point, 1987), 117–31, at 123.

39. Ted Kerasote, *Bloodties: Nature, Culture, and the Hunt* (New York: Random House, 1993), 225.

40. See Sherwood.

41. See Aldo Leopold, *A Sand County Almanac: With Other Essays on Conservation from Round River* (New York: Oxford University Press, 1966), 260.

42. See Dale Bartlett, Susan Hagood, and John W. Grandy, *Learn the Facts about Hunting: Answers to Commonly Asked Questions* (booklet) (Washington, D.C.: HSUS, 1997), 12.

43. See Guy A. Baldassarre and Eric G. Bolen, *Waterfowl Ecology and Management* (New York: John Wiley & Sons, 1994), 357.

44. So that hunters will target does, state "wildlife" departments sometimes attempt to ban the killing of bucks. Typically, hunters squelch such efforts through vehement protest. For an instance of such protest in Wisconsin, see "Addenda," *Washington Post*, 30 Mar. 1996, A11.

45. *Hunting—The Facts*, 16.

46. *This Is Foxhunting* (pamphlet) (London: Countryside Alliance, [1997]), 1.

47. *Hunting—The Facts*, 16; Bob Baskerville quoted in Paul Brown.

48. Irvin R. Savidge and J. Scott Ziesenis, "Sustained Yield Management," in *Wildlife Management Techniques Manual*, 4th ed., ed. Sanford D. Schemnitz (Washington, D.C.: Wildlife Society, 1980), 405–9, at 405.

49. Quoted in Ted Williams, "Alaska's War on the Wolves," *Audubon*, May/June 1993, 44+, at 48; quoted in Ron Baker, *The American Hunting Myth* (New York: Vantage, 1985), 49.

50. Brian Stangeland, "Meet the Congressional Sportsmen's Caucus," *Hand-Gunning*, Nov./Dec. 1992, 26–27, at 26.

51. Clyde Ormond, *Complete Book of Hunting*, 2d ed. (New York: Outdoor Life and Harper & Row, 1972), 4.

52. Ted Williams, "Low-Down Humbugs and Frauds," *Fly Rod & Reel*, Apr. 1994, 57+, at 58.

53. Helgeland, 210.
54. George Reiger, "Academic Allies," *Field & Stream*, Sept. 1990, 12, 14, at 14.
55. Quoted in T. H. Watkins, "The Thin Green Line," *Audubon*, Sept. 1980, 68–87, at 85.
56. Vern Edewaard quoted in "Safari Club International," *Animals' Voice*, July/Aug. 1990, 55.
57. Bill Morrill, "No Friend of the Polar Bear," *Washington Post*, 10 May 1994, A17.
58. See Carl Bakal, *The Right to Bear Arms* (New York: McGraw-Hill, 1966), 316–19.
59. O'Connor, 393.
60. See Lewis Regenstein, "The End of the Game," *Animals' Voice*, Nov./Dec. 1989, 44–45; "Safari Club International."
61. See Ted Williams, "Open Season on Endangered Species," *Audubon*, Jan. 1991, 26+.
62. *American Heritage Dictionary*, 3d ed., under *conserve*.
63. See Jack Anderson and Dale van Atta, "The Poaching Boom," *Washington Post*, 22 Dec. 1991, C7.
64. See George Reiger, "Our Achilles' Heel," *Field & Stream*, Jan. 1991, 8–9.
65. Beverly Conner, "Hunter Harassment: Plaguing Our American Heritage," *Outdoor Life*, Oct. 1990, 82+, at 83.
66. James B. Whisker, *The Right to Hunt* (Croton-on-Hudson, N.Y.: North River, 1981), 97.
67. Peter R. Currie, "Young Ideas" (letter), *Outdoor Life*, Dec. 1994, 6; Frank Woolner, *Grouse and Grouse Hunting* (New York: Crown, 1970), 161.
68. Dale R. Potter, John C. Hendee, and Roger N. Clark, "Hunting Satisfaction: Game, Guns, or Nature?" *Transactions of the Thirty-eighth North American Wildlife and Natural Resources Conference* (1973): 62–71, at 68; Clare Conley, "How to Fight Back," *Outdoor Life*, June 1990, 77, 81, at 77; Gary Randall, "On Bear Hunting with Hounds" (letter), *Field & Stream*, Aug. 1993, 4.
69. Ali Üstay quoted in Kerasote, 115, 117.
70. Sydney P. Jarkow, *Having It All* (New York: Vantage, 1992), 53.
71. Christopher Michaels, "Stalking the 'Perilous' Peccary," *Field & Stream*, Apr. 1991, 38+, at 39.
72. Edwin Way Teale, *Wandering through Winter: A Naturalist's Record of a 20,000-Mile Journey through the North American Winter* (New York: Dodd, Mead, 1965), 161.
73. Sam Fadala, *Successful Deer Hunting* (Northfield, Ill.: DBI, 1983), 10, 81.
74. Whisker, 96.
75. Theodore Vitali quoted in Alfred Lubrano, "Killing Animals," *Sunday Star-Ledger* (Newark, N.J.), 11 Feb. 1996, sec. 1, pp. 39–40, at 40.
76. Thomas McIntyre, *The Way of the Hunter: The Art and the Spirit of Modern Hunting* (New York: E. P. Dutton, 1988), 101, 104; Doug Townson quoted in Mark Binelli, "In Alabama, Hunting Deer with Spears," *Washington Post*, 17 May 1997, A3.
77. Whisker, 136, 137.
78. See "News Shorts," *Animals' Agenda*, Jan./Feb. 1990, 43.

79. David James, "Is Hunting Cruel?" in *In Praise of Hunting*, 9–27, at 11; Ormond, 227, 219, 220, 226; Paul Joslin quoted in Barbara Sleeper, "Vanishing Wild Cats," *Animals*, July/Aug. 1991, 24–28, at 27.

80. Vinson, 237; Bob McNally, "Boars: Bad to the Bone," *Outdoor Life*, Dec. 1992, 78+, at 122.

81. Bert Popowski, *The Varmint and Crow Hunter's Bible* (Garden City, N.Y.: Doubleday, 1962), 75.

82. Quoted in O'Connor, 211.

83. Robert Ruark, *Use Enough Gun* (New York: New American Library, 1966), 91.

84. Harold F. Blaisdell, "Woodcock Lore," in *Hunting Secrets*, 125–35, at 129.

85. Bourjaily, "Hunting Is Humane," 6.

86. John K. Beene, "In Defense of Hunting" (letter), *Field & Stream*, Dec. 1990, 10; John Reiger, *American Sportsmen and the Origins of Conservation* (New York: Winchester, 1975), 14.

87. Richard Hummel, *Hunting and Fishing for Sport: Commerce, Controversy, Popular Culture* (Bowling Green, Ohio: Bowling Green State University Popular Press, 1994), 16; Kerasote, 90.

88. See *The Merriam-Webster Concise Handbook for Writers* (Springfield, Mass.: Merriam-Webster, 1991), 83.

89. Peter H. Capstick, *Last Horizons: Hunting, Fishing, and Shooting on Five Continents* (New York: St. Martin's, 1988), 90.

90. Harold E. Anthony, "But It's Instinctive," *Saturday Review*, 17 Aug. 1957, 9+, at 9.

91. Peter H. Capstick, *Death in a Lonely Land: More Hunting, Fishing, and Shooting on Five Continents* (New York: St. Martin's, 1990), 57; Bradford Angier, "Moose Can Be Tough," in *Hunting Secrets*, 193–204, at 204.

92. Larry Brown, *From a Pheasant Hunter's Notebook* (Ames: Iowa State University Press, 1992), 51.

93. Hummel, 12.

94. Leonard Read quoted in George K. Russell, Editorial, *Orion*, spring 1990, 3; Leopold, 260; Hummel, 23.

95. Quoted in Stephen R. Kellert, "From Kinship to Mastery: A Study of American Attitudes toward Animals" (report to FWS, 1974), 176.

96. Popowski, 29; Fadala, 189.

97. Whisker, 40.

98. Quoted in Bob Brister, "Cutting Our Losses," *Field & Stream*, Nov. 1989, 74+, at 74.

99. See Amory, 172.

100. Greg Miller, "Trophies in Transition," *Outdoor Life*, Feb. 1990, 51+, at 75.

101. Gene Hill, "What Makes a Hunter?" *Field & Stream*, Feb. 1981, 20, 22, at 22.

102. John Barsness, "Grand-Slam Flim-Flams and Record-Book Bunco," *Field & Stream*, May 1991, 48–49, at 49.

103. Jarkow, 100.

104. Popowski, 131, 80, 120, 125, 121, 80, 48, 50, 120, 21, 123.

105. William Thompson quoted in Pope, 114.

106. Whisker, 13.

107. Bob Kubick quoted in Kerasote, 129; Hansen, 26.

108. Quoted in Amory, 185; Vance Bourjaily, *The Unnatural Enemy* (New York: Dial, 1963), 169.

109. Popowski, 45.

110. Jarkow, 80; Smith, 97.

111. David E. Petzal, "Two Modest Proposals," *Field & Stream*, July 1990, 26, 35, at 26.

5 Cruelty by Deception: The Language of Sportfishing

Epigraph: George Gordon Byron, "Don Juan" (1819–24), canto 13, stanza 106, n. 2.

1. See Ted Williams, "Fishing to Win," *Audubon*, May 1984, 82–95.

2. See *Fisheries of the United States, 1997* (Silver Spring, Md.: National Marine Fisheries Service, 1998), 32; U.S. Fish and Wildlife Service (FWS) and U.S. Bureau of the Census, *1996 National Survey of Fishing, Hunting, and Wildlife-Associated Recreation* (Washington, D.C.: FWS, 1997), 8, 12.

3. See Peter Spinks, "Fear of Fishing," *New Scientist*, 2 Apr. 1987, 25.

4. John Buckland, *The Game Fishing Bible* (New York: Prentice Hall, 1991), 189.

5. John Goddard and Brian Clarke, *The Trout and the Fly: A New Approach* (New York: Nick Lyons, 1980), 183.

6. See Maurice I. Muoneke and W. Michael Childress, "Hooking Mortality: A Review for Recreational Fisheries," *Reviews in Fisheries Science* 2, no. 2 (1994): 123–56.

7. See Ray Troll and Brad Matsen, *Ray Troll's Shocking Fish Tales* (Berkeley: Ten Speed, 1993), 32.

8. See Spinks.

9. See Bob Stearns, "Turning Up the Heat," *Field & Stream*, July 1990, 70+.

10. Jim Harrison, "Ice Fishing, the Moronic Sport," in *Silent Seasons: 21 Fishing Adventures by 7 American Experts*, ed. Russell Chatham (New York: E. P. Dutton, 1978), 162–71, at 165.

11. Bruce Nash, Allan Zullo, and Ray Villwock, *Amazing but True Fishing Stories* (Kansas City: Andrews & McMeel, 1993), 48.

12. Göran Cederberg, "Fishing after the Catch," in *The Complete Book of Sportfishing*, ed. Göran Cederberg (New York: Bonanza, 1988), 272–81, at 274.

13. Ken Schultz, "Will That Bass Live?" *Field & Stream*, Oct. 1980, 60+, at 64; Larry Larsen, "Proud as a Peacock Bass," *Outdoor Life*, Oct. 1990, 82+, at 118.

14. See Muoneke and Childress.

15. George Langley quoted in Steve Heiting, *Musky Mastery: The Techniques of Top Guides* (Iola, Wis.: Krause, 1992), 9.

16. See George W. Sandell, *Half a Million Muskie-Catching Fishing Facts* (Eden Prairie, Minn.: Muskie Memories, 1994), 219.

17. See Jim Bashline, *The Fly Fisherman's Bible* (New York: Doubleday, 1993), 156, 138.

18. See Muoneke and Childress.

19. Duncan Barnes, Up Front, *Field & Stream*, Nov. 1994, 5.

20. See Gilbert B. Pauley and G. L. Thomas, "Mortality of Anadromous Coastal

Cutthroat Trout Caught with Artificial Lures and Natural Bait," *North American Journal of Fisheries Management* 13, no. 2 (1993): 337–45; Doug Vincent-Lang, Marianna Alexandersdottir, and Doug McBride, "Mortality of Coho Salmon Caught and Released Using Sport Tackle in the Little Susitna River, Alaska," *Fisheries Research* 15, no. 4 (1993): 339–56; John Daily quoted in Jeff Murray, "How to Let Go," *Outdoor Life*, Apr. 1993, 57+, at 57.

21. See "Annual [Fish Hatchery] Summary by Species: April 1, 1994–March 31, 1995," New York State Department of Environmental Conservation; *Fish and Fish Egg Distribution Report, Fiscal Year 1996* (Arlington, Va.: FWS, 1997).

22. See Tom Fuller, "Endangered, Threatened, or Status Quo?" *Field & Stream* (East edition), Dec. 1994, 71.

23. See Leigh Dayton, "Save the Sharks," *New Scientist*, 15 June 1991, 34–38; Frank Sargeant, *The Tarpon Book: A Complete Angler's Guide* (Lakeland, Fla.: Larsen's Outdoor Publishing, 1991), 111, 137; Ted Williams, "The Last Bluefin Hunt," *Audubon*, July/Aug. 1992, 14+; George Reiger, "The Way We Were," *Field & Stream*, Sept. 1992, 10, 12; Sandell, 204–5.

24. See Darwin Lambert, "Cruelty for Fun," *National Parks and Conservation Magazine*, June 1975, 15–16.

25. See Duncan Barnes, Up Front, *Field & Stream*, Jan. 1991, 5.

26. See Nash, Zullo, and Villwock, 14–15.

27. W. Horace Carter, *W. Horace Carter's Crappie Secrets and Techniques for Catching Other Panfish* (Tabor City, N.C.: Atlantic, 1991), 349; Sandell, 213.

28. Wade Bourne, *Fishing Fundamentals* (Brainerd, Minn.: In-Fisherman, 1988), 13.

29. See Kathy Hobbs, "Fish Story" (letter), *Field & Stream*, Oct. 1990, 7.

30. Ken Schultz, "'Nuisance' Fish," *Field & Stream*, Sept. 1992, 116.

31. B. R. Peterson, *Buck Peterson's Complete Guide to Fishing* (Berkeley: Ten Speed, 1991), 25; Seth Norman, "Carp—Fish of Your Future," *Field & Stream*, July 1990, 22, 24, at 24.

32. Nash, Zullo, and Villwock, 6.

33. Edward C. Migdalski, *The Inquisitive Angler* (New York: Lyons & Burford, 1991), 157.

34. W. D. Wetherell, *Upland Stream: Notes on the Fishing Passion* (Boston: Little, Brown, 1991), 96.

35. A. A. Luce, *Fishing and Thinking* (1959; reprint, Camden, Maine: Ragged Mountain, 1993), 174–90, at 174.

6 Freedom Denied: The Language of Zoos

Epigraph: David Hancocks, "An Introduction to Reintroduction," in *Ethics on the Ark: Zoos, Animal Welfare, and Wildlife Conservation*, ed. Bryan G. Norton et al. (Washington, D.C.: Smithsonian Institution Press, 1995), 181–83, at 181.

1. Gary K. Clarke, "Zoo Behavior: Animals and Visitors," *Kansas School Naturalist* 28, no. 3 (1982): 3–15, at 6.

2. See Bob Reiss, "Merv Larson's Team Takes Nature to the Animals," *Smithsonian*, Feb. 1987, 106+.

3. Brian Rutledge quoted in Reiss, 107.

4. Vicki Croke, "Zoo Wrangler," *Boston Globe*, 10 Aug. 1996, C1, C4, at C1.

5. See *Animal Welfare Report, Fiscal Year 1998* (Washington, D.C.: Animal and Plant Health Inspection Service, 1999), 11; "AZA Accredited Zoos and Aquariums" (sheet) (Bethesda, Md.: American Zoo and Aquarium Association, 1999).

6. See David Lewis, "The Concrete Jungle," *CNN News*, 11, 13, and 16 Oct. 1994, Transcripts 750–17, 752–12, and 405–2; John Gripper, *Florida Zoo Inquiry* (London: World Society for the Protection of Animals [WSPA] and Born Free Foundation, 1996). Abysmal conditions also are common in Canadian and British zoos. See John Gripper, *Zoos in Maritime Canada: An Investigative Report* (Toronto: WSPA and Zoocheck Canada, 1996); *Pitiful "Exhibits": The State of British Zoos* (pamphlet) (Tonbridge, England: Animal Aid, 1994).

7. See Hancocks.

8. See Gripper, *Florida Zoo Inquiry*, 63.

9. Quoted in Jeffrey P. Cohn, "Decisions at the Zoo," *BioScience*, Oct. 1992, 654–59, at 659.

10. Quoted in Jeffrey Cohn, 659.

11. At I.Q. Zoo (Scottsdale, Ariz.), Scotch Plains Zoo (Scotch Plains, N.J.), and Flag Acres Zoo (Hoosick Falls, N.Y.). See Kris Weatherly, "I.Q. Zoo Saddening" (letter), *Arizona Republic/Phoenix Gazette*, 24 Sept. 1993, 2; Judy Peet, "Out of Style," *Sunday Star-Ledger* (Newark, N.J.), 7 Apr. 1996, sec. 1, pp. 1+; Stefan Ormrod, "Showboat as Ark," *BBC Wildlife*, July 1994, 40–44.

12. Author's observations, 30 Sept. 1999.

13. Quoted in Bernard Gavzer, "Are Our Zoos Humane?" *Parade Magazine*, 26 Mar. 1989, 4–9, at 5.

14. Clayton Freiheit quoted in Dick Kreck, "This Place Is a Real Zoo," *Denver Post*, 24 Mar. 1996, sec. EMP, pp. 16+, at 30.

15. *American Heritage Dictionary*, 3d ed., under *freedom*.

16. See John Sedgwick, *The Peaceable Kingdom: A Year in the Life of America's Oldest Zoo* (New York: William Morrow, 1988), 62, 123.

17. George Orwell, *1984* (1949; reprint, New York: New American Library, 1961), 218; Clarke, 6; quoted in Gavzer, 5.

18. See Philip P. Pan, "Two Rare Zebras Succumb to Cold," *Washington Post*, 26 Feb. 2000, B1, B5.

19. See D'Vera Cohn, "Vandals' Rock Crushes Black Swan at Zoo," *Washington Post*, 24 May 1994, C1, C4.

20. Judith Gaines, "New Bedford Police Seek Leads in Rape, Killing of Deer at Zoo," *Boston Globe*, 28 July 1991, 24.

21. See Don Gold, *Zoo: A Behind-the-Scenes Look at the Animals and the People Who Care for Them* (Chicago: Contemporary, 1988), 110.

22. See Louise Sloan, "Dumbo the Elephant: What's in a Name?" *AAZPA Annual Conference Proceedings* (American Association of Zoological Parks and Aquariums) (1991): 182–86.

23. See Sedgwick, 142–45, 206.

24. Stephen St C. Bostock, *Zoos and Animal Rights: The Ethics of Keeping Animals* (London: Routledge, 1993), 46, 49.

25. At Dallas Zoo, Cincinnati Zoo, and Noell's Ark—The Chimp Farm (Tarpon Springs, Fla.). See Steven R. Reed, "A Matter of Survival," *Houston Chronicle*, 18 Sept. 1994, 1D, 6D; Mary Kane, "Thrills and Spills of the Harried Whistleblower,"

Sunday Star-Ledger (Newark, N.J.), 11 Feb. 1996, 54; Betsy Swart, "The Chimp Farm," in *The Great Ape Project: Equality beyond Humanity*, ed. Paola Cavalieri and Peter Singer (New York: St. Martin's, 1993), 291–95.

26. See Cynthia Hubert, "Zoo's Care of Animals Criticized," *Sacramento Bee*, 12 May 1996, A1, A19.

27. At Pioneer Park (Zolfo Springs, Fla.) and Everglades Wonder Gardens (Bonita Springs, Fla.). See Gripper, *Florida Zoo Inquiry*, 64, 38.

28. Thomas Althaus quoted in William Johnson, *The Rose-Tinted Menagerie* (London: Heretic, 1990), 120; Bostock, 123; Michael H. Robinson, "Zoo and Aquarium Messages, Meanings and Contexts," in *The Ark Evolving: Zoos and Aquariums in Transition*, ed. Christen M. Wemmer (Front Royal, Va.: Smithsonian Institution Conservation and Research Center, 1995), 1–24, at 16.

29. Robinson, "Zoo and Aquarium Messages," 13; Colin Tudge, *Last Animals at the Zoo: How Mass Extinction Can Be Stopped* (Washington, D.C.: Island, 1992), 1.

30. Robinson, "Zoo and Aquarium Messages," 13; Sedgwick, 149; see Cathryn McCue, "Federal Complaints Nothing New," *Roanoke Times and World-News* (Va.), A1–A2.

31. Quoted in Michael Hornsby, "Trauma of Captivity 'Sends Animals Mad,'" *The Times* (London), 23 Mar. 1993, 6.

32. Ginger Alexander quoted in Gold, 148.

33. Elizabeth O'Hara quoted in Karen Kucher, "Polar Bears' Problems Cast Chill on Zoo Exhibit," *San Diego Union-Tribune*, 18 Aug. 1996, B1, B4, at B4.

34. JoAnne Simerson quoted in Matthew Fordahl, "Pacing Polar Bears Puzzle Zookeepers," *Charleston Gazette*, 2 Sept. 1996, 2B.

35. See Kucher; Shelley Caudill, "Zookeepers Give Bear Prozac," *Indianapolis News*, 14 Jan. 1995, A1–A2.

36. Pam Dunn quoted in Gold, 248.

37. See Gavzer.

38. See Dale Tuttle, "Elephant Management in Changing Times," *AAZPA Regional Conference Proceedings* (1989): 611–15.

39. See Jane Fritsch, "Elephants in Captivity: A Dark Side," *Los Angeles Times*, 5 Oct. 1988, sec. 1, pp. 1+.

40. See Jane Fritsch, "Zoo Official Says Wild Animal Park Trainers Injured Aggressive Elephant," *Los Angeles Times*, 25 May 1988, sec. 1, pp. 3, 20; Jane Fritsch, "Keepers Struck Elephant More Than 100 Times, Trainer Says," *Los Angeles Times*, 26 May 1988, sec. 1, pp. 3, 33.

41. Tom Hanscom quoted in Fritsch, "Zoo Official," 3.

42. Douglas Myers quoted in Fritsch, "Zoo Official," 3.

43. Alan Roocroft quoted in Gavzer, 8.

44. Alan Roocroft quoted in Fritsch, "Zoo Official," 3, 20.

45. See Michael Winikoff, "Lota Lost?" *HSUS News* (Humane Society of the United States), spring 1992, 22–26; also reported by eyewitness Rachel N. Anastasi, telephone conversation with author, 31 May 1997.

46. "Loading Lota," *Milwaukee Sentinel*, 28 Nov. 1990, sec. 1, p. 1.

47. See Rachel N. Anastasi, "Lota Falls to Her Knees but Is Banished Anyway," *Milwaukee Sentinel*, 28 Nov. 1990, sec. 1, p. 5.

48. See Elizabeth S. Frank, "Elephant Management under Public Scrutiny: Is Your Staff Prepared?" *AAZPA Regional Conference Proceedings* (1991): 778–80.

49. Anastasi, "Lota Falls."

50. Cecilia Tom, "Lota Hefty, Happy, New Owner Says," *Milwaukee Sentinel*, 18 Sept. 1991, 6.

51. See Rachel N. Anastasi, e-mail to author, 6 Aug. 1997.

52. See Paula A. Poda, "Zoo Official Says Reports that Elephant Fell Are Wrong," *Milwaukee Sentinel*, 29 Nov. 1990, sec. 1, p. 8. Like other media outlets, the *Milwaukee Journal Sentinel* (the result of a *Milwaukee Journal/Milwaukee Sentinel* merger) has a cozy relationship with its local zoo. As of 1997, Robert Kahlor was both the chairman of the company that owns the newspaper and an honorary director of the society that runs the Milwaukee County Zoo. In 1996 *Journal Sentinel* in-kind contributions to the zoo totaled between \$50,000 and \$100,000. See the *Journal Sentinel*'s 7 Sept. 1997 masthead; *Zoological Society* (brochure) (Milwaukee: Zoological Society of Milwaukee County, 1996); "Serengeti Circle," *Alive* (Milwaukee County Zoological Gardens), spring 1997, 15.

53. Frank, 778.

54. Laura Pedriani, "A Lota Due about Nothing," *AAZPA Annual Conference Proceedings* (1991): 273–76, at 273.

55. Craig Perry, affidavit submitted to U.S. Department of Agriculture investigator K. James Carter, 5 Mar. 1992.

56. Mark Rosenthal quoted in Virginia Mullery, "Jo-Don Farms Provides Some True Adventure," *Chicago Tribune* (Lake edition), 27 June 1993, sec. 18, p. 5.

57. Quoted in Vicki Croke, *The Modern Ark: The Story of Zoos* (New York: Scribner, 1997), 171.

58. See Stephen Bitgood and Arlene Benefield, *Visitor Behavior: A Comparison across Zoos*, Technical Report 86–20 (Jacksonville, Ala.: Psychology Institute, Jacksonville State University, 1987); Dale L. Marcellini and Thomas A. Jenssen, "Visitor Behavior in the National Zoo's Reptile House," *Zoo Biology* 7, no. 4 (1988): 329–38.

59. See Stephen R. Kellert and Julie Dunlap, "Informal Learning at the Zoo: A Study of Attitude and Knowledge Impacts" (report to the Zoological Society of Philadelphia, 1989), 66–71.

60. See Kellert and Dunlap.

61. D. L. Rhoads and R. J. Goldsworthy, "The Effects of Zoo Environments on Public Attitudes toward Endangered Wildlife," *International Journal of Environmental Studies* 13, no. 4 (1979): 238–87, at 283.

62. See Gripper, *Zoos in Maritime Canada*, Appendix D.

63. See Croke, *Modern Ark*, 14, 75.

64. Karen Asis, "Wildlife Conservation: Public Relations' Ticket to the Future," *AAZPA Regional Proceedings* (1989): 189–92, at 189, 192, 190; Robert A. Ramin, "Promoting the AZA and Member Zoos and Aquariums as Conservation Organizations through Cause-Related Marketing," *AZA Annual Conference Proceedings* (1995): 438–40, at 438; quoted in Jim White, "The Zoo Lives," *Independent* (London), 19 Nov. 1993, 21.

65. See International Union of Directors of Zoological Gardens and Captive Breeding Specialist Group, *The World Zoo Conservation Strategy: The Role of Zoos and Aquaria of the World in Global Conservation* (Brookfield, Ill.: Chicago Zoological Society, 1993), 44.

66. See Lee Werle, Curator of Mammals, Woodland Park Zoo, letter to author, 5 Aug. 1997; Nanette Bragin, Phoenix Zoo registrar, e-mail to author, 31 July 1997; Carmi Penny, Curator of Mammals, San Diego Zoo, e-mail to author, 10 Sept. 1997.

67. Jill Mellen quoted in Croke, *Modern Ark*, 191.

68. See Andrew Balmford, Nigel Leader-Williams, and M. J. B. Green, "Parks or Arks: Where to Conserve Threatened Mammals?" *Biodiversity and Conservation* 4, no. 6 (1995): 595–607.

69. See Kes Smith and Fraser Smith, "Conserving Rhinos in Garamba National Park," in *Rhinoceros Biology and Conservation*, ed. Oliver A. Ryder (San Diego: Zoological Society of San Diego, 1993), 166–77.

70. See Alan Rabinowitz, "Helping a Species Go Extinct: The Sumatran Rhino in Borneo," *Conservation Biology* 9, no. 3 (1995): 482–88. Transport also killed five of twenty black rhinos sent from Zimbabwe to the U.S. and New South Wales in 1992. See Polly Ghazi, "Threatened Black Rhinos Fly to Safety in Australia," *Observer* (London), 14 Mar. 1993, 11.

71. Quoted in Croke, *Modern Ark*, 171.

72. Asis, 190.

73. See Benjamin Beck, "Reintroduction, Zoos, Conservation, and Animal Welfare," in *Ethics on the Ark*, 155–63, at 155, 156.

74. See Michael H. Robinson, "The Shape of Things to Come," in *Keepers of the Kingdom: The New American Zoo* (New York: Thomasson-Grant & Lickle, 1996), 45–51.

75. For the zoo-as-showboat metaphor, I'm indebted to Ormrod.

76. Brian Joseph quoted in Gestin Suttle, "Walrus' Deathly Illness Puzzles Keepers," *News Tribune* (Tacoma, Wash.), 7 Nov. 1996, B7.

77. Thomas Meehan quoted in Cheryl terHorst, "The Doctor Will See You Now," *Daily Herald* (Arlington Heights, Ill.), 23 Sept. 1996, sec. 3, pp. 1, 3, at 3.

78. Victor Camp quoted in Joe Kimball, "Sunny the Giraffe Dies Unexpectedly," *Star Tribune* (Minneapolis), 9 May 1996, B1.

79. See Kevin Duchschere, "Giraffe Is Third to Die at Como Zoo in '96," *Star Tribune* (Minneapolis), 5 Sept. 1996, B3.

80. Sharon Pickett quoted in Linda Wheeler and Scott Bowles, "National Zoo's Baby Elephant Dies Suddenly," *Washington Post*, 27 Apr. 1995, C1, C6, at C6.

81. Charles Wikenhauser quoted by Rachel N. Anastasi in notes taken during Nov. 1990 interview and provided to author.

82. Bostock, 117.

83. At Louisiana Purchase Gardens and Zoo. Bob Powell quoted in Lewis, 16 Oct.

84. See D'Vera Cohn.

85. See Chris Crystal, "Moving Josephine from Zoo Home Stirs Protest," United Press International, 21 June 1988.

86. See "San Francisco Zoo Breaks Up Orang-utan Couple," *IPPL Newsletter* (International Primate Protection League), Aug. 1988, 6.

87. Saul Kitchener quoted in Crystal.

88. Andy Baker quoted in Daniel Rubin, "Zoo Mulls How to Replace the Irreplaceable," *Philadelphia Inquirer*, 31 Dec. 1995, B1, B7, at B7.

89. See Croke, *Modern Ark*, 216.

90. See Gretchen Schuldt, "Ament Demands Return of Lota's Ownership," *Milwaukee Journal Sentinel*, 25 Jan. 1997, 1B, 4B; "PAWS Discovers Lota at the Walker Brothers Circus," *Sanctuary* (Performing Animal Welfare Society), winter 1996, 4.

91. See Steve Graham, "Issues of Surplus Animals," in *Wild Mammals in Cap-*

tivity: Principles and Techniques, ed. Devra G. Kleiman et al. (Chicago: University of Chicago Press, 1996), 290–96; Jason Shepard, "Banned UW Studies Used 65 Zoo Monkeys," *Capital Times* (Madison, Wis.), 13 Aug. 1997, 1A, 4A.

92. Among others, these zoos include the Birmingham Zoo; Busch Gardens (Tampa, Fla.); the Cleveland Metroparks, Franklin Park (Boston), Gladys Porter (Brownsville, Tex.), Greater Baton Rouge (Baker, La.), Irvine Park (Chippewa Falls, Wis.), Knoxville, Lincoln Park (Chicago), Los Angeles, Lowry Park (Tampa, Fla.), Memphis, Mesker Park (Evansville, Ind.), National (Washington, D.C.), Philadelphia, and San Antonio Zoos; the San Diego Wild Animal Park (Escondido, Calif.); and the San Diego, San Francisco, Stone (Boston), and Wildlife World (Litchfield Park, Ariz.) Zoos. See "Law Sought on Sales of Zoo Animals," *Los Angeles Times*, 27 Feb. 1990, B2; Dianne Dumanoski, "Advocates Demand to Know Animals' Fate," *Boston Globe*, 20 Dec. 1990, 33, 41; Lisa A. Landres, "Exposing the Zoo–Hunting Ranch Connection," *Act'ionLine* (Friends of Animals), Nov./Dec. 1991, 5–9; "Zoos Sell to Hunters, Group Says," *Arizona Republic*, 3 Sept. 1994, A10; Steve Nidetz, "Channel 2's Mendte in the Cross Hairs over Zoo Report," *Chicago Tribune*, 5 Mar. 1995, sec. 5, p. 7; Janean Marti, "Zoo Review," *Leader-Telegram* (Eau Claire, Wis.), 14 July 1996, 1A–2A; Linda Goldston, "Where Zoo Animals Become Fair Game," *San Jose Mercury News*, 8 Feb. 1999, 15A.

93. See Marti.

94. Bostock, 148.

95. See Croke, *Modern Ark*, 217.

96. Graham, 294.

97. Quoted in Bill Bruns, *A World of Animals: The San Diego Zoo and the Wild Animal Park* (New York: Abrams, 1983), 152.

98. Bostock, 133.

99. See Bob Mullan and Garry Marvin, *Zoo Culture* (London: Weidenfeld & Nicolson, 1987), 11.

100. Maya Bell, "A Tiger Named Natasha Breaks a Zoo's Heart," *Orlando Sentinel*, 2 Sept. 1991, A1, A7.

101. Christine Simonetti quoted in Kurt Chandler, "All in a Day's Work," *Star Tribune* (Minneapolis), 26 Feb. 1995, 1E, 8E, at 1E.

102. See Sedgwick, 143–44; Sloan, 183.

103. William Conway quoted in Douglas Martin, "Much More Than a Zoo," *New York Times*, 25 Apr. 1995, B1, B3, at B3.

104. Quoted in Jeffrey Cohn, 659.

7 More Speciesism on Display: The Language of "Aquariums" and "Marine Parks"

Epigraph: Richard O'Barry quoted in Patricia Corrigan, "Making Waves at Sea World," *St. Louis Post-Dispatch*, 8 Oct. 1990, 1BP+, at 1BP.

1. See David Weddle, "Loving Dolphins to Death," *Los Angeles Times Magazine*, 7 Apr. 1991, 22+.

2. Vicki Aversa, "Taking Control of the Animal Rights Challenge," *AAZPA Annual Conference Proceedings* (American Association of Zoological Parks and Aquariums) (1991): 252–55, at 253. Before its 1981 opening, the National Aquarium in Baltimore (NAIB) captured four Atlantic bottlenose dolphins: Gretel, Kibby,

Aphrodite, and Mimi. Suffering from poor appetite, lymph-node abscesses, and a heart-valve cyst, Gretel was brought to the NAIB "against medical advice." She died two months later. Kibby, Aphrodite, and Mimi developed bleeding ulcers and were transferred to other facilities. See Edward F. Gibbons Jr. and Michael K. Stoskopf, "An Interdisciplinary Approach to Animal Medical Problems," in *Animal Care and Use in Behavioral Research: Regulations, Issues, and Applications*, ed. Janis W. Driscoll (Beltsville, Md.: Animal Welfare Information Center, 1989), 60–68, quotation at 61.

3. See *Marine Mammal Inventory Report* (Silver Spring, Md.: National Marine Fisheries Service, 1997), under "National Aquarium in Baltimore."

4. "Terminology to Consider When Speaking with the Public or Press," NAIB in-house sheet in use as of May 1997.

5. See Richard O'Barry with Keith Coulbourn, *Behind the Dolphin Smile* (Chapel Hill, N.C.: Algonquin, 1989), 112.

6. Quoted in Jeremy Cherfas, *Zoo 2000: A Look beyond the Bars* (London: British Broadcasting Corporation, 1984), 207.

7. See O'Barry with Coulbourn, 66.

8. See "Chickens of the Sea," *Harper's*, May 1992, 35.

9. See John Camper, "Canada Tells Aquarium It Can Capture Two Whales," *Chicago Tribune*, 27 July 1989, sec. 2, pp. 1, 6; William Mullen, "Caught in the Middle," *Chicago Tribune Magazine*, 12 Nov. 1989, 16+.

10. See "List of Officers, Directors, Trustees, and Key Employees," *1992 Form 990: John G. Shedd Aquarium*; *The Journey Forward: 1998 Annual Report* (Chicago: John G. Shedd Aquarium, 1999), 9.

11. William Mullen, "Two Shedd Whales Splash into New Home," *Chicago Tribune*, 4 Aug. 1989, sec. 1, p. 5.

12. Betsy Raymond quoted in Nichole M. Christian, "Shedd Will Retrieve Whales from Canada," *Chicago Tribune*, 2 Aug. 1992, sec. 2, p. 3.

13. See Craig Kasnoff, "Captive Marine Mammals Deserve Better Conditions," *Seattle Times*, 25 Mar. 1991, A9.

14. William Mullen, "What Weighs a Ton, Can Swim and Flies?" *Chicago Tribune*, 5 Mar. 1991, sec. 1, pp. 1, 10, at 1.

15. See Mullen, "Caught in the Middle."

16. Patrick T. Reardon, "You Can Send One Whale of a Holiday Card," *Chicago Tribune*, 5 Dec. 1990, sec. 2, pp. 1, 10, at 1.

17. See "Aquarium Beluga Whale Dies," *Washington Post*, 28 Dec. 1999, A11.

18. "Spoiling the Good News about Belugas" (editorial), *Chicago Tribune*, 13 Jan. 1992, sec. 1, p. 14.

19. See Mullen, "What Weighs a Ton?" 10; Debbie Leahy, "Captive Shedd Envoys Send Message" (letter), *Chicago Sun-Times*, 23 May 1993, 40.

20. Jack Kisling, "One Phony Habitat Much Like Another," *Denver Post*, 19 Sept. 1995, 2D.

21. See John Gripper, *Florida Zoo Inquiry* (London: World Society for the Protection of Animals and Born Free Foundation, 1996), 69.

22. See "Chickens of the Sea."

23. *Monterey Bay Aquarium: Annual Review 1995* (Monterey, Calif.: Monterey Bay Aquarium, 1996), 7; see Robin Roy Gress, "Immersion Experience," *Los Angeles Times*, 10 Mar. 1996, L5.

24. See Gress.

25. See "Second Blue Shark Found Dead at Aquarium," *San Diego Union-Tribune*, 28 Feb. 1996, A3.

26. See Helaine Olen, "New Baltimore Home for Dolphins, Whales Angers Animal-Rights Groups," *Wall Street Journal*, 28 Dec. 1990, 17; Fern Shen, "Do Dolphins Dream of Return to the Deep?" *Washington Post*, 13 Dec. 1993, D3.

27. Aversa, 253.

28. See Shen; "National Aquarium Euthanizes Dolphin," *Washington Post*, 26 May 1999, B3.

29. "Terminology to Consider."

30. See "Counting Noses," *Shorelines* (Monterey Bay Aquarium), fall/winter 1995, 6–7.

31. George N. Lundskow, "The New Orleans Aquarium of the Americas: A Deconstruction Analysis" (master's thesis, University of New Orleans, 1992), 85.

32. Michael Stoskopf quoted in David Riley, "Our Love of Dolphins Has Turned Into a Questionable Affair," *Smithsonian*, Jan. 1993, 58+, at 63; Brad Andrews quoted in Weddle, 64; Danielle Oki, *Animal Training at Sea World*, 2d ed. (Orlando, Fla.: Sea World, 1995), 20.

33. See Weddle. Newly captured belugas too are force-fed, including via a stomach tube. See "One-Month Report, Beluga Live Capture, Churchill, Manitoba, August 13–17, 1992" (Shedd Aquarium report to Canadian Department of Fisheries and Oceans, Sept. 1992), 18–19, 20, 23, 24.

34. See "Chickens of the Sea"; "Terminology to Consider."

35. See Deborah Schoch, "Sink or Swim," *Los Angeles Times*, 19 Mar. 1994, B1–B2.

36. Mike Schaadt quoted in J. Michael Kennedy, "Octavia the Octopus Dies as Tank Empties," *Los Angeles Times*, 12 Apr. 1994, B1, B3, at B3.

37. See Jim McCartney, "UnderWater World Officials Deny Claims by Specialist," *Saint Paul Pioneer Press*, 11 June 1996, 1A, 8A.

38. John Hewitt quoted in Anne Brataas, "Ex-employee: Shortcuts in Care Led to 30% Death Rate for Fish," *Saint Paul Pioneer Press*, 11 June 1996, 1A, 8A, at 8A.

39. Quoted in Lisa Friedman Miner, "Scaling Back," *Daily Herald* (Arlington Heights, Ill.), 13 Sept. 1993, sec. 4, pp. 1–2, at 2; Steve Dale, "The New Marine Corps," *Chicago Tribune*, 26 Apr. 1991, sec. 7, pp. 34–35, at 34; conditions visible in Shedd Aquarium photos taken by Debbie Leahy in August 1993 and provided to author.

40. See Weddle.

41. See Erich Hoyt, *The Performing Orca—Why the Show Must Stop* (Bath, England: Whale and Dolphin Conservation Society, 1992), 42.

42. Jim McBain quoted in LEXIS®/NEXIS® version of Richard Core, "Killer Whale's Death Shocks Sea World," *Tribune* (San Diego), 22 Aug. 1989, A1, A8; Sea World officials quoted in H. G. Reza, "Whales Collide, One Is Fatally Injured in Sea World Tank," *Los Angeles Times*, 22 Aug. 1989, sec. 1, pp. 3, 20, at 3; Sea World cashier quoted in Mike McIntyre, "PR Campaign Order of Day at Sea World," *San Diego Union*, 23 Aug. 1989, A6–A7, at A7.

43. See Hoyt, *Performing Orca*, 49–50, 55; Craig Dezern and Cindy Schreuder, "Dolphins in Captivity," *Orlando Sentinel*, 10 June 1990, A1+. Captive belugas, too, receive anti-ulcer medication. See "One-Month Report," 7, 19, 20.

44. See Hoyt, *Performing Orca*, 50; Dezern and Schreuder.

45. Thomas H. Woodley, Janice L. Hannah, and David M. Lavigne, "A Comparison of Survival Rates for Captive and Free-Ranging Bottlenose Dolphins (*Tursiops truncatus*), Killer Whales (*Orcinus orca*), and Beluga Whales (*Delphinapterus leucas*)," Draft Technical Report No. 93–01 (Guelph, Ontario: International Marine Mammal Association, 1994), 21.

46. See Kendrick Blackwood, "Zoo Aquarium Trying to Get Its Sea Legs," *Omaha World-Herald* (Metropolitan edition), 19 Apr. 1995, 1–2, at 1.

47. See Erich Hoyt, *Orca: The Whale Called Killer*, 2d ed. (Camden East, Ontario: Camden House, 1990), 205, 238–51.

48. See Hoyt, *Orca*, 246.

49. See Hoyt, *Orca*, 238–51; Hoyt, *Performing Orca*, 65; William Johnson, *The Rose-Tinted Menagerie* (London: Heretic, 1990), 187.

50. See *Marine Mammal Inventory*, under "Sea World."

51. See "Chickens of the Sea."

52. Murray Newman, *Life in a Fishbowl: Confessions of an Aquarium Director* (Vancouver: Douglas & McIntyre, 1994), 68.

53. Quoted in Miner, 2.

54. See Sam Walker, "An Aquatic Abode," *Christian Science Monitor*, 24 June 1994, 10–11.

55. Quoted in Russell Working, "Sick Walrus 'Andy' Dies at Point Defiance," *News Tribune* (Tacoma, Wash.), 9 Nov. 1996, B1, B3, at B3.

56. See "Sea World and Busch Gardens Adventures: Alien Vacation!" prod. Busch Entertainment Corporation, televised on CBS-TV, 10 June 1997.

57. See Lundskow, 84.

58. Mac Rawls quoted in Katherine Calos, "Reach Out and Touch Flora and Fauna of 'Deep,'" *Richmond Times-Dispatch* (Va.), 16 June 1996, H1, H8, at H1.

59. Quoted in William A. Davis, "No Ocean? A Minor Detail," *Boston Globe*, 8 Sept. 1991, 89, 102, at 102.

60. See "Chickens of the Sea."

61. Jim McBain quoted in Karen Kucher, "This Vet Has a Huge Practice," *San Diego Union-Tribune*, 9 Jan. 1994, B1–B2, at B2. As reported by a former orca "trainer," Sealand of the Pacific (Victoria, British Columbia) has used food deprivation to keep marine mammals performing on cue (see Hoyt, *Performing Orca*, 28, 35).

62. George Millay quoted in "Aquatic Theme Park Celebrates Silver Anniversary," 21 Mar. 1989, *Times-Advocate* (Escondido, Calif.), B2.

63. See Riley, 66.

64. See Robert Jenkins, "Testimony of the American Zoo and Aquarium Association and the Alliance of Marine Mammal Parks and Aquariums," in House Committee on Merchant Marine and Fisheries, *Marine Mammal Protection Act, Part 3: Hearing before the Subcommittee on Environment and Natural Resources*, 103d Cong., 1st sess., 10 Feb. 1994, 18–20, 89–103; Cindy Schreuder and Craig Dezern, "Still Waiting for Rules on Sea Mammals," *Orlando Sentinel*, 6 Jan. 1991, A1, A8.

65. See Cindy Schreuder and Craig Dezern, "U.S. Lifts Ban on Capturing Dolphins," *Orlando Sentinel*, 16 Mar. 1990, A1, A13.

66. See John A. Hodges, prepared statement on behalf of the Marine Mammal Coalition regarding the 44th annual meeting of the International Whaling Commis-

sion (IWC), presented at a meeting of the IWC Interagency Committee (National Oceanic and Atmospheric Administration), Washington, D.C., 30 Mar. 1992; "Whale of a Client," *Legal Times* (Washington, D.C.), 22 Jan. 1990, 3.

67. See Dianne Dumanoski, "Catching Wild Dolphins: Is It Right?" *Boston Globe*, 1 Oct. 1990, 25–26.

68. See Kent A. Fanning, "The Living Ocean," *St. Petersburg Times*, 7 Mar. 1995, 1D, 3D; Dan Moreau, "Dream Jobs," *Kiplinger's Personal Finance Magazine*, May 1996, 75–79; Debbi Wilgoren, "Couple Makes Fish a Family Affair," *Washington Post*, 22 Mar. 1990, Howard County Weekly sec., pp. Md. 1, Md. 3; Walker; Vincenza Scarpaci and Gordy Slack, *California Academy of Sciences: Annual Report 1995* (San Francisco: California Academy of Sciences, 1996), 8.

69. See Andrea Conley-Early, "The Great Tuna Chase," *Sea Frontiers*, fall 1995, 38–42.

70. See Philip Wechsler, "Staff at Camden Aquarium Has 'Gone Fishing,'" *New York Times*, 20 Oct. 1991, New Jersey Weekly sec., p. 16.

71. Timothy Hurley, "Taking a Walk into the Deep," *Maui News* (Wailuku, Hawaii), 11 Feb. 1996, A1, A5, at A5.

72. See Bruce V. Bigelow, "Sea World Displays Resolve, Snags Great White Shark," *San Diego Union-Tribune*, 28 July 1994, A1, A17.

73. Quoted in Lundskow, 81, 82.

74. Kevin Calhoon, "Field Collection of Native Birds for the Tennessee Aquarium," *AZA Regional Conference Proceedings* (American Zoo and Aquarium Association) (1995): 399–402, at 399, 402.

75. William P. Braker, "Conservation Value of Zoos, Aquariums" (letter), *Chicago Tribune*, 20 Feb. 1992, sec. 1, p. 18; quoted in Sharon E. Dean, "Aquariums: Emerging Leaders in the Environmental Conservation Movement," in *The Ark Evolving: Zoos and Aquariums in Transition*, ed. Christen M. Wemmer (Front Royal, Va.: Smithsonian Institution Conservation and Research Center, 1995), 221–58, at 257.

76. Karen Furnweger and Carol Garfinkel, *A Walk along the Coast: A Guide to the Oceanarium* (Chicago: John G. Shedd Aquarium, 1991 [still being distributed as of 2000]), 7; also see 11, 14, 37.

77. See "Statement of Net Assets," *1991 Form 990: John G. Shedd Aquarium*; *Toxics Release Inventory, 1987–1994 CD-ROM*, EPA Publication 749–C–96–003 (Washington, D.C.: U.S. Environmental Protection Agency, 1996).

78. See Stevenson Swanson, "$3 Million Fine Assessed for Incinerator Violations," *Chicago Tribune*, 23 June 1992, sec. 2, p. 6.

79. See "List of Officers"; *Journey Forward*, 9.

80. See Newman, 43, 96–97.

81. Newman, 4.

82. See Newman, 43, 96–97; Howard Schneider, "Loggers, Environmentalists vs. B.C.," *Washington Post*, 22 Apr. 1997, A15.

83. See Lundskow, 84–90.

84. Steve Bailey et al., "Husbandry of One Species of Squid in Captivity," in *Proceedings of the Third International Aquarium Congress*, ed. Chris Barrett (Boston: New England Aquarium, 1995), 277–88, at 277; see John Dayton et al., "Collection, Transport, and Care of Bluefin Tuna, *Thunnus thynnus*, at the New England Aquarium," in *Aquarium Congress*, 469–76.

85. See Woodley, Hannah, and Lavigne, 34.

86. See Linda Woo and Martha Brockenbrough, "Beluga Baby Loses Fight for Life," *News Tribune* (Tacoma, Wash.), 16 July 1994, A1, A8.

87. Rob Carson, "Baby Whale's Death Mourned," *Orange County Register* (Santa Ana, Calif.), 18 July 1994, 18.

88. Tom Otten quoted in Woo and Brockenbrough, A8.

8 In the Name of Science: The Language of Vivisection

Epigraph: George Bernard Shaw, "Preface on Doctors," in *The Doctor's Dilemma: A Tragedy* (1911; reprint, Baltimore: Penguin, 1954), 7–88, at 55.

1. Andrew N. Rowan, *Of Mice, Models, and Men: A Critical Evaluation of Animal Research* (Albany: State University of New York Press, 1984), 3; also see 23.

2. See Peter Singer, *Animal Liberation*, 2d ed. (New York: New York Review of Books, 1990), 36–37.

3. Adrian R. Morrison, "Improving the Image of Biomedical Research," *Lab Animal*, Apr. 1994, 36–39, at 37. Over decades, Morrison has vivisected at least hundreds of cats. Largely to see the effects on their sleep patterns, he has electrically burned and suctioned out portions of their brains, subjected them to heat and cold, crushed their spinal cords, put cylinders on their eyes so they can't be closed, and blinded them. See John McArdle, "The Research Career of Adrian Morrison," parts 4 and 5, *AV Magazine* (American Anti-Vivisection Society), Jan. 1991, 10–14, and Mar. 1991, 8–14.

4. Gregory A. Maas, "Public Relations and Animal Research," *Lab Animal*, Apr. 1994, 28–31, at 30; Susan E. Paris, letter, *Washington Post*, 10 June 1995, A16; Frankie L. Trull, "The Research Movement," *Lab Animal*, Apr. 1994, 23–26, at 25. Similarly, vivisectionists refer to product testing on nonhuman animals as "product safety testing" in general.

5. See "Molecules and Markets: A Survey of Pharmaceuticals," *Economist*, 7 Feb. 1987, 14-page insert between pp. 50 and 51; John Schwartz, "Fat-Fighting Drug Shows Results in First Human Trial," *Washington Post*, 15 June 1998, A14.

6. Alan M. Goldberg, "Presentation on Acceptance of Russell and Burch Award" (speech delivered at Humane Society of the United States symposium "Animals in Research," Washington, D.C., 11 Oct. 1991), 6.

7. See F. Barbara Orlans, *In the Name of Science: Issues in Responsible Animal Experimentation* (New York: Oxford University Press, 1993), 72.

8. Morrison, 36; *Animal Research: The Search for Life-Saving Answers*, Department of Health and Human Services (DHHS) Publication No. (ADM) 92–1771 (Rockville, Md.: National Institute of Mental Health, 1992), 6.

9. See Susan E. Lederer, "Political Animals: The Shaping of Biomedical Research Literature in Twentieth-Century America," *ISIS* 83, no. 1 (1992): 61–79.

10. "Points to Look Out For in Connection with the Antivivisectionists" (undated memo listing in-house publication guidelines for *Journal of Experimental Medicine*), Record Group 517, Box 1, Folder 3, Rockefeller Archive Center, North Tarrytown, N.Y., 2.

11. J. Bruce Overmier and Martin E. P. Seligman, "Effects of Inescapable Shock upon Subsequent Escape and Avoidance Responding," *Journal of Comparative and Physiological Psychology* 63, no. 1 (1967): 28–33, at 30, 31.

12. See Steven F. Maier, Martin E. P. Seligman, and Richard L. Solomon, "Pavlovian Fear Conditioning and Learned Helplessness: Effects on Escape and Avoidance Behavior of (a) the CS–US Contingency and (b) the Independence of the US and Voluntary Responding," in *Punishment and Aversive Behavior*, ed. Byron A. Campbell and Russell M. Church (New York: Appleton-Century-Crofts, 1969), 299–342.

13. See Martin E. P. Seligman and Steven F. Maier, "Failure to Escape Traumatic Shock," *Journal of Experimental Psychology* 74, no. 1 (1967): 1–9.

14. Steven F. Maier and Martin E. P. Seligman, "Learned Helplessness: Theory and Evidence," *Journal of Experimental Psychology: General* 105, no. 1 (1976): 3–46, at 7.

15. Martin E. P. Seligman, *Learned Optimism* (New York: Alfred A. Knopf, 1991), 20.

16. Perry Grigsby and Yosh Maruyama, letter, *British Journal of Radiology* 55, no. 651 (1982): 250–51, at 251; Robert J. White, "Antivivisection: The Reluctant Hydra," *American Scholar*, summer 1971, 503–7, at 506.

17. Quoted in Mary T. Phillips, "Savages, Drunks, and Lab Animals: The Researcher's Perception of Pain," *Society and Animals* 1, no. 1 (1993): 61–81, at 67.

18. Orlans, 130; see Arnold Arluke, "Trapped in a Guilt Cage," *New Scientist*, 4 Apr. 1992, 33–35; "Researchers Said to Be Minimizing 'Suffering' of Laboratory Animals," *Birmingham News*, 2 Feb. 1986, 23A.

19. Quoted in Bernard E. Rollin, *The Unheeded Cry: Animal Consciousness, Animal Pain and Science* (New York: Oxford University Press, 1989), 29; Craig W. Stevens, "Alternatives to the Use of Mammals for Pain Research," *Life Sciences* 50, no. 13 (1992): 901–12, at 903, 902.

20. Francis Rioux and Margot Lemieux, "Behavioral Responses Elicited by Intraperitoneal Neurotensin in Guinea Pigs," *Peptides* 13, no. 4 (1992): 841–42, at 842; Francoise Bayart et al., "Influence of Maternal Proximity on Behavioral and Physiological Responses to Separation in Infant Rhesus Monkeys (*Macaca mulatta*)," *Behavioral Neuroscience* 104, no. 1 (1990): 98–107, at 107.

21. "Points to Look Out For," 2; Editorial ledger (1930–48) for *Journal of Experimental Medicine*, Record Group 517, Box 1, Folder 3, Rockefeller Archive Center, North Tarrytown, N.Y., 45.

22. Alice Heim, "The Proper Study of Psychology," *New Universities Quarterly* 32, no. 2 (1979): 135–54, at 143; Patrick D. Wall, Editorial, *Pain* 1, no. 1 (1975): 1–2, at 2; Richard A. Sternbach, "The Need for an Animal Model of Chronic Pain," *Pain* 2, no. 1 (1976): 2–4, at 2.

23. Monika Remy and H. Philip Zeigler, "Classical Conditioning of Jaw Movements in the Pigeon: Acquisition and Response Topography," *Animal Learning and Behavior* 21, no. 2 (1993): 131–37.

24. Shanaz M. Tejani-Butt, William P. Paré, and J. Yang, "Effect of Repeated Novel Stressors on Depressive Behavior and Brain Norepinephrine Receptor System in Sprague-Dawley and Wistar Kyoto (WKY) Rats," *Brain Research* 649, nos. 1–2 (1994): 27–35, at 28, 32; Benjamin H. Natelson et al., "Hamsters with Coronary Vasospasm Are at Increased Risk from Stress," *Psychosomatic Medicine* 53, no. 3 (1991): 322–31, at 322, 323.

25. J. S. Schwartzbaum and Todd O. Leventhal, "Neural Substrates of Behavioral Aversion in Lateral Hypothalamus of Rabbits," *Brain Research* 507, no. 1 (1990): 85–91, at 88; Bart P. Vos, Andrew M. Strassman, and Raymond J. Maciewicz, "Be-

havioral Evidence of Trigeminal Neuropathic Pain Following Chronic Constriction Injury to the Rat's Infraorbital Nerve," *Journal of Neuroscience* 14, no. 5 (1994): 2707–23, at 2710, 2711; Michael J. Gentle and Fiona L. Hill, "Oral Lesions in the Chicken: Behavioural Responses Following Nociceptive Stimulation," *Physiology and Behavior* 40, no. 6 (1987): 781–83; Leonard L. Howell and Larry D. Byrd, "Characterization of the Effects of Cocaine and GBR 12909, a Dopamine Uptake Inhibitor, on Behavior in the Squirrel Monkey," *Journal of Pharmacology and Experimental Therapeutics* 258, no. 1 (1991): 178–85, at 179.

26. Home Office, *Statistics of Experiments on Living Animals, Great Britain, 1986* (London: Her Majesty's Stationery Office [HMSO], 1987), 13; Home Office, *Statistics of Scientific Procedures on Living Animals, Great Britain, 1987* (London: HMSO, 1988), 22.

27. Christopher J. Gordon, Lela Fogelson, and Jerry W. Highfill, "Hypothermia and Hypometabolism: Sensitive Indices of Whole-Body Toxicity Following Exposure to Metallic Salts in the Mouse," *Journal of Toxicology and Environmental Health* 29, no. 2 (1990): 185–200, at 185, 199; John Crabbe, Emmett R. Young, and Janet Dorow, "Effects of Dizocilpine in Withdrawal Seizure-Prone (WSP) and Withdrawal Seizure-Resistant (WSR) Mice," *Pharmacology, Biochemistry and Behavior* 47, no. 3 (1994): 443–50, at 445.

28. See Vance Packard, *The People Shapers* (Boston: Little, Brown, 1977), 319.

29. Fabrizio Benedetti, "The Development of the Somatosensory Representation in the Superior Colliculus of Visually Deprived Mice," *Developmental Brain Research* 65, no. 2 (1992): 173–78, at 177, 178.

30. "Points to Look Out For," 3; Bradford Waters et al., "Effect of Route of Nutrition on Recovery of Hepatic Organic Anion Clearance after Fasting," *Surgery* 115, no. 3 (1994): 370–74; Perry Grigsby and Yosh Maruyama, "Modification of the Oral Radiation Death Syndrome with Combined WR–2721 and Misonidazole," *British Journal of Radiology* 54, no. 647 (1981): 969–72, at 969.

31. J. Bruce Overmier and Robert Murison, "Poststress Effects of Danger and Safety Signals on Gastric Ulceration in Rats," *Behavioral Neuroscience* 103, no. 6 (1989): 1296–1301, at 1297. I use *he* for each vivisected rat because all of the rats were male.

32. J. Bruce Overmier and Robert Murison, "Temporal Location of Contextual Exposure Determines Whether Shocks Influence Later Ulcer Vulnerability," *Learning and Motivation* 24, no. 3 (1993): 282–92, at 286.

33. Mark I. Talan, Hal M. Tatelman, and Bernard T. Engel, "Cold Tolerance and Metabolic Heat Production in Male C57BL/6J Mice at Different Times of Day," *Physiology and Behavior* 50, no. 3 (1991): 613–16, at 614.

34. Ling-Ling Tsai, Bernard M. Bergmann, and Allan Rechtschaffen, "Sleep Deprivation in the Rat: XVI. Effects in a Light–Dark Cycle," *Sleep* 15, no. 6 (1992): 537–44, at 538; Roland R. Griffiths et al., "Self-Injection of Barbiturates, Benzodiazepines and Other Sedative-Anxiolytics in Baboons," *Psychopharmacology* 103, no. 2 (1991): 154–61, at 155 (for a description of the restraint chair, see J. D. Findley, W. W. Robinson, and W. Gilliam, "A Restraint System for Chronic Study of the Baboon," *Journal of the Experimental Analysis of Behavior* 15, no. 1 [1971]: 69–71); "Let's Visit a Research Laboratory" (poster), in *Let's Visit a Research Laboratory: Introduction and Lesson Plans*, DHHS Publication No. (ADM) 92–1811 (Rockville, Md.: Alcohol, Drug Abuse, and Mental Health Administration, 1991).

35. Steve Reilly, Ralph Norgren, and Thomas C. Pritchard, "A New Gustometer for Testing Taste Discrimination in the Monkey," *Physiology and Behavior* 55, no. 3 (1994): 401–6, at 403; J. Kim et al., "A Standard Experimental 'Chemical Burn,'" *Burns* 20, no. 3 (1994): 200–201, at 200.

36. T. J. MacVittie et al., "The Relative Biological Effectiveness of Mixed Fission-Neutron-γ Radiation on the Hematopoietic Syndrome in the Canine: Effect of Therapy on Survival," *Radiation Research (Supplement)* 128, no. 1 (1991): S29–S36, at S30.

37. Quoted in Lloyd G. Stevenson, "Religious Elements in the Background of the British Anti-Vivisection Movement," *Yale Journal of Biology and Medicine* 29 (Nov. 1956): 125–57, at 126.

38. Ghanta N. Rao, letter, *Laboratory Animal Science* 38, no. 5 (1988): 558.

39. Quoted in Mary T. Phillips, "Constructing Laboratory Animals: An Ethnographic Study in the Sociology of Science" (Ph.D. diss., New York University, 1991), 217.

40. See Harold Herzog, "Tangled Lives: Human Researchers and Animal Subjects" (commentary), *Anthrozoös* 3, no. 2 (1989): 80–82.

41. Joseph D. McInerney, "Animals in Education: Are We Prisoners of False Sentiment?" *American Biology Teacher*, May 1993, 276–80, at 276.

42. Lisa J. Raines, "Animal Patents Should Be Allowed," in *Genetic Engineering: Opposing Viewpoints*, ed. William Dudley (San Diego: Greenhaven, 1990), 196–201, at 197, 199.

43. Quoted in "Animal Group Information Misleading" (press release), Hershey Medical Center, Pennsylvania State University, 15 Apr. 1994, 3.

44. See Reilly, Norgren, and Pritchard; Thomas C. Pritchard, Robert B. Hamilton, and Ralph Norgren, "Neural Coding of Gustatory Information in the Thalamus of *Macaca mulatta*," *Journal of Neurophysiology* 61, no. 1 (1989): 1–14.

45. Dennis W. Blick et al., "Behavioral Toxicity of Anticholinesterases in Primates: Effects of Daily Repeated Soman Exposure," *Pharmacology, Biochemistry and Behavior* 48, no. 3 (1994): 643–49, at 643; Kenneth H. Muhvich, Loraine H. Anderson, and William J. Mehm, "Evaluation of Antimicrobials Combined with Hyperbaric Oxygen in a Mouse Model of Clostridial Myonecrosis," *Journal of Trauma* 36, no. 1 (1994): 7–10, at 7; quoted in Arnold Arluke, "Uneasiness among Laboratory Technicians," *Lab Animal*, May/June 1990, 20+, at 29; see "Meetings and CE Offerings," *Journal of the American Veterinary Medical Association* 206, no. 8 (1995): 1242–45, at 1242.

46. See Arnold Arluke, "'We Build a Better Beagle': Fantastic Creatures in Lab Animal Ads," *Qualitative Sociology* 17, no. 2 (1994): 143–58.

47. Mitchell L. Henry et al., "Antibody Depletion Prolongs Xenograft Survival," *Surgery* 115, no. 3 (1994): 355–61, at 356.

48. Arthur Kling quoted in "Workshop I: Instinctual and Environmental Learning," ed. Harry F. Harlow and Stephen J. Suomi, in *Animal Models in Human Psychobiology*, ed. George Serban and Arthur Kling (New York: Plenum, 1976), 61–74, at 69.

49. Roy Henrickson quoted in Deborah Blum, "Both Sides Using Moral Arguments," *Sacramento Bee*, 24 Nov. 1991, A1, A10, at A10.

50. Thomas Gonda quoted in Lise Giraud, "'Denial, Dishonesty' Mark Animal Research," *Stanford University Campus Report*, 18 May 1988, 17.

51. Quoted in Phillips, "Constructing Laboratory Animals," 124.

52. Crabbe, Young, and Dorow, 444.

53. Robert A. Yokel, "Aluminum Produces Age Related Behavioral Toxicity in the Rabbit," *Neurotoxicity and Teratology* 11, no. 3 (1989): 237–42, at 238.

54. Quoted in Stephen R. Kellert, "From Kinship to Mastery: A Study of American Attitudes toward Animals" (report to the U.S. Fish and Wildlife Service, 1974), 129.

55. See Mary T. Phillips, "Proper Names and the Social Construction of Biography: The Negative Case of Laboratory Animals," *Qualitative Sociology* 17, no. 2 (1994): 119–42.

56. Robert B. Hamilton, Thomas C. Pritchard, and Ralph Norgren, "Central Distribution of the Cervical Vagus Nerve in Old and New World Primates," *Journal of the Autonomic Nervous System* 19, no. 2 (1987): 153–69, at 165.

57. "Points to Look Out For," 1.

58. See Joan Margules (my birth name) and C. R. Gallistel, "Heading in the Rat: Determination by Environmental Shape," *Animal Learning and Behavior* 16, no. 4 (1988): 404–10.

59. See Phillips, "Proper Names."

60. See Arnold Arluke, "Sacrificial Symbolism in Animal Experimentation: Object or Pet?" *Anthrozoös* 2, no. 2 (1988): 98–117; Phillips, "Constructing Laboratory Animals," 128.

61. See *Inside Biosearch*, videocassette (Washington, D.C.: People for the Ethical Treatment of Animals [PETA], [1988]); [Virginia L. Bollinger], "PETA Investigator's Log Notes: Wright State University," 24 Aug.–21 Oct. 1992, 7; Peter Hamilton, "Broken Promises: Vivisection Harms Animals and People," letter to members of Lifeforce (Vancouver), Aug. 1986; Richard D. Ryder, *Animal Revolution: Changing Attitudes towards Speciesism* (Oxford: Basil Blackwell, 1989), 250.

62. In *Products of Pain*, videotape filmed by PETA undercover investigator Leslie Fain, compiled by Lori Gruen and Ken Knowles (Washington, D.C.: Ark II, 1986); *"Unnecessary Fuss"*, videocassette (Washington, D.C.: PETA, 1984).

63. Quoted in Phillips, "Proper Names," 138.

64. Kathleen A. Mahon et al., "Oncogenesis of the Lens in Transgenic Mice," *Science*, 27 Mar. 1987, 1622–28, at 1622; quoted in Arnold Arluke, "Going into the Closet with Science: Information Control among Animal Experimenters," *Journal of Contemporary Ethnography* 20, no. 3 (1991): 306–30, at 311; David Brown and Malcolm Gladwell, "Customizing Lab Mice," *Washington Post*, 21 Aug. 1992, A1, A4, at A4; Barbara Bentley, "Animal Use in the Classroom," review of *The Responsible Use of Animals in Biology Classrooms—Including Alternatives to Dissection*, edited by Rosalina V. Hairston, *Quarterly Review of Biology* 66, no. 4 (1991): 475–77, at 476.

65. R. Douglas Fields, Theodore H. Bullock, and G. David Lange, "Ampullary Sense Organs, Peripheral, Central and Behavioral Electroreception in Chimeras (*Hydrolagus*, Holocephali, Chondrichthyes)," *Brain, Behavior and Evolution* 41, no. 6 (1993): 269–89, at 270, 276, 279.

66. Quoted in Phillips, "Proper Names," 135.

67. William Lane-Petter, preface to *Animals for Research: Principles of Breeding and Management*, ed. William Lane-Petter (London: Academic, 1963), vii–viii, at viii.

68. In *Products of Pain*; quoted in Arluke, "Going into the Closet," 319.

69. J. L. Katz, E. Tirelli, and J. M. Witkin, "Stereoselective Effects of Cocaine," *Behavioural Pharmacology* 1, no. 4 (1990): 347–53, at 347; D. A. Powell et al., "On the Generality of Conditioned Bradycardia in Rabbits: Assessment of CS and US Modality," *Animal Learning and Behavior* 21, no. 4 (1993): 303–13, at 304; W. Joseph Messick et al., "Differential Changes in Intestinal Permeability Following Burn Injury," *Journal of Trauma* 36, no. 3 (1994): 306–12, at 307.

70. Muhvich, Anderson, and Mehm, 8.

71. Dennis J. Mujsce, Javad Towfighi, and Robert C. Vannucci, "Physiologic and Neuropathologic Aspects of Hypothermic Circulatory Arrest in Newborn Dogs," *Pediatric Research* 28, no. 4 (1990): 354–60, at 354; Edward R. Gruberg et al., "Behavioral and Physiological Consequences of Unilateral Ablation of the Nucleus Isthmi in the Leopard Frog," *Brain, Behavior and Evolution* 37, no. 2 (1991): 92–103, at 93.

72. L. Martineau et al., "Clenbuterol, a β_2-Adrenergic Agonist, Reverses Muscle Wasting Due to Scald Injury in the Rat," *Burns* 19, no. 1 (1993): 26–34, at 32; Kim et al., 200.

73. Gordon C. Bayliss and Beth O. Moore, "Hippocampal Lesions Impair Spatial Response Selection in the Primate," *Experimental Brain Research* 98, no. 1 (1994): 110–18, at 111; Priscilla J. Slanetz et al., "Hemoglobin Blood Substitutes in Extended Preoperative Autologous Blood Donation: An Experimental Study," *Surgery* 115, no. 2 (1994): 246–54; Paul Schnur, Manuel Espinoza, and Ryan Flores, "Context-Specific Sensitization to Naloxone-Precipitated Withdrawal in Hamsters: Effect of Pimozide," *Pharmacology, Biochemistry and Behavior* 48, no. 3 (1994): 791–97, at 792.

74. Elizabeth O'Byrne quoted in Cathy Fernandez, "Scientist Defends Responsible Use of Animals in Research," *Independent Press* (Bloomfield, N.J.), 21 Nov. 1990, 5–6, at 5; see Susan Rich, "An Investigative Report by In Defense of Animals on Brain Damage/Amputation Experiments on Kittens, Cats, and Monkeys Conducted at the Uniformed Services University of the Health Sciences" (Silver Spring, Md.: In Defense of Animals, [1992]); Sharon L. Juliano, "Use of Laboratory Animals Supplement to PHS Form 398/2590," in "Federal Grant Application PHS NS–24014: Structural Correlates of Cortical Information Processing" (application to DHHS), Oct. 1988; quoted in Sandra Arnoult, "Protesters Target Researcher," *Montgomery Journal* (Rockville, Md.), 17 July 1991, A8; Sharon L. Juliano et al., "Determinants of Patchy Metabolic Labeling in the Somatosensory Cortex of Cats: A Possible Role for Intrinsic Inhibitory Circuitry," *Journal of Neuroscience* 9, no. 1 (1989): 1–12, at 9.

75. Bill Seay, Bruce K. Alexander, and Harry F. Harlow, "Maternal Behavior of Socially Deprived Rhesus Monkeys," *Journal of Abnormal and Social Psychology* 69, no. 4 (1964): 345–54, at 347, 351, 353; Harry F. Harlow, "Love and Aggression," in *From Learning to Love: The Selected Papers of H. F. Harlow*, ed. Clara Mears Harlow (New York: Praeger, 1986), 307–17, at 314; Harry F. Harlow and Stephen J. Suomi, "Induced Psychopathology in Monkeys," *Engineering and Science* 33, no. 6 (1970): 8–14, at 10, 11.

76. M. Potegal and M. M. Myers, "Spontaneously Hypertensive Wistar-Derived Male Rats Are More Aggressive than Those of Their Normotensive Progenitor Strain," *Behavioral and Neural Biology* 51, no. 2 (1989): 247–61, at 251.

77. Thomas A. Tatham, Ann M. Gyorda, and James E. Barrett, "Shock Postpone-

ment Reverses the Effects of Cocaine on the Punished Pecking of Pigeons," *Pharmacology, Biochemistry and Behavior* 48, no. 2 (1994): 491–95.

78. Arluke, "Uneasiness among Laboratory Technicians," 34.

79. See Arluke, "Trapped in a Guilt Cage," 33.

80. Quoted in Arluke, "Trapped in a Guilt Cage," 34.

81. Douglas Hogg, in "Animal Experiments (Cosmetics)," *Parliamentary Debates*, Commons, 6th ser., vol. 149 (23 Mar. 1989): 1255–61, at 1260.

82. Wise Young quoted in Katherine Greene and Richard Greene, "Necessary Evil?" *Redbook*, Sept. 1989, 160+, at 160; see Murry J. Cohen et al., "A Critique of Neurology Experiments at Northwestern University," in *Perspectives on Medical Research*, vol. 4, ed. Stephen R. Kaufman and Kathryn Hahner (New York: Medical Research Modernization Committee, 1993), 22–27; quoted in Michael Specter, "Animal-Research Labs Increasingly Besieged," *Washington Post*, 30 May 1989, A1, A6, at A6.

83. Frederick K. Goodwin and Adrian R. Morrison, "In Animal Rights Debate, the Only Valid Moderates Are Researchers," *Scientist*, 6 Sept. 1993, 12; William R. Hendee et al., *Use of Animals in Biomedical Research: The Challenge and Response* (position statement) (Chicago: American Medical Association, 1988), 9; Susan E. Paris, letter, *Nature*, 5 May 1994, 10.

84. See Stephen J. Suomi and Harry F. Harlow, "Depressive Behavior in Young Monkeys Subjected to Vertical Chamber Confinement," *Journal of Comparative and Physiological Psychology* 180, no. 1 (1972): 11–18; Stephen J. Suomi and Harry F. Harlow, "Apparatus Conceptualization for Psychopathological Research in Monkeys," *Behavior Research Methods and Instrumentation* 1, no. 7 (1969): 247–50, at 247, 248, 249; Stephen J. Suomi, "Surrogate Rehabilitation of Monkeys Reared in Total Social Isolation," *Journal of Child Psychology and Psychiatry* 14, no. 1 (1973): 71–77.

85. Quoted in Colleen Cordes, "Suomi Heads New Primate Center," *APA Monitor* (American Psychological Association), Aug. 1984, 10.

86. Quoted in Kellert, 139; Shaw, 56, 42.

87. Seligman, 22, 21.

88. See Seligman, 23, 28–30.

89. See Shaw. "If a guinea pig may be sacrificed for the sake of the very little that can be learnt from it, shall not a man be sacrificed for the sake of the great deal that can be learnt from him?" Shaw challenged (Shaw, 53).

9 Feeding on Flesh, Milk, Eggs, and Lies: The Language of "Animal Agriculture"

Epigraph: Carol J. Adams, "Feeding on Grace: Institutional Violence, Feminist Ethics, and Vegetarianism," in *Neither Man nor Beast: Feminism and the Defense of Animals* (New York: Continuum, 1994), 162–78, at 167.

1. See "Just Say NO to Drugs . . . and Other Words That Don't Send a Positive Image to the General Public," *Texas Longhorn Trails* (Texas Longhorn Breeders Association of America), June 1992, 27. In a 1996 merger the National Cattlemen's Association and National Live Stock and Meat Board became the National Cattlemen's Beef Association.

2. See "Just Say NO."

3. See William Lutz, *Doublespeak: From "Revenue Enhancement" to "Terminal Living"* (New York: Harper & Row, 1989), 205.

4. Seaton Baxter, *Intensive Pig Production: Environmental Management and Design* (London: Granada, 1984), 405.

5. See G. M. Cronin, "The Development and Significance of Abnormal Stereotyped Behaviours in Tethered Sows" (Ph.D. diss., Agricultural University of Wageningen, the Netherlands, 1985), 25, 29, 40.

6. *Animal Welfare Position Statements and Background Information* (Schaumburg, Ill.: American Veterinary Medical Association, 1993), 15.

7. Boars and pregnant sows fed amounts "typical of commercial conditions" experience "a high level of hunger throughout the day," industry researchers have reported (A. B. Lawrence, Michael C. Appleby, and H. A. Macleod, "Measuring Hunger in the Pig Using Operant Conditioning: The Effect of Food Restriction," *Animal Production* 47, no. 1 [1988]: 131–37, at 132, 136).

8. Russel R. Weisensel, letter, *Vealer USA*, July/Aug. 1982, 24–25, at 25.

9. See Gail A. Eisnitz, *Slaughterhouse: The Shocking Story of Greed, Neglect, and Inhumane Treatment inside the U.S. Meat Industry* (Amherst, N.Y.: Prometheus, 1997), 220.

10. Kathy Kellogg and Bob Kellogg, *Raising Pigs Successfully* (Charlotte, Vt.: Williamson, 1985), 159.

11. See "Largest Slaughter Check Ever Finds Respiratory Disease to Be Widespread," *Feedstuffs*, 7 Jan. 1985, 8, 25.

12. Compare the June 1985 version of Fact Sheet No. 75 ("Pork Production Systems with Business Analyses"), *Pork Industry Handbook* (West Lafayette, Ind.: Purdue University and U.S. Department of Agriculture [USDA] Cooperative Extension Service), by David G. Spruill and Clyde R. Weathers, with the February 1996 version by Raymond E. Massey et al.

13. Wilson G. Pond, Jerome H. Maner, and Dewey L. Harris, *Pork Production Systems: Efficient Use of Swine and Feed Resources* (New York: Van Nostrand Reinhold, 1991), 52.

14. Richard E. Austic and Malden C. Nesheim, *Poultry Production*, 13th ed. (Philadelphia: Lca & Febiger, 1990), 243.

15. See *Chickens and Eggs* (National Agricultural Statistics Service [NASS]), Feb. 2000, 2; Donald Bell, "Egg Industry Technology Today," *Poultry Digest*, Jan. 1992, 10+.

16. *Animal Agriculture Myths and Facts* (pamphlet) (Arlington, Va.: Animal Industry Foundation, [1988]), 2.

17. Dan Ross quoted in Richard Conniff, "Superchicken: Whose Life Is It Anyway?" *Discover*, June 1988, 32+, at 40.

18. Bobby D. Barnett, "Humane Treatment of Farm Animals," *Feedstuffs*, 6 Apr. 1981, 24–25, at 25; *Animal Welfare Position Statements*, 18.

19. See Mack O. North and Donald D. Bell, *Commercial Chicken Production Manual*, 4th ed. (New York: Van Nostrand Reinhold, 1990), 441.

20. North and Bell, 440.

21. Austic and Nesheim, 257.

22. *In Depth: 6–10 Days Old Precision Debeaking*, Bulletin No. 281–184 (Chula Vista, Calif.: Lyon Electric Co., 1990), 1; North and Bell, 635.

23. James V. Craig, *Domestic Animal Behavior: Causes and Implications for Animal Care and Management* (Englewood Cliffs, N.J.: Prentice-Hall, 1981), 243; North and Bell, 249.

24. Robert W. Berg and David A. Halvorson, *Turkey Management Guide* (St. Paul: Minnesota Turkey Growers Association, 1985), 19; Craig, 243, 244.

25. Richard A. Battaglia, "Goat Management Techniques," in *Handbook of Livestock Management Techniques*, ed. Richard A. Battaglia and Vernon B. Mayrose (Minneapolis: Burgess, 1981), 411–63, at 445.

26. Jerry Belanger, *Raising Milk Goats the Modern Way*, 2d ed. (Pownal, Vt.: Storey Communications, 1990), 77, 78.

27. Verl M. Thomas, *Beef Cattle Production: An Integrated Approach* (Philadelphia: Lea & Febiger, 1986), 46.

28. David P. Hutcheson, "Stress Influences Nutritional Requirements of Receiving Cattle," *Feedstuffs*, 27 Jan. 1992, 13+, at 13.

29. See "Just Say NO."

30. See "Just Say NO."

31. John B. Herrick, "We Must Take a Stand on Controversial Issues," *Journal of the American Veterinary Medical Association* (*JAVMA*) 197, no. 4 (1990): 458–59, at 459.

32. Betsy M. Farr and Richard G. Warner, "Rearing Dairy Calves—An Animal Welfare Issue?" in *Proceedings, 1982 Cornell Nutrition Conference for Feed Manufacturers* (Ithaca, N.Y.: Cornell University, 1982), 46–52, at 50.

33. Quoted in Jim Mason and Peter Singer, *Animal Factories*, 2d ed. (New York: Harmony, 1990), 28; Anthony Schwartz, "The Politics of Formula-Fed Veal Calf Production," *JAVMA* 196, no. 10 (1990): 1578–86, at 1581; Barbara Huffman, prepared statement on behalf of the American Veal Association, in House Committee on Agriculture, *Veal Calf Protection Act: Hearings on H.R. 84*, 101st Cong., 1st sess., 6 June 1989, 341–45, at 341, 342.

34. Steve Bjerklie, "How Will Seafood Grow?" *Meat & Poultry*, Mar. 1991, 25+, at 32.

35. See *Catfish and Trout Production* (NASS), Feb. 2000, 6–9; Debra Sloan, president, U.S. Trout Farmers Association, telephone conversation with author, 20 Mar. 1998.

36. See *Catfish Production* (NASS), July 1990, 7, and Feb. 1991, 4, 6, 10.

37. *Animal Welfare Position Statements*, 12; Baxter, 249.

38. Thomas H. Jukes, "Today's Non-Orwellian Animal Farm," *Nature*, 13 Feb. 1992, 582.

39. See Andrew Johnson, *Factory Farming* (Oxford: Basil Blackwell, 1991), 123; North and Bell, 840.

40. See A. J. F. Webster, "Meat and Right: Farming as if the Animal Mattered," *Canadian Veterinary Journal* 28, no. 8 (1987): 462–65.

41. Webster, 463.

42. See Barbara E. Straw, "Performance Measured in Pigs with Pneumonia and Housed in Different Environments," *JAVMA* 198, no. 4 (1991): 627–30.

43. Betsy Freese, "Production," *Successful Farming*, May/June 1990, 25.

44. Henny Adams, "A Fun Journey into the World of Fiber," *Sheep Producer*, June/July 1992, 11; Jane Lindgren, "Testimony on Behalf of the American National CattleWomen, Inc.," in House Committee on Agriculture, 346–50, at 348.

45. Steve Bjerklie, "Rights and Welfare," *Meat & Poultry*, May 1990, 6.

46. See Eisnitz, 100–103, 125, 132–33, 211.

47. See Eisnitz, 46, 100, 130, 132, 188.

48. See *The Down Side of Livestock Marketing*, videotape compiled by Farm Sanctuary and Becky Sandstedt (Watkins Glen, N.Y.: Farm Sanctuary, 1991); Eisnitz, 45–46, 99–100, 130, 132, 145, 188, 196, 199–200, 211, 215.

49. See "Just Say NO"; Mike Lyons, "Animal Activists Cause for Alarm by Farm Bureau," *Daily Journal* (Kankakee, Ill.), 1 Dec. 1991, 41–42.

50. See *Livestock Slaughter: 1999 Summary* (NASS), Mar. 2000, 3; *Poultry Slaughter* (NASS), Feb. 2000, 2–3; *Catfish and Trout Production*, Feb. 2000, 10, 12, 18, 20–21.

51. See Eisnitz, 46, 124, 130, 132, 145, 188, 195, 197, 216.

52. See Eisnitz, 20, 25, 28–29, 41–44, 120–24, 126–30, 132–33, 144–45, 197–98, 200, 203–4, 215–17, 223. In kosher slaughter, which forbids stunning, all animals are fully conscious when they're shackled and hoisted and their throat is slit.

53. See Eisnitz, 68, 81–82, 94, 98, 100, 102, 113, 124–25, 132, 267.

54. See Eisnitz, 66–75, 80, 83–88, 90–94, 97–98, 133, 143–44, 237, 265–66; Temple Grandin, "Euthanasia and Slaughter of Livestock," *JAVMA* 204, no. 9 (1994): 1354–60.

55. See Eisnitz, 93–94, 98, 144–45; Temple Grandin, "Behavior of Slaughter Plant and Auction Employees toward the Animals," *Anthrozoös* 1, no. 4 (1988): 205–13.

56. Quoted in Grandin, "Slaughter Plant and Auction Employees," 210; quoted in Eisnitz, 87.

57. See John Ezard, "Getting Meat's Image off Hook," *Guardian* (London), 30 Nov. 1984, 1.

58. Pond, Maner, and Harris, 46; Kevin Bartells quoted in Steve Bjerklie, "'Fututech': Australia's Plant of the Future," *Meat & Poultry*, Sept. 1990, 24.

59. Grandin, "Slaughter Plant and Auction Employees," 208–9; Grandin, "Euthanasia and Slaughter."

60. Dan Murphy, "Let's Kill 'Slaughtering'" (editorial), *Meat Processing*, Apr. 1990, 4.

61. See "Just Say NO."

62. Quoted in "The Things They Say," *Agscene* (Compassion in World Farming), summer 1992, 12.

63. See Steve Kestin, Research Fellow, Division of Food Animal Science, University of Bristol, e-mail to author, 6 Apr. 2000.

64. See Kestin.

65. See Jasper S. Lee, *Commercial Catfish Farming*, 3d ed. (Danville, Ill.: Interstate, 1991), 294. A veterinarian notes, "An apparatus that applies electrodes to opposite sides of the head, or in another way directs electric current immediately through the brain, is necessary to induce immediate unconsciousness" (John C. Thurmon, "Euthanasia of Food Animals," *Veterinary Clinics of North America: Food Animal Practice* 2, no. 3 [1986]: 743–56, at 753–54). In a 13 June 1995 telephone interview, Marty Brunson, a catfish specialist, professor at Mississippi State University, and USDA Cooperative Extension Service leader, told me he's quite certain that catfishes feel the electric shock they receive during the slaughter process, which he has repeatedly witnessed.

66. Leon Fuksman, "Group Protests 'Slaughtering' of Chickens," *Daily Times* (Salisbury, Md.), 20 June 1993, A1.

67. See Eisnitz, 166, 194, 280. The least cruel way of slitting someone's throat, by severing both carotid arteries with a sharp blade, is standard only in kosher slaughter.

68. Belanger, 145.

69. Donna Lopez, "A Goat Named Kevin," *Dairy Goat Guide*, Mar. 1984, 18–19, at 19.

70. Ewe Notes by Martha Mutton, *Sheep Breeder and Sheepman*, Aug. 1991, 20.

71. See Lorri Bauston, "A Special Place for Kids and Critters," *Sanctuary News* (Farm Sanctuary), fall 1992, 3.

72. Quoted in Michael W. Fox, *Inhumane Society: The American Way of Exploiting Animals* (New York: St. Martin's, 1990), 25.

73. Thomas Wagner quoted in Gene Bylinsky, "Here Come the Bionic Piglets," *Fortune*, 26 Oct. 1987, 74+, at 80.

74. Austic and Nesheim, 232.

75. Michael C. Appleby, Barry O. Hughes, and H. Arnold Elson, *Poultry Production Systems: Behaviour, Management and Welfare* (Wallingford, England: C.A.B. International, 1992), 85–86.

76. Ted Needham, "Sea Water Cage Culture of Salmonids," in *Salmon and Trout Farming*, ed. Lindsay M. Laird and Ted Needham (Chichester, England: Ellis Horwood, 1988), 126.

77. Keith A. Wilson, "Veterinarians on Call," *National Hog Farmer*, 15 Mar. 1995, 34.

78. Leonard S. Mercia, *Raising Your Own Turkeys* (Charlotte, Vt.: Garden Way, 1981), 49; Henny Adams.

79. Jenny Neal, *Goatkeeping for Profit* (Newton Abbot, England: David & Charles, 1988), 141; Barbara Rota, "A Goatkeeper's First Year," *Dairy Goat Journal*, Apr. 1986, 22+, at 22; Kellogg and Kellogg, 13; Rick Luttmann and Gail Luttmann, *Chickens in Your Backyard: A Beginner's Guide* (Emmaus, Pa.: Rodale, 1976), 101.

80. Eric C. Gonder, "An Inside Look at Integration," *JAVMA* 202, no. 10 (1993): 1589–90, at 1590.

81. Quoted in William Hedgepeth, *The Hog Book* (New York: Doubleday, 1978), 100.

82. Lee McTier and anonymous shochet quoted in Michael Lesy, *The Forbidden Zone* (New York: Farrar, Straus & Giroux, 1987), 84, 130. In attempting to justify slaughter, the shochet stated his belief that humans possess souls whereas other animals don't. The belief that *anyone* (human or nonhuman) possesses a soul lacks the support of evidence or logic. In any case, if nonhuman animals experience only life on Earth (that is, aren't compensated, in an afterlife, for suffering), there's all the more reason to spare them suffering and avoid ending their lives prematurely.

83. A. William Jasper, "Marketing," in *American Poultry History, 1823–1973*, ed. Oscar A. Hanke, John L. Skinner, and James H. Florea (Madison, Wis.: American Poultry Historical Society, 1974), 306–69, at 367; "Texel: 'The Lean Meat Machine,'" *Sheep Producer*, June/July 1992, cover, 1; Bob Bohlender quoted in Joel Achenbach, "Graze Anatomy," *Washington Post*, 19 Aug. 1994, G5; New Growers Ask, *Vealer USA*, Jan./Feb. 1981, 37; Charles W. Towne and Edward N. Wentworth, *Pigs: From Cave to Corn Belt* (Norman: University of Oklahoma Press, 1950), 265; L. J. Taylor quoted in "British Observer Praises U.S. Boars, Says Sows Are the Worst," *National Hog Farmer*, Mar. 1978, 27; John Byrnes, "Raising Pigs

by the Calendar at Maplewood Farm," *Hog Farm Management*, Sept. 1976, 30+, at 30.

84. Byrnes, 30.

85. Belanger, 142.

86. Henry Pace quoted in John Robbins, *Diet for a New America* (Walpole, N.H.: Stillpoint, 1987), 104.

87. Quoted in Grandin, "Slaughter Plant and Auction Employees," 210.

88. Ceil Wright, Ceil's Veal Letter, *Vealer USA*, Mar./Apr. 1982, 42–43, at 42.

89. James R. Borcherding, "Her Date Book Filled through 1991," *Successful Farming*, Aug. 1990, 34.

90. In *Humans and Other Animals: Beyond the Boundaries of Anthropology* ([London: Pluto, 1989], 16–21), Barbara Noske insightfully compares the factory exploitation of humans and the factory enslavement of nonhumans.

91. Jan C. Gawthrop, prepared statement, in House Committee on Agriculture, 215–17, at 215.

92. Kent Britt, "The Joy of Pigs," *National Geographic*, Sept. 1978, 398–415, at 411.

93. Robert Greene, "Humane Slaughter," Associated Press, 2 Oct. 1994; Conniff, 33.

94. Richard Goings and Charles Sniffen, "What Makes Some Cows Last Longer?" *Hoard's Dairyman*, 25 Feb. 1992, 141; "Keeping Sows Working," *National Hog Farmer: Blueprint Series for Top Managers*, fall 1992, 3.

95. See Conniff.

96. Cathryn Baskin, "Confessions of a Chicken Farmer," *Country Journal*, Apr. 1978, 37–41.

97. In defense of keeping calves in the dark, a *Vealer USA* editor has remarked, "Who wants to add the cost of a year's electricity to the cost of meat?" ("Vealer Has Had Numerous Inquiries about How a Grower Can Deal with Charges that Veal Production Is a Cruel and Inhuman Process," *Vealer USA*, Mar./Apr. 1980, 28–29, at 28).

98. Bill Uckele, "New Mineral Technology: Time-Released Biotechnology Breakthrough," *Vealer*, July 1986, 20–22, at 22.

99. Ceil Wright, Ceil's Veal Letter, *Vealer USA*, Jan. 1983, 6–7, at 6.

100. Herb Ley, "Why Don't Some Baby Calves Eat?" *Vealer USA*, May/June 1979, 12.

101. New Growers Ask, *Vealer USA*, Jan./Feb. 1980, 20; Ceil Wright, Ceil's Veal Letter, *Vealer USA*, Sept./Oct. 1981, 30.

102. Freese; quoted in Eisnitz, 100 (also see 267).

103. Sarah Muirhead, "Breast Blisters, Buttons Continue to Be Costly for Turkey Industry," *Feedstuffs*, 3 Oct. 1994, 12, 25, at 25.

104. Stephanie Brush, "When the Fur Starts to Fly," *Washington Post*, 13 Aug. 1989, F1, F8, at F8; Jon Margolis, "Radical Protectors of Animals Are Wrong about Rights," *Chicago Tribune*, 19 Mar. 1991, sec. 1, p. 19.

105. Quoted in "Statement of Principles," *Meat & Poultry*, Apr. 1990, 102.

106. Carol J. Adams, "The Feminist Traffic in Animals," in *Ecofeminism: Women, Animals, Nature*, ed. Greta Gaard (Philadelphia: Temple University Press, 1993), 195–218, at 202.

107. Michael Thompson quoted in Katherine Bishop, "U.S.A.'s Culinary Rule: Hot Dogs Yes, Dogs No," *New York Times*, 5 Oct. 1989, A22.

108. See Nick Fiddes, *Meat: A Natural Symbol* (London: Routledge, 1991), 132.

109. Gilbert Le Coze quoted in Molly O'Neill, "What to Put in the Pot: Cooks Face Challenge over Animal Rights," *New York Times*, 8 Aug. 1990, C1, C6, at C6.

10 Pronoun Politics

Epigraph: Frederick Douglass, *My Bondage and My Freedom* (1855; reprint, New York: Arno and New York Times, 1968), 360.

1. Douglass, 360.

2. See Tom Biracree and Nancy Biracree, *The Parents' Book of Facts: Child Development from Birth to Age Five* (New York: Facts on File, 1989), 118.

3. "Zookeepers Kill Escaped White Rhinoceros," *Washington Post*, 27 Dec. 1996, A15.

4. See Mary T. Phillips, "Constructing Laboratory Animals: An Ethnographic Study in the Sociology of Science" (Ph.D. diss., New York University, 1991), 173–76.

5. See Carol N. Hopper, "Choosing Your Words: Toward a Language of Respect in Conservation Education," *AZA Annual Conference Proceedings* (American Zoo and Aquarium Association) (1996): 148–50; Karin Hostetter, "Anthropomorphism in Graphics: How Much Is Enough—Or Too Much?" *AZA Regional Conference Proceedings* (1996): 584–85, at 584.

6. "Points to Look Out For in Connection with the Antivivisectionists" (undated memo listing in-house publication guidelines for *Journal of Experimental Medicine*), Record Group 517, Box 1, Folder 3, Rockefeller Archive Center, North Tarrytown, N.Y., 2; Karen Pryor, Richard Haag, and Joseph O'Reilly, "The Creative Porpoise: Training for Novel Behavior," *Journal of the Experimental Analysis of Behavior* 12, no. 4 (1969): 653–61, at 656; Karen Pryor, *Lads before the Wind: Adventures in Porpoise Training* (New York: Harper & Row, 1975), 240 n; Jane Goodall, *Through a Window: My Thirty Years with the Chimpanzees of Gombe* (Boston: Houghton Mifflin, 1990), 15.

7. Joan Margules and C. R. Gallistel, "Heading in the Rat: Determination by Environmental Shape," *Animal Learning and Behavior* 16, no. 4 (1988): 404–10, at 410.

8. James L. Gould and Carol Grant Gould, *The Honey Bee* (New York: Scientific American Library, 1988), 63.

9. See Goodall, 15.

10. "Points to Look Out For," 2.

11. "Points to Look Out For," 2.

12. Hugh Glass quoted in James Hall, "The Missouri Trapper," in *Letters from the West; Containing Sketches of Scenery, Manners, and Customs; and Anecdotes Connected with the First Settlements of the Western Sections of the United States* (1828; reprint, Gainesville, Fla.: Scholars' Facsimiles & Reprints, 1967), 293–305, at 304.

13. Mark Twain, *The Adventures of Huckleberry Finn* (1885; reprint in *The Unabridged Mark Twain*, vol. 1, ed. Lawrence Teacher, Philadelphia: Running, 1976), 746–956, at 905.

14. Larry Armer quoted in Michael Goodman, "Caged Animals, Wild Hunters," *Los Angeles Times Magazine*, 10 Nov. 1991, 30+, at 51.

15. Quoted in Jeanie Kasindorf, "The Fur Flies: The Cold War over Animal Rights," *New York*, 15 Jan. 1990, 27–33, at 33.
16. See Sharon Voas, "To Fur or Not to Fur," *Pittsburgh Post-Gazette Magazine*, 2 Jan. 1992, 15–17.
17. See Kasindorf.
18. Phil McCombs, "An Endangered Species," *Washington Post*, 6 Dec. 1992, F1+, at F7.

11 "Bitches," "Monkeys," and "Guinea Pigs": "Animal" Metaphors

Epigraph: Ray Smith, cartoon, *Vegan* (Vegan Society, Oxford), Feb./Mar. 1987, 11.
1. Haig A. Bosmajian, *The Language of Oppression* (Washington, D.C.: Public Affairs, 1974), 6.
2. Quoted in H. R. Hays, *The Dangerous Sex: The Myth of Feminine Evil* (New York: G. P. Putnam's Sons, 1964), 201; see Robert Baker, "'Pricks' and 'Chicks': A Plea for 'Persons,'" in *Philosophy and Sex*, ed. Robert Baker and Frederick Elliston (Buffalo, N.Y.: Prometheus, 1975), 45–64.
3. Saul D. Schor, "Bulldogs: Breeding Instructions," *Pure-Bred Dogs—American Kennel Gazette*, Dec. 1989, 139–40, at 140; "New Claims Reveal the Endless Potential for Human Injury," *Professional Liability: The AVMA Trust Report* (American Veterinary Medical Association), Sept. 1991, 1.
4. Alleen Pace Nilsen, "Sexism as Shown through the English Vocabulary," in *Sexism and Language*, ed. Alleen Pace Nilsen et al. (Urbana, Ill.: National Council of Teachers of English, 1977), 27–41, at 29.
5. Baker, 56.
6. Each year, more than 200,000 foxes are killed by U.S. trappers (estimate provided by Norm Phelps of The Fund for Animals, 29 Mar. 2000, and based primarily on 1996–97 data from state "wildlife" agencies); untold other foxes are killed on U.S. "fur farms."
7. See Sharon Voas, "To Fur or Not to Fur," *Pittsburgh Post-Gazette Magazine*, 2 Jan. 1992, 15–17.
8. See Voas.
9. See Andrée Collard with Joyce Contrucci, *Rape of the Wild: Man's Violence against Animals and the Earth* (Bloomington: Indiana University Press, 1989), 55 n. 34.
10. Stephanie Ross, "How Words Hurt: Attitudes, Metaphor and Oppression," in *Sexist Language: A Modern Philosophical Analysis*, ed. Mary Vetterling-Braggin (Totowa, N.J.: Rowman & Littlefield, 1981), 194–216, at 199.
11. See Winthrop D. Jordan, *White over Black: American Attitudes toward the Negro, 1550–1812* (Chapel Hill: University of North Carolina Press, 1968), 508, 510.
12. Language modernized; quoted in Jordan, 238.
13. See Edward Long, "Observations on the Gradation in the Scale of Being between the Human and Brute Creation, Including Some Curious Particulars Respecting Negroes," part 2, *Columbian Magazine* 2, no. 2 (1788): 70–75; Prospero [pseud.], *Caliban: A Sequel to "Ariel"* (1868; reprint in *The "Ariel" Controversy*, vol. 5 of *Anti-Black Thought, 1863–1925: An Eleven-Volume Anthology of Racist Writings*, ed. John David Smith, New York: Garland, 1993), 191–222, at 197;

quoted in Ernst Haeckel, *The History of Creation; or, The Development of the Earth and Its Inhabitants by the Action of Natural Causes*, vol. 2, trans. Ray Lankester (New York: D. Appleton, 1893), 492–93.

14. Charles Carroll, *The Negro a Beast; or, In the Image of God* (1900; reprint, Miami: Mnemosyne, 1969), 289, 290; Charles Carroll, *The Tempter of Eve; or, The Criminality of Man's Social, Political, and Religious Equality with the Negro, and the Amalgamation to Which These Crimes Inevitably Lead* (1902; reprint in *The Biblical and "Scientific" Defense of Slavery*, vol. 6 of *Anti-Black Thought*), 296–793, at 579, 581.

15. Quoted in Stanley Feldstein, ed., *The Poisoned Tongue: A Documentary History of American Racism and Prejudice* (New York: William Morrow, 1972), 322, 320.

16. Quoted in Mary Ellen Gale, "On Curbing Racial Speech," *Responsive Community*, winter 1990/1991, 47–58, at 47.

17. Jordan, 156.

18. George M. Fredrickson, *The Black Image in the White Mind: The Debate on Afro-American Character and Destiny, 1817–1914* (Middletown, Conn.: Wesleyan University Press, 1971), 56.

19. [Theodore D. Weld], *American Slavery as It Is: Testimony of a Thousand Witnesses* (1839; reprint, New York: Arno and New York Times, 1968), 110.

20. Joseph Henry Allen, "Africans in America, and Their New Guardians," *Christian Examiner* 73 (July 1862): 96–133, at 114; Benjamin Tillman quoted in Feldstein, 192; Paul B. Barringer, *The Sacrifice of a Race* (1900; reprint in *The "Benefits" of Slavery*, vol. 4 of *Anti-Black Thought*), 211–40, at 216; William Benjamin Smith, *The Color Line: A Brief in Behalf of the Unborn* (1905; reprint in *Racial Determinism and the Fear of Miscegenation, Post-1900*, vol. 8 of *Anti-Black Thought*), 45–315, at 112.

21. Quoted in "When a University Is Forced to Examine Its Very Soul," *Pennsylvania Gazette* (University of Pennsylvania), May 1993, 15–19, at 19.

22. Colleen Bonnicklewis et al., in "The Complainants Withdraw Their Grievance and Call the Judicial System Corrupt," *Pennsylvania Gazette*, May 1993, 18.

23. Bonnicklewis et al.

24. Peggy Reeves Sanday, in "Complainants Withdraw."

25. Tony Auth, cartoon, *Philadelphia Inquirer*, 26 May 1993, A14.

26. See Raymond S. Franklin, *Shadows of Race and Class* (Minneapolis: University of Minnesota Press, 1991), 96.

27. George T. Winston, "The Relation of the Whites to the Negroes," *Annals of the American Academy of Political and Social Science* (July 1901): 105–18, at 109; Robert Bingham, *An Ex-slaveholder's View of the Negro Question in the South* (1900; reprint in *"Benefits" of Slavery*), 241–56, at 253; Mrs. L. H. Harris, "A Southern Woman's View" (letter), *Independent* (New York), 18 May 1899, 1354–55, at 1355.

28. Quoted in Laura M. Rose, *The Ku Klux Klan; or, Invisible Empire* (1914; reprint in *Disenfranchisement Proposals and the Ku Klux Klan*, vol. 9 of *Anti-Black Thought*), 423–520, at 475.

29. Quoted in Feldstein, 322.

30. Quoted in Barry H. Lopez, *Of Wolves and Men* (New York: Charles Scribner's Sons, 1978), 170; Cotton Mather, *Decennium Luctuosum: An History of Re-*

markable Occurrences in the Long War Which New England Hath Had with the Indian Savages, from the Year 1688 to the Year 1698 (1699; reprint in *Narratives of the Indian Wars, 1675–1699*, ed. Charles H. Lincoln [New York: Charles Scribner's Sons, 1913], 179–300), at 193; Cotton Mather, *Magnalia Christi Americana; or, The Ecclesiastical History of New England*, vol. 1 (1702; reprint, Hartford, Conn.: Silas Andrus & Son, 1855), 55; Washington to James Duane, 7 Sept. 1783, *The Writings of George Washington*, vol. 27, ed. John C. Fitzpatrick (Washington, D.C.: U.S. Government Printing Office, 1938), 133–40, at 140; Jackson to John Calhoun, 16 Dec. 1817, *Correspondence of Andrew Jackson*, vol. 2, ed. John Spencer Bassett (Washington, D.C.: Carnegie Institution of Washington, 1927), 340.

31. Harold W. Thompson, *Body, Boots, and Britches: Folktales, Ballads and Speech from Country New York* (1939; reprint, Syracuse, N.Y.: Syracuse University Press, 1979), 67.

32. Language standardized; Adam Poe quoted in Frank Triplett, *Conquering the Wilderness; or, New Pictorial History of the Life and Times of the Pioneer Heroes and Heroines of America* (New York: N. D. Thompson, 1883), 329.

33. Language modernized; quoted in Francis Parkman, *The Conspiracy of Pontiac and the Indian War after the Conquest of Canada*, vol. 2 (Boston: Little, Brown, 1905), 44 n.

34. Quoted in Parkman, 45.

35. John House quoted in Cecil Eby, *"That Disgraceful Affair," the Black Hawk War* (New York: W. W. Norton, 1973), 253; J. M. Chivington quoted in William Meyer, *Native Americans: The New Indian Resistance* (New York: International, 1971), 32.

36. See Robert Sommer, "The Personality of Vegetables: Botanical Metaphors for Human Characteristics," *Journal of Personality* 56, no. 4 (1988): 665–83.

37. The term *scapegoat* apparently derives from an ancient Hebrew ritual (described in Leviticus 16) in which a goat was slaughtered, a priest verbally transferred the Hebrews' sins to another goat, and this second goat (the "escaped goat") was taken into the wilderness and abandoned.

12 Persons of Other Species: Toward Legal Redefinition

Epigraph: Oren Lyons quoted in David Gucwa and James Ehmann, *To Whom It May Concern: An Investigation of the Art of Elephants* (New York: W. W. Norton, 1985), 208.

1. See *Gluckman v. American Airlines, Inc.*, 844 Federal Supplement 151–63 (S.D.N.Y. 1994), quotations at 155, 156, 159.

2. See Victoria Benning, "Front Royal Magistrate Faces Cat-Nabbing Charges," *Washington Post*, 7 Aug. 1996, D2; Michael deCourcy Hinds, "Among Amish, Suspect in Arson Is Well Known," *New York Times*, 25 Nov. 1993, A16.

3. See *Bailey et al. v. Poindexter's Executor*, 54–56 Reports of Cases in the Supreme Court of Appeals of Virginia (14 Grattan's Virginia Reports) 428–55 (1858), quotations at 432, 434; Mark Twain, *The Adventures of Huckleberry Finn* (1885; reprint in *The Unabridged Mark Twain*, vol. 1, ed. Lawrence Teacher, Philadelphia: Running, 1976), 746–956, at 905.

4. See *Commonwealth v. Welosky*, 177 North Eastern Reporter 656–65 (1931),

quotations at 659, 660. For similar cases, see *In re Goodell*, 39 Wisconsin Reports 232–46 (1875); *In re Lockwood*, Petitioner, 154 United States Reports 116–18 (1894).

5. See *Sierra Club v. Morton*, 405 United States Reports 727–60 (1972), quotation at 745.

6. Christopher D. Stone, "Should Trees Have Standing?—Toward Legal Rights for Natural Objects," *South California Law Review* 45, no. 2 (1972): 450–501.

7. See Gavin Daws, "'Animal Liberation' as Crime: The Hawaii Dolphin Case," in *Ethics and Animals*, ed. Harlan B. Miller and William H. Williams (Clifton, N.J.: Humana, 1983), 361–71; *State v. LeVasseur*, 613 Pacific Reporter, 2d ser., 1328–35 (Hawaii App. 1980), quotations at 1330. I wholeheartedly support the illegal liberation of oppressed nonhumans. But someone must provide for liberated animals' safety and well-being if they seem unable to fend for themselves. Kea and Puka were released—while debilitated—into the Pacific rather than their native Atlantic. No one prepared them for freedom or took measures to protect them. Almost certainly they soon died.

8. See *Corso v. Crawford Dog and Cat Hospital, Inc.*, 415 New York Supplement, 2d ser., 182–83 (City Civ. Ct. 1979), quotation at 183.

9. See *Citizens to End Animal Suffering and Exploitation v. New England Aquarium*, 836 Federal Supplement 45–59 (D. Mass. 1993).

10. See *Gluckman v. American Airlines*, quotations at 158.

11. See *Bueckner v. Hamel*, 886 South Western Reporter, 2d ser., 368–78 (Tex. App.—Houston [1st Dist.] 1994), quotations at 377, 378.

Select Bibliography

Philosophy of Animal Equality

Pluhar, Evelyn B. *Beyond Prejudice: The Moral Significance of Human and Nonhuman Animals*. Durham, N.C.: Duke University Press, 1995.

Rachels, James. *Created from Animals: The Moral Implications of Darwinism*. Oxford: Oxford University Press, 1990.

Regan, Tom. *The Case for Animal Rights*. Berkeley: University of California Press, 1983.

Rollin, Bernard. *Animal Rights and Human Morality*. 2d ed. Buffalo, N.Y.: Prometheus, 1992.

Salt, Henry S. *Animals' Rights—Considered in Relation to Social Progress*. 3d ed. 1922. Reprint, Clarks Summit, Pa.: Society for Animal Rights, 1980.

Sapontzis, Steve F. *Morals, Reason, and Animals*. Philadelphia: Temple University Press, 1987.

Singer, Peter. *Animal Liberation*. 2d ed. New York: New York Review of Books, 1990.

Nonhuman Intelligence and Emotion

Barber, Theodore X. *The Human Nature of Birds: A Scientific Discovery with Startling Implications*. New York: St. Martin's, 1993.

Burton, Maurice. *Just Like an Animal*. New York: Charles Scribner's Sons, 1978.

Cavalieri, Paola, and Peter Singer, eds. *The Great Ape Project: Equality beyond Humanity*. New York: St. Martin's, 1993.

Fouts, Roger, with Stephen Tukel Mills. *Next of Kin: What Chimpanzees Have Taught Me about Who We Are*. New York: William Morrow, 1997.

Gonzalez, Philip, and Leonore Fleischer. *The Dog Who Rescues Cats: The True Story of Ginny*. New York: HarperCollins, 1995.

Green, Susan Kohn. *Gentle Gorilla: The Story of Patty Cake*. New York: Richard Marek, 1978.

Griffin, Donald R. *Animal Minds*. Chicago: University of Chicago Press, 1992.

Hart, Martin. *Rats*. Translated by Arnold Pomerans. London: Allison & Busby, 1982.

Hendrickson, Robert. *More Cunning than Man: A Social History of Rats and Men*. New York: Stein & Day, 1983.

Howard, Len. *Birds as Individuals*. New York: Doubleday, 1953.

Macphail, Euan M. *Brain and Intelligence in Vertebrates*. Oxford: Clarendon, 1982.

Masson, Jeffrey M., and Susan McCarthy. *When Elephants Weep: The Emotional Lives of Animals*. New York: Delacorte, 1995.

Patterson, Francine, and Eugene Linden. *The Education of Koko*. New York: Holt, Rinehart & Winston, 1981.

Romanes, George J. *Animal Intelligence*. London: Kegan Paul, Trench, & Co., 1882.

Ryden, Hope. *Lily Pond: Four Years with a Family of Beavers*. New York: William Morrow, 1989.

Thomas, Elizabeth Marshall. *The Hidden Life of Dogs*. Boston: Houghton Mifflin, 1993.

Hunting

Amory, Cleveland. *Man Kind? Our Incredible War on Wildlife*. New York: Dell, 1974.

Baker, Ron. *The American Hunting Myth*. New York: Vantage, 1985.

Benke, Adrian. *The Bowhunting Alternative*. San Antonio: B. Todd, 1989.

Report of the Panel of Enquiry into Shooting and Angling (1976–1979). Horsham, England: Panel of Enquiry into Shooting and Angling, 1980.

Sportfishing

Migdalski, Edward C. *The Inquisitive Angler*. New York: Lyons & Burford, 1991.

Muoneke, Maurice I., and W. Michael Childress. "Hooking Mortality: A Review for Recreational Fisheries." *Reviews in Fisheries Science* 2, no. 2 (1994): 123–56.

Report of the Panel of Enquiry into Shooting and Angling (1976–1979). Horsham, England: Panel of Enquiry into Shooting and Angling, 1980.

Sosin, Mark, and John Clark. *Through the Fish's Eye: An Angler's Guide to Gamefish Behavior*. New York: Harper & Row, 1973.

Spinks, Peter. "Fear of Fishing." *New Scientist* (2 Apr. 1987): 25.

Williams, Ted. "Frankenstein's Fish." *Audubon* (Sept. 1987): 74–77.

Zoos

Cohn, Jeffrey P. "Decisions at the Zoo." *BioScience* (Oct. 1992): 654–59.

Croke, Vicki. *The Modern Ark: The Story of Zoos*. New York: Scribner, 1997.

Gold, Don. *Zoo: A Behind-the-Scenes Look at the Animals and the People Who Care for Them*. Chicago: Contemporary, 1988.

Green, Alan, and The Center for Public Integrity. *Animal Underworld: Inside America's Black Market for Rare and Exotic Species*. New York: Public Affairs, 1999.

Gripper, John. *Florida Zoo Inquiry*. London: World Society for the Protection of Animals (WSPA) and Born Free Foundation, 1996.

———. *Zoos in Maritime Canada: An Investigative Report*. Toronto: WSPA and Zoocheck Canada, 1996.

Hornsby, Michael. "Trauma of Captivity 'Sends Animals Mad.'" *The Times* (London) (23 Mar. 1993): 6.

Norton, Bryan G., Michael Hutchins, Elizabeth F. Stevens, and Terry L. Maple, eds. *Ethics on the Ark: Zoos, Animal Welfare, and Wildlife Conservation*. Washington, D.C.: Smithsonian Institution Press, 1995.

Pitiful "Exhibits": The State of British Zoos (pamphlet). Tonbridge, England: Animal Aid, 1994.

Sedgwick, John. *The Peaceable Kingdom: A Year in the Life of America's Oldest Zoo*. New York: William Morrow, 1988.

Aquaprisons

Dezern, Craig, and Cindy Schreuder. "Dolphins in Captivity." *Orlando Sentinel* (10 June 1990): A1+.
Hoyt, Erich. *The Performing Orca—Why the Show Must Stop*. Bath, England: Whale and Dolphin Conservation Society, 1992.
Johnson, William. *The Rose-Tinted Menagerie*. London: Heretic, 1990.
Riley, David. "Our Love of Dolphins Has Turned Into a Questionable Affair." *Smithsonian* (Jan. 1993): 58+.
Rogers, David K. "Marine Mammals Face Threats in Captivity." *St. Petersburg Times* (15 Apr. 1990): 1A–2A.
Rose, Naomi A., and Richard Farinato. *The Case against Marine Mammals in Captivity*. Washington, D.C.: Humane Society of the United States, 1995.
Weddle, David. "Loving Dolphins to Death." *Los Angeles Times Magazine* (7 Apr. 1991): 22+.

Vivisection

Cohen, Murry J., Stephen R. Kaufman, Rhoda Ruttenberg, and Alix Fano. *A Critical Look at Animal Experimentation*. 5th ed. New York: Medical Research Modernization Committee, 1998.
Fano, Alix. *Lethal Laws: Animal Testing, Human Health and Environmental Policy*. London: Zed, 1997.
Greek, C. Ray, and Jean Swingle Greek. *Sacred Cows and Golden Geese: The Human Cost of Experiments on Animals*. New York: Continuum, 2000.
Inside Biosearch. Videocassette. Washington, D.C.: People for the Ethical Treatment of Animals (PETA), [1988].
Kaufman, Stephen R. "Does Vivisection Pass the Utilitarian Test?" *Public Affairs Quarterly* 9, no. 2 (1995): 127–37.
LaFollette, Hugh, and Niall Shanks. "Animal Models in Biomedical Research: Some Epistemological Worries." *Public Affairs Quarterly* 7, no. 2 (1993): 113–30.

Ruesch, Hans. *Slaughter of the Innocent.* 1978. Reprint, Swain, N.Y.: Civitas, 1983.

Sharpe, Robert. *The Cruel Deception: The Use of Animals in Medical Research.* Wellingborough, England: Thorsons, 1988.

———. *Science on Trial: The Human Cost of Animal Experiments.* Sheffield, England: Awareness, 1994.

Shaw, George Bernard. "Preface on Doctors." In *The Doctor's Dilemma: A Tragedy.* 1911. Reprint, Baltimore: Penguin, 1954.

———. *Shaw on Vivisection.* Edited by G. H. Bowker. London: Allen & Unwin, 1949.

Singer, Peter. "Tools for Research." Chapter 2 in *Animal Liberation,* 2d ed. New York: New York Review of Books, 1990.

"Unnecessary Fuss". Videocassette. Washington, D.C.: PETA, 1984.

Food-Industry Enslavement and Slaughter

Coats, C. David. *Old MacDonald's Factory Farm: The Myth of the Traditional Farm and the Shocking Truth about Animal Suffering in Today's Agribusiness.* New York: Continuum, 1989.

Davis, Karen. *Prisoned Chickens, Poisoned Eggs: An Inside Look at the Modern Poultry Industry.* Summertown, Tenn.: Book Publishing Company, 1996.

The Down Side of Livestock Marketing. Videotape compiled by Farm Sanctuary and Becky Sandstedt. Watkins Glen, N.Y.: Farm Sanctuary, 1991.

Eisnitz, Gail A. *Slaughterhouse: The Shocking Story of Greed, Neglect, and Inhumane Treatment inside the U.S. Meat Industry.* Buffalo, N.Y.: Prometheus, 1997.

Fox, Michael W. *Farm Animals: Husbandry, Behavior, and Veterinary Practice.* Baltimore: University Park Press, 1984.

Humane Slaughter? Videocassette. Watkins Glen, N.Y.: Farm Sanctuary, 1991.

Mason, Jim, and Peter Singer. *Animal Factories.* 2d ed. New York: Harmony, 1990.

Robbins, John. *Diet for a New America.* Walpole, N.H.: Stillpoint, 1987.

Singer, Peter. "Down on the Factory Farm." Chapter 3 in *Animal Liberation,* 2d ed. New York: New York Review of Books, 1990.

Speciesism and Human Oppression

Adams, Carol J. *Neither Man nor Beast: Feminism and the Defense of Animals*. New York: Continuum, 1994.

———. *The Sexual Politics of Meat: A Feminist-Vegetarian Critical Theory*. 2d ed. New York: Continuum, 2000.

Adams, Carol J., and Josephine Donovan, eds. *Animals and Women: Feminist Theoretical Explorations*. Durham, N.C.: Duke University Press, 1995.

Collard, Andrée, with Joyce Contrucci. *Rape of the Wild: Man's Violence against Animals and the Earth*. Bloomington: Indiana University Press, 1989.

Mason, Jim. *An Unnatural Order: Uncovering the Roots of Our Domination of Nature and Each Other*. New York: Simon & Schuster, 1993.

Spiegel, Marjorie. *The Dreaded Comparison: Human and Animal Slavery*. 3d ed. New York: Mirror, 1996.

Nonhuman Animals and the Law

Francione, Gary L. *Animals, Property, and the Law*. Philadelphia: Temple University Press, 1995.

Tischler, Joyce S. "Rights for Nonhuman Animals: A Guardianship Model for Dogs and Cats." *San Diego Law Review* 14, no. 2 (1977): 484–506.

Wise, Steven M. *Rattling the Cage: Toward Legal Rights for Animals*. Cambridge, Mass.: Perseus, 2000.

Wolfson, David J. *Beyond the Law: Agribusiness and the Systemic Abuse of Animals Raised for Food or Food Production*. New York: Archimedian/Coalition for Non-Violent Food, 1996.

Index

Throughout this index, a slash between two page references means "in conjunction with." For example, "215(n 25)/76" means "note 25 on page 215, in conjunction with page 76."